THE ESSENTIAL ANTIFEDERALIST

THE ESSENTIAL ANTIFEDERALIST

edited by
W. B. Allen
HARVEY MUDD COLLEGE
and
Gordon Lloyd
UNIVERSITY OF REDLANDS

ASSOCIATE EDITOR
Margie Lloyd

UNIVERSITY
PRESS OF
AMERICA

LANHAM • NEW YORK • LONDON

University Press of America,® Inc.

4720 Boston Way
Lanham, MD 20706

3 Henrietta Street
London WC2E 8LU England

Co-published by arrangement with the
Center for the Study of the Constitution

Library of Congress Cataloging in Publication Data
Main entry under title:

The Essential antifederalist.

  1. Political science—United States—History—Sources.
2. United States—Constitutional history—Sources.
3. United States—Constitutional law. I. Allen, W. B.
(William Barclay), 1944-   . II. Lloyd, Gordon,
1942-   . III. Lloyd, Margie.
JK155.E84   1985   342.73'029   85-5303
                         347.30229
ISBN 0-8191-4631-5 (alk. paper)
ISBN 0-8191-4632-3 (pbk. : alk. paper)

All University Press of America books are produced on acid-free
paper which exceeds the minimum standards set by the National
Historical Publications and Records Commission.

EDITORS' NOTE

This volume of essays offers a readily accessible version of essential Antifederalist thought. We made it with the undergraduate in mind, designing to provide an introduction to Antifederalist thought, which nonetheless touches upon the critical issues in a comprehensive manner. We mean it to be easily readable. Accordingly, we have standardized spelling, grammar, and syntax (wherever permissible) throughout. Because our goal has been to present this work in a simplified format, we have avoided adding notes and editorial apparatus. Notes attached to the essays are the work of the authors themselves. We have relied mainly on the texts established in Herbert Storing's *The Complete Antifederalist* as the definitive guide for the identification of authors and the order of their works. We follow, for example, his renumeration of the "Agrippa" essays. We have also drawn material from versions of Antifederalist writings published in Jonathan Elliot's *Debates*, *The Writings of James Monroe* (1898), Jensen/Kaminski's *Documentary History of the Ratification of the Constitution*, Max Farrand's *Records of the Constitutional Convention*, and *Writings of Thomas Jefferson* (Boyd).

TABLE OF CONTENTS

Editors' Note   v

Interpretative Essay   viii

Timeline   xv

Chapter One: The Origin of Antifederalist Thought   3
   Z   4
   John Lansing, George Mason and Luther Martin, 20 June, 1787   7
   George Mason, "Objections"   11
   Robert Yates and John Lansing, "Reasons of Dissent"   14
   Luther Martin, 27-28 June, 1787   16
   Elbridge Gerry, "Objections"   20
   Richard Henry Lee, Letter to Edmund Randolph   22
   Old Whig Essay, Essay VII   27
   Plebian (excerpts)   31
   Agrippa, Letters XV and XVI   41
   Sidney, Essay II   50
   Pennsylvania Minority Report (excerpts)   53
   Thomas Jefferson, Letter to Alexander Donald,
      February, 1788 (excerpts)   70

Chapter Two: The Antifederalist Views of Federalism   73
   Federal Farmer, Letters I and XVII   75
   Centinel, Letter I   93
   Brutus, Letters I and V   102
   Maryland Farmer, Letter III, 7 March, 1788   117
   Agrippa, Letter IV   121
   Patrick Henry, speeches given in the
      Virginia Ratifying Convention, 4-5 June, 1788 (excerpts)   123

Chapter Three: The Antifederalist View of Republicanism   137
   James Monroe, "Observations on the Constitution"   139
   John DeWitt, Essay V   153
   Cato, Essays V, VI, VII   159
   John Lansing, 24 June, 1788   169
   Melancton Smith, 20 June, 1788   171

Federal Farmer, Letters II, III, XII   177
Brutus, Essays IV,XI,XII, XV   201

Chapter Four: Antifederalist Support
   of Capitalism and Democracy   225
A Georgian (excerpts)   226
Agrippa, Essays VII, IX, XII, XIV   228
Centinel, Letters III, IV, VII, VIII   242
Maryland Farmer, Essays III (part II), and VII   254
Federal Farmer, Letters VII, VIII, IX   261
Brutus, Essay III   269

INTERPRETATIVE ESSAY

"The Antifederalists" is the name commonly used to designate those people who opposed the ratification of the Constitution. This negative nomenclature was not consciously chosen by the opposition; they would have preferred the positive image of Republicans. Our surest guide to understanding how the Antifederalists received their name is to recognize in the term a political concept immediately applicable in the context of American politics. From the adoption of the Articles of Confederation in 1781, and coming to a head in 1783–85, those who aimed to "cement," "support," or "protect" the Confederation (in which they identified the Union) were perceived as federal-minded as opposed to state-minded. By 1787, those who opposed the movement to strengthen the Confederation were being widely described as "antifederal men" with an "unfederal disposition."

Federal-minded men finally persuaded the Confederation Congress in February 1787 to call a Constitutional Convention to revise the Articles of Confederation. They proposed a plan for a strengthened union which radically departed from the Articles. The antifederal men countered the nationalism of the new Constitution by emphasizing the extent to which it departed from the federal principles of the Articles. This position is manifest above all in the pre-eminent Antifederalist, Richard Henry Lee, whose "Federal Farmer" essays sought to arrogate to himself a title which for four years past he energetically resisted. A common Antifederalist argument during the ratification struggle of 1787–88 was that they were the true federalists because they took their bearings from the principles of federalism laid down in the Articles. They accused the Federalists of abandoning the principles of federalism and instead substituting a consolidated system.

Each side in the debate over the ratification of the Constitution was known by the reputation which it had earned in the struggles of the 1780's over strengthening the Union, rather than in terms of the principles which they articulated in the post-convention struggle. The initial argument for strengthening the Confederation was reinforced by Alexander Hamilton, John Jay, and James Madison in the eighty-five essays which they wrote urging ratification of the Constitution. These essays, known as *The Federalist*, presented the choice in terms of the survival or dismemberment of the union. The opposition was accused of disunion sentiment, being self-serving, uninformed, and inconsistent. Despite the best efforts of opposition leaders to shed the "anti" image, the nomenclature "Antifederalist" was preserved for posterity.

Despite recent efforts to retrieve Antifederalist thought from oblivion, the Antifederalists are still widely viewed as irrelevant and disorganized. They even receive a negative evaluation from those scholars who give the Antifederalists a comprehensive and sympathetic treatment. Their opposition is viewed as "piecemeal," their attitude one "of little faith," and their perspective "reactionary." Their legacy to the American political tradition is viewed as minimal and inconsequential. We believe, however, that Antifederalist Melancton Smith was correct when he argued that "there is a remarkable uniformity in the objections made to the constitution, *on the most important points.*"

When the leading Antifederalists are permitted to speak for themselves on these important points, a hitherto unappreciated positive critique and coherent alternative emerges.

The task of evaluating Antifederalist thought would be much easier had three people sat down and written *The Antifederalist*. Instead, the Antifederalist literature (as is the case with most of the Federalist literature other than *The Federalist*) is immense and heterogeneous, encompassing speeches, pamphlets, essays, and letters. Tensions, inconsistencies, and disagreements among the Antifederalists over a particular issue can easily be discovered. The same is true for the "other" Federalists. There is a sense in which *The Federalist* has made our understanding of the founding too easy. Its coherence and coverage have lulled us into the belief that these easily accessible essays contain all we need to know.

But *The Federalist* represents only one side of the debate, presenting the opposition in the worst possible light. Unfortunately, much subsequent scholarship has accepted *The Federalist*'s view of the Antifederalists at face value. Although the Federalists won the debate, they did not get everything that they desired. Antifederalist political theory entered the very nature of the American system, for example, by virtue of its adherents' successful appeal for a bill of rights. This victory was less than they would have liked, but more than can justify rejection as insignificant by their inheritors. Precisely because American politics is so often a debate over the possibilities and limitations of the separation of powers, an independent judiciary, federalism, and representative government, it is vital that the potentcy of Antifederalist political analysis be restored. A healthy appreciation for "the other side" completes the picture of our founding, a drama which has yet to be equalled in the political world.

The Antifederalists did not sense a need to fundamentally change the government under the Articles of Confederation. They liked the union as it was: well-constructed and protective of its citizens' liberties. What and where was the danger in letting the people enjoy the fruits of their labors, protected by state laws against private violence? Faction, majority or minority, was troublesome, and many Antifederalists thought that it could have been better contained under the Articles; but wasn't that the reason the Philadelphia convention was called?—to preserve or enhance the present condition of liberty with "the least burdensome system which shall defend those rights."[1]

The Antifederalists admitted that the Articles were weak but they believed that the political and economic conditions did not approach the crisis proportions portrayed by those who wanted a radical overhauling of the Articles. The Antifederalist position on the eve of the Constitutional Convention in May 1787 was to grant more power to Congress over domestic commerce and foreign affairs without abandoning the structure of the Articles (which guaranteed the traditional assumption that republicanism can only thrive in a small territorial orbit). With the emergence of the new plan of government from Philadelphia in September 1787, the Antifederalists fleshed out this argument in order to warn their fellow citizens that the new plan departed radically from traditional republicanism.

Two principles formed the basis of the Antifederalist idea for the American republic: the people are the sovereigns of the government; and an express reservation of powers qualified the government by affirming the people's sovereignity. Once the people proclaimed their power, they appointed a select few to administer that power, which filtered back to the people. They declared their rules, taking into account the chief negative feature of civil society—minority faction—and turned out a positive yet minimal framework which enabled them to govern themselves by honesty and virtue. Minority faction could not possibly exist in a government where all interests of the people were represented:

> The perfection of government depends on the equality of its operation, as far as human affairs admit, upon all the parts of the empire, and upon all the citizens. Some inequalities indeed will take place. One man will be obliged to travel a few miles further than another man to procure justice. But when he has traveled, the poor man ought to have the same measure of justice as the rich one. Small inequalities may be compensated.[2]

The publication of the Constitution signalled an onslaught of Antifederalist literature throughout the nation for the next nine months. They agreed that four basic questions were inadequately addressed in the document; the Antifederalists wanted the answers built into the Constitution, or they would encourage the delegates to their respective state ratifying conventions to oppose the Constitution. The first problem they had was with the notion of a strong central government. The Constitution provided neither recall elections nor frequent rotation in office. The Antifederalists feared that once elected and comfortable in his job, the representative would not relinquish his power. Being some distance away from his district would alienate him from his constituents' wishes; he would be inclined to favor his own affairs and those of the national city. Another shortcoming of the strong central government would be governing the regional differences between the states and their inhabitants. Making general laws that would apply to the needs of Maine or Georgia would not address the important local needs of either state. The new government would have to become more tolerant to the local issues (as under the Articles) for the people not to be suspicious of its huge power.

The Antifederalists understood the basic choice facing mankind to be either republicanism or despotism. The operating principle of republicanism was self government while that of despotism was force. They believed that republics fell into despotism if the principle of self-government became corrupted. Thus, special care must be taken regarding those things which constitute the pillars of self government. They believed that if the pillar of small size was to be removed then it became imperative to erect an alternative system of support. They believed that special attention should be given to the habits and customs of the people on the one hand and to securing the dependency of the representatives on the other hand. The problem with the new plan was that it neglected the mores of the people, and it bestowed more power on the representatives without providing for the corresponding checks on that power.

A big complaint of the Antifederalists was the actual framework of the Constitution; it seemed to encourage the growth of minority faction. Remember, the Antifederalists were very suspicious of privilege, and the proposed Constitution appeared to offer plenty of public jobs for an aristocracy. There were no places in the government for the yeoman middle class, and no checks upon those civil servants who would not govern in the interests of the middle class. Wealthy officeholders would appoint their wealthy friends to public office. Instead of a governmental framework based on the middle class values of hon-

esty and virtue, the proposed framework would be based on and
encourage the love of wealth and greed. A lack of checks against this
problem would allow a tyranny of minority faction over majority
values. The Antifederalists wanted a middle class government, where

> ... the people are sovereign and their sense or opinion is the criterion
> of every public measure ... if you vest all the legislative power in one
> body of men (separating the executive and judicial) elected for a short
> period, and necessarily excluded by rotation from permanency, and
> guarded from precipitancy and surprise by delays imposed on its pro-
> ceedings, you will create the most perfect responsibility.[3]

The third problem of the proposed Constitution was that Congress
had the power to impose barriers against commerce. Antifederalists
believed that commerce should remain free to pursue natural courses.
Since commercial interests would not be supported by the government, trade would have to be allowed to develop new interests, thus
benefitting more people. To this end, the Antifederalists pushed for
either more checks on Congress or less power of Congress over the
people and their affairs. Following Montesquieu, the Antifederalists
believed that those governments which favored commerce seemed
better suited to ameliorate the human condition, while those which
most favored commerce served *best* of all. They feared that the power
to regulate interstate commerce and foreign trade as well as the power
over internal taxation granted to the Congress under the new plan
would produce a restrictive and burdensome economy. They felt that
Congress would use its authority to grant monopolies, thereby reducing economic opportunity even further. The Antifederalists were appre-
hensive about the restrictive economic message that America would be
sending the world. More policy control over our markets would mean
less productivity, less business, and less prosperity to reinvest into the
businesses overseas. This unfriendliness to trade would be a signal to
Europe that the new nation would not be working in congruence with
its markets at home and abroad.

The key criticism the Antifederalists had with the Constitution was
the representation issue. In order to truly represent the interests of the
people and reduce the possibility of governmental corruption, the
proposed government had to increase the number of representatives in
proportion to the size of the nation (or conversely, decrease the size of
the nation in proportion to the number of representatives now planned
in the Constitution). For the nation to be flexible to the demands of
representation and successful in maintaining a good government, the

scheme of representation had to expand in size along with the population. While it is true that aristocrats and demagogues would be elected over the middling class as a matter of course, expanding the representation meant that the majority opinion—middle class in this instance—would be guaranteed an ear in Congress. Antifederalists noted that under the proposed scheme of representation, the power of recall, frequent elections, and rotation of office were not built into the model. Their fear from this omission was that the local interests of the citizens would not be kept before Congress, thus causing their frustration with the new centralized government: the power of the representative would constantly rest over the peoples' heads, and not vice versa. If the proposed government had restored this power to the people, then minority tyranny, represented by aristocratic public servants, would be dissipated (if not completely done away with) by the majority opinion and/or representatives.

> By widening the class of those with power we approach republican perfection.[4]

The stability of the country will be encouraged by the yeoman or small businessman as he has the nation's interests at heart; let him and the many others like him, thought the Antifederalists, represent the positive middling interests of this country.

The Antifederalists wanted a national government to reply to the peoples' local needs. Under the Articles, the people had a voice in the national government and they had basic freedoms to enjoy the results of their hard work. When the new government scrapped the Articles in the summer of 1787 for a more centralized framework, the Antifederalists reacted strongly, warning citizens of what freedoms and power they had before the new plan, and how quickly they would lose what had been fought for and cherished. The pamphlet war the opponents waged lasted until the adoption of the Bill of Rights, when the Antifederalists were placated with certain freedoms and powers built into the Constitution.

Therefore, respecting the main points, the Antifederalists were not only in agreement but their position was coherent. They believed that republican liberty was best preserved in small units where the people had an active and continuous part to play in government. They thought that the Articles secured this concept of republicanism. They argued that the Constitution placed republicanism in danger because it undermined the prop of small size. As a consequence, they argued that the system of representation under the new plan must be altered to secure what was formerly secured by small size. They believed that under the new plan the representatives would become independent from rather than dependent on the people. Lastly, they warned that unless restrictions were placed on the powers of the Congress, the Executive, and the Judiciary, the potentiality for the abuse of power would become a reality. These various approaches culminated in their insistence on a Bill of Rights which they saw satisfying the same function that small territory, representative dependency, and strict construction would perform for republicanism.

The Antifederalist perspective and recommendations are still alive in the American political tradition. When we hear the argument that the Founding Fathers feared power and thus separated government into three branches and tried to ensure that no one branch would dominate, we are in fact hearing what the Antifederalists feared and desired. Their perspective did *not* prevail in 1787; nevertheless, the contemporary argument that the Founding Fathers created a "dead-locked" system is in fact assuming that the Founding Fathers were Antifederalists. And when we hear the argument that the Founding Fathers were wealthy and ambitious men who designed an undemocratic government in secret for their own benefit, we are in fact hearing a vulgarization of the Antifederalist critique of the leading proponents of change. Moreover, when we hear the claim that our representatives are drawn from a minority of the population, that they operate in a manner which is independent of the people, and that the Congress does not represent the broad cross-section of interests which it is supposed to represent, we are in fact repeating the Antifederalist critique of the scheme of representation found in the Constitution. When we hear the argument that the federal government is out of control, that it interferes too much with the life of American citizens and that state and local officials understand the needs of the people far better than do representatives in Washington, we are in fact echoing the warnings of the Antifederalists. Finally, when Americans instinctively associate the Constitution and the meaning of democracy with the Bill of Rights, we are in fact honoring the essential contribution of the Antifederalists.

Notes

1. Agrippa: Essay III.
2. Agrippa: Essay VII.
3. Centinel: Letter I
4. Melancton Smith, 20 June, 1788.

TIMELINE

1776

Declaration of Independence

1781

Articles of Confederation effective

1783

Peace with England; United States independence recognized

1786

September 14	Annapolis Convention: request for Constitutional Convention
October 16	Virginia selects seven delegates
November 23	New Jersey selects five delegates
December 30	Pennsylvania selects eight delegates

1787

January 6	North Carolina selects five delegates
January 17	New Hampshire selects four delegates
February 3	Delaware selects five delegates
February 4	Shays rebellion ends
February 10	Georgia selects four delegates
February 21	Confederation Congress approves Constitutional Convention
February 28	New York selects three delegates
March 8	South Carolina selects four delegates
March 10	Massachusetts selects four delegates
March 14	Rhode Island rejects to send delegates
May 5	Rhode Island again rejects to send delegates
May 14	Constitutional Convention meets with only five states present
May 21	Connecticut selects three delegates
May 25	Constitutional Convention begins after quorum of seven states is reached
May 29	Virginia Plan introduced
June 13	Virginia Plan amended

June 15	New Jersey Plan introduced
June 16	Rhode Island again rejects to send delegates
June 19	New Jersey Plan rejected
July 13	Northwest Ordinance adopted
July 16	Connecticut Compromise
July 26	Convention adjourns for rest and deliberation
August 6	Convention reconvenes: Committee of Detail reports on first draft of Constitution
September 12	Committee of Style reports on final draft of Constitution
September 17	Constitution signed
September 20	Congress reads Constitution
September 26–28	Congress debates Constitution
September 28	Call for state ratifying conventions by Congress: nine states needed to ratify Constitution
September 28	Pennsylvania calls for state convention
October 17	Connecticut calls for state convention
October 25	Massachusetts calls for state convention
October 26	Georgia calls for state convention
October 31	Virginia calls for state convention
November 1	New Jersey calls for state convention
November 6	Pennsylvania elects delegates
November 10	Delaware calls for state convention
November 12	Connecticut elects delegates
November 19–January 7	Massachusetts elects delegates
November 20–December 15	Pennsylvania ratifying convention meets
November 26	Delaware elects delegates
November 27	Maryland calls for state convention
November 27–December 1	New Jersey elects delegates
December 3–7	Delaware ratifying convention meets
December 4–5	Georgia elects delegates
December 6	North Carolina calls for state convention
December 7	Delaware ratifies 30-0
December 11–20	New Jersey ratifying convention meets
December 12	Pennsylvania ratifies 46-23
December 14	New Hampshire calls for state convention
December 18	New Jersey ratifies 38-0
December 25–January 5	Georgia ratifying convention meets
December 31	Georgia ratifies 26-0
December 31	New Hampshire elects delegates

1788

January 3–9	Connecticut ratifying convention meets
January 9	Connecticut ratifies 128-40

January 9–February 7	Massachusetts ratifying convention meets
January 30	Massachusetts Compromise proposed (ratify now, amend later)
February 1	New York calls for state convention
February 6	Massachusetts ratifies 187-168 with nine proposed amendments
February 13–22	New Hampshire ratifying convention meets and votes for adjournment until June 18
March 24	Rhode Island votes to have a state ratifying convention: measure is rejected as only half of voters turn out and of that amount (2711) only 237 favor Constitution
March 28–29	North Carolina elects delegates
April 7	Maryland elects delegates
April 11–12	South Carolina elects delegates
April 21–29	Maryland ratifying convention meets
April 26	Maryland ratifies 63-11
April 29–May 3	New York elects delegates
May 12–24	South Carolina ratifying convention meets
May 23	South Carolina ratifies 149–73
June 2–27	Virginia ratifying convention meets
June 17–July 26	New York ratifying convention meets
June 18–21	New Hampshire ratifying convention: second session
June 21	New Hampshire ratifies 57-47 with twelve proposed amendments
June 25	Virginia ratifies 89-79 with proposed bill of rights of 20 amendments
July 2	Congress of the Confederation accepts new Constitution as ratified and appoints committee to put Constitution in operation
July 21–August 4	North Carolina ratifying convention meets
July 25	New York votes for a conditional ratification: plan rejected
July 26	New York ratifies 30-27
August 2	North Carolina ratifying convention decides not to ratify until a bill of rights and other amendments are incorporated into the Constitution
September 13	Congress prepares for a new government
November 30	North Carolina calls for a second constitutional convention

1789

January 7	Presidential electors chosen

February 4	Election of senators, representatives, and president
March 4	First Congress
April 1	House of Representatives organized
April 6	Senate organized
April 8	House begins work
April 30	First inaugural
August 21–22	North Carolina elects delegates to second convention
September 9	Bill of Rights introduced
October 10	Last business under Articles of Confederation
November 16–23	North Carolina ratifying convention meets
November 21	North Carolina ratifies 194-77
December 23	Maryland cedes ten square miles for building of new federal city on the Potomac

1790

January 17	Rhode Island calls for state convention
February 8	Rhode Island elects delegates
March 1–6	Rhode Island convention: first session
May 26–29	Rhode Island convention: second session
May 29	Rhode Island ratifies 34-32 and proposes amendments

1791

December 15	Bill of Rights is incorporated into Constitution

THE ESSENTIAL ANTIFEDERALIST

Chapter I.

The Origin of Antifederalist Thought

Seventy-four delegates were chosen by twelve states to attend the Constitutional Convention in Philadelphia during the summer of 1787. (Rhode Island did not participate.) Of this number, nineteen declined their appointments, thirteen left early, and three refused to sign on September 17, 1787. It would be erroneous to infer that the failure of these thirty-six delegates to either participate or concur meant that they opposed the Constitution. The overwhelming majority cited personal reasons for their limited involvement and in fact worked hard for the adoption of the Constitution. However, at least eleven did oppose the Constitution and they became the original nucleus of the Antifederalist opposition.

Richard Henry Lee, the presumed author of the "Federal Farmer" essays, and Patrick Henry refused their appointments because they did not want to be associated with any attempt to radically alter the Articles of Confederation. Lee tried unsuccessfully to abort the plan when it was discussed in the Confederation Congress in late September of 1787 and he circulated letters to leading politicians urging that the plan be amended prior to adoption. Henry led the opposition to the new system in the Virginia Ratifying Convention in June of 1787. Like Lee and Henry, George Mason was a prominent revolutionary hero from Virginia. His refusal to sign the document proved a serious obstacle to the Federalists. Together, these three Antifederalists turned Virginia's convention into a close race. Another non-signer from Virginia was Edmund Randolph; he is difficult to place since he introduced the radical Virginia Plan at the Constitutional Convention and ultimately supported ratification in Virginia. However, his objections played an important role in the Antifederalist litany of complaints.

Another influential non-signer was Elbridge Gerry from Massachusetts. Like Lee and Mason he had signed the Declaration of Independence and his refusal to support the Constitution gave credence to the Antifederalist claim that the new plan betrayed the revolution of 1776. This theme receives careful articulation by "A Georgian." Gerry was certainly influential in encouraging the opposition to wage a

3

tough campaign in Massachusetts. He also influenced John Winthrop, whose "Agrippa" essays are among the most coherent of all in the Antifederalist literature. John Lansing and Robert Yates, presumed author of the "Brutus" essays and possible author of the "Sidney" essays, left the convention early and joined Governor George Clinton, author of the "Cato" letters, in an all-out assault on the Constitution in New York. They received considerable assistance from Melancton Smith, author of the "Plebian" essay. John Francis Mercer and Luther Martin left early and played a prominent part in the Maryland Ratifying Convention. Willie Jones and Richard Caswell from North Carolina refused their appointments. Along with Alexander Martin, who left early, they were successful in preventing adoption in North Carolina in August of 1788.

The "Dissent of the Pennsylvania Minority", written by George Bryan, author of the "Centinel" essays, captures the original Antifederalist argument concerning republicanism, federalism, capitalism, and democracy.

Z
(Philadelphia) Freeman's Journal
16 May, 1787

It seems to be generally felt and acknowledged, that the affairs of this country are in a ruinous situation. With vast resources in our hands, we are impoverished by the continual drain of money from us in foreign trade; our navigation is destroyed; our people are in debt and unable to pay; industry is at a stand; our public treaties are violated, and national faith, solemnly plighted to foreigners and to our own citizens, is no longer kept. We are discontented at home, and abroad we are insulted and despised.

In this exigency people naturally look up to the continental Convention, in hopes that their wisdom will provide some effectual remedy for this complication of disorders. It is perhaps the last opportunity which may be presented to us of establishing a permanent system of Continental Government; and, if this opportunity be lost, it is much to be feared that we shall fall into irretrievable confusion.

How the great object of their meeting is to be attained is a question which deserves to be seriously considered. Some men, there is reason to believe, have indulged the idea of reforming the United States by means of some refined and complicated schemes of organizing a future

Congress in a different form. These schemes, like many others with which we have been amused in times past, will be found to be merely visionary, and produce no lasting benefit. The error is not in the form of Congress, the mode of election, or the duration of the appointment of the members. The source of all our misfortunes is evidently in the want of power in Congress. To be convinced of this, we need only recollect the vigor, the energy, the unanimity of this country a few years past, even in the midst of a bloody war, *when Congress governed the continent*. We have gradually declined into feebleness, anarchy and wretchedness, from that period in which the several States began to exercise the sovereign and absolute right of treating the recommendations of Congress with contempt. From that time to the present, we have seen the great Federal Head of our union clothed with the authority of making treaties without the power of performing them; of contracting debts without being able to discharge them, or to bind others to discharge them; of regulating our trade, and providing for the general welfare of the people, in their concerns with foreign nations, without the power of restraining a single individual from the infraction of their orders, or restricting any trade, however injurious to the public welfare.

To remedy these evils, some have weakly imagined that it is necessary to annihilate the several States, and vest Congress with the absolute direction and government of the continent, as one single republic. This, however, would be impracticable and mischievous. In so extensive a country many local and internal regulations would be required, which Congress could not possibly attend to, and to which the States individually are fully competent; but those things which alike concern all the States, such as our foreign trade and foreign transactions, Congress should be fully authorized to regulate, and should be invested with the power of enforcing their regulations.

The ocean, which joins us to other nations, would seem to be the scene upon which Congress might exert its authority with the greatest benefit to the United States, as no one State can possibly claim any exclusive right in it. It has been long seen that the States individually cannot, with any success, pretend to regulate trade. The duties and restrictions which one State imposes, the neighboring States enable the merchants to elude; and besides, if they could be enforced, it would be highly unjust, that the duties collected in the port of one State should be applied to the sole use of that State in which they are collected, whilst the neighboring States, who have no ports for foreign commerce, consume a part of the goods imported, and thus in effect pay a part of the duties. Even if the recommendation of Congress had been attended to, which proposed the levying for the use of Congress five per centum on goods imported, to be collected by officers to be appointed by the individual States, it is more than probable that the laws would have been feebly executed. Men are not apt to be sufficiently attentive to the business of those who do not appoint, and cannot remove or control them; officers would naturally look up to the State which appointed them, and it is past a doubt that some of the States would esteem it no unpardonable sin to promote their own particular interest, or even that of particular men, to the injury of the United States.

Would it not then be right to vest Congress with the sole and exclusive power of regulating trade, of imposing port duties, of appointing officers to collect these duties, of erecting ports and deciding all questions by their own authority, which concern foreign trade and navigation upon the high seas? Some of those persons, who have conceived a narrow jealousy of Congress, and therefore have unhappily obstructed their exertions for the public welfare, may perhaps be startled at the idea, and make objections. To such I would answer, that our situation appears to be sufficiently desperate to justify the hazarding an experiment of anything which promises immediate relief. Let us try this for a few years; and if we find it attended with mischief, we can refuse to renew the power. But it appears to me to be necessary and useful; and I cannot think that it would in the least degree endanger our liberties. The representatives of the States in Congress are easily changed as often as we please, and they must necessarily be changed often. They would have little inclination and less ability to enterprise against the liberties of their constituents. This, no doubt, would induce the necessity of employing a small number of armed vessels to enforce the regulations of Congress, and would be the beginning of a Continental Navy; but a navy was never esteemed, like a standing army, dangerous to the liberty of the people.

To those who should object that this is too small a power to grant to Congress; that many more are necessary to be added to those which they already possess, I can only say, that perhaps they have not sufficiently reflected upon the great importance of the power proposed. That it would be of immense service to the country I have no doubt, as it is the only means by which our trade can be put on a footing with other nations; that it would in the event greatly strengthen the hands of Congress, I think is highly probable.

John Lansing, George Mason
and Luther Martin
(from Madison's records of the Federal Convention)
20 June, 1787

Mr. Lansing observed that the true question here was, whether the Convention would adhere to or depart from the foundation of the present Confederacy; and moved instead of the second resolution "that the powers of legislation be vested in the United States in Congress." He had already assigned two reasons against such an innovation as was proposed: first, the want of competent powers in the convention, and second, the state of the public mind. It had been observed by Mr. Madison in discussing the first point, that in two states the delegates to Congress were chosen by the people. Notwith-standing the first appearance of this remark, it had in fact no weight, as the delegates however chosen, did not represent the people merely as so many individuals; but as forming a sovereign state. Mr. Randolph put it, he said, on its true footing, namely, that the public safety superceded the scruple arising from the review of our powers. But in order to feel the force of this consideration, the same impression must be had of the public danger. He had not himself the same impression, and could not therefore dismiss his scruple. Mr. Wilson contended that as the convention were only to recommend, they might recommend what they pleased. He differed much from him; any act whatever of so respectable a body must have a great effect, and if it does not succeed, will be a source of great dissensions. He admitted that there was no certain criterion of the public mind on the subject. He therefore recurred to the evidence of it given by the opposition in the states to the scheme of an impost. It could not be expected that those possessing sovereignty could ever voluntarily part with it. It was not to be expected from any one state, much less from thirteen. He proceeded to make some observations on the plan itself and the arguments urged in support of it. The point of representation could receive no elucidation from the case of England. The corruption of the boroughs did not proceed from their comparative smallness: but from the actual fewness of the inhabitants, some of them not having more than one or two: a great inequality existed in the counties of England. Yet the like com-plaint of peculiar corruption in the small ones had not been made. It had been said that Congress represents the state prejudices; will not any other body whether chosen by the legislatures or people of the states, also represent their prejudices? It had been asserted by his colleague Colonel Hamilton, that there was no coincidence of interests among the large states that ought to excite fears of oppression in the smaller. If it were true that such a uniformity of interests existed among the states, there was equal safety for all of them, whether the representation remained as heretofore, or were proportioned as now proposed. It is proposed that the general legislature shall have a negative on the laws of the states. Is it conceivable that there will be leisure for such a task? There will on the most moderate calculation, be as many acts sent up from the states as there are days in the year. Will the members of the general legislature be competent judges? Will a gentleman from Georgia be a judge of the expediency of a law which is to operate in New Hampshire? Such a negative would be more injurious than that of Great Britain heretofore was. It is said that the national government must have the influence arising from the grant of offices and honors. In order to render such a government effectual he believed such an influence to be necessary. But if the states will not agree to it, it is in vain; worse than in vain to make the proposition. If this influence is to be attained, the states must be entirely abolished. Will anyone say this would ever be agreed to? He doubted whether any general government equally beneficial to all can be attained. That now under consideration, he is sure, must be utterly unattainable. He had another objection. The system was too novel and complex. No man could foresee what its operation will be either with respect to the general government or the state governments. One or other it has been surmised must absorb the whole.

Col. Mason did not expect this point would have been reagitated. The essential differences between the two plans, had been clearly stated. The principal objections against that of Mr. Randolph were the *want of power* and the *want of practicability*. There can be no weight in the first as the fiat is not to be *here*, but in the people. He thought with his colleague, Mr. Randolph, that there were besides certain crises, in which all the ordinary cautions yielded to public necessity. He gave as example the eventual treaty with Great Britain in forming which the commissioners of the United States had boldly disregarded the improvident shackles of Congress and given to their country an honorable and happy peace, and instead of being censured for the transgression of their powers, had raised to themselves a monument more durable than brass. The *impracticability* of gaining the public concurrence he thought was still more groundless. Mr. Lansing had cited the attempts of Congress to gain an enlargement of their powers, and had inferred from the miscarriage of these attempts, the hopelessness of the plan which he (Mr. Lansing) opposed. He thought a very different inference ought to have been drawn, *viz.*, that the plan which he espoused, and which proposed to augment the powers of Congress, never could be expected to succeed. He meant not to throw any reflections on Congress as a body, much less on any particular members of it. He meant however to speak his sentiments without reserve on this subject; it was a privilege of age, and perhaps the only compensation which nature had given for the privation of so many other enjoyments; and he should not scruple to exercise it freely. Is it to be thought that the people of America, so watchful over their interests, so jealous of their liberties, will give up their all, will surrender both the sword and the purse, to the same body, and that too not chosen immediately by themselves? They never will. They never ought. Will they trust such a body with the regulation of their trade, with the regulation of their taxes, with all the other great powers which are in contemplation? Will they give unbounded confidence to a secret journal—to the intrigues—to the factions which in the nature of things appertain to such an Assembly? If any man doubts the existence of these characters of Congress, let him consult their journals for the years '78, '79, and '80. It will be said, that if the people are averse to parting with power, why is it hoped that they will part with it to a national legislature? The proper answer is that in this case they do not part with power; they only transfer it from one set of immediate representatives to another set. Much has been said of the unsettled state of the mind of the people. He believed the mind of the people of America, as elsewhere, was unsettled as to some points, but settled as to others. In two points he was sure it was well settled: first, in an attachment to republican government, and second, in an attachment to more than one branch in the legislature. Their constitutions accord so generally in both these circumstances, that they seem almost to have been preconcerted. This must either have been a miracle, or have resulted from the genius of the people. The only exceptions to the establishment of two branches in the legislatures are the state of Pennsylvania and Congress and the latter the only single one not chosen by the people themselves. What has been the consequence? The people have been constantly averse to giving that body further powers. It was acknowledged by Mr. Paterson that his plan could not be enforced without military coercion. Does he consider the force of this concession? The most jarring elements of nature, fire and water themselves, are not more incompatible than such a mixture of civil liberty and military execution. Will the militia march from one state to another in order to collect the arrears of taxes from the delinquent members of the republic? Will they maintain an army for this purpose?

Will not the citizens of the invaded state assist one another till they rise as one man, and shake off the Union altogether? Rebellion is the only case in which the military force of the state can be properly exerted against its citizens. In one point of view he was struck with horror at the prospect of recurring to this expedient. To punish the nonpayment of taxes with death was a severity not yet adopted by despotism itself; yet this unexampled cruelty would be mercy compared to a military collection of revenue, in which the bayonet could make no discrimination between the innocent and the guilty. He took this occasion to repeat that notwithstanding his solicitude to establish a national government, he never would agree to abolish the state governments or render them absolutely insignificant. They were as necessary as the general government and he would be equally careful to preserve them. He was aware of the difficulty of drawing the line between them, but hoped it was not insurmountable. The convention, though comprising so many distinguished characters, could not be expected to make a faultless government. And he would prefer trusting to posterity the amendment of its defects, rather than push the experiment too far.

Mr. Luther Martin agreed with Col. Mason as to the importance of the state governments. He would support them at the expense of the general government which was instituted for the purpose of that support. He saw no necessity for two branches, and if it existed Congress might be organized into two. He considered Congress as representing the people, being chosen by the legislatures, who were chosen by the people. At any rate, Congress represented the legislatures; and it was the legislatures not the people who refused to enlarge their powers. Nor could the rule of voting have been the ground of objection; otherwise ten of the states must always have been ready to place further confidence in Congress. The causes of repugnance must therefore be looked for elsewhere. At the separation from the British Empire, the people of America preferred the establishment of themselves into thirteen separate sovereignties instead of incorporating themselves into one; to these they look up for the security of their lives, liberties and properties; to these they must look. The federal government they formed to defend the whole against foreign nations in case of war, and to defend the lesser states against the ambition of the larger. They are afraid of granting powers unnecessarily, lest they should defeat the original end of the union, lest the powers should prove dangerous to the sovereignties of the particular states which the union was meant to support, and expose the lesser to being swallowed up by the larger. He conceived also that the people of the states having already vested their powers in their respective legislatures, could not resume them without a dissolution of their governments. He was against conventions in the states, but was not against assisting states against rebellious subjects. He thought the *federal* plan of Mr. Paterson did not require coercion more than the *national one*, as the latter must depend for the deficiency of its revenues on requisitions and quotas, and that a national judiciary extended into the states would be ineffectual, and would be viewed with a jealousy inconsistent with its usefulness.

George Mason
Objections to the Constitution of Government formed by the Convention
1787

There is no declaration of rights; and, the laws of the general government being paramount to the laws and constitutions of the several states, the declarations of rights in the separate states are no security. Nor are the people secured even in the enjoyment of the benefit of the common law, which stands here upon no other foundation than its having been adopted by the respective acts forming the constitutions of the several states.

In the House of Representatives there is not the substance, but the shadow only of representation, which can never produce proper information in the legislature, or inspire confidence in the people. The laws will, therefore, be generally made by men little concerned in, and unacquainted with, their effects and consequences.*

The Senate have the power of altering all money bills, and of originating appropriations of money, and the salaries of the officers of their own appointment, in conjunction with the President of the United States, although they are not the representatives of the people, or amenable to them. These, with their other great powers, (*viz.*, their powers in the appointment of ambassadors, and all public officers, in making treaties, and in trying all impeachments) their influence upon, and connection with, the supreme executive from these causes; their duration of office; and their being a constant existing body, almost

---

*This Objection has been in some Degree lessened by an Amendment, often before refused, and at last made by an Erasure, after the Engrossment upon Parchment, of the word *forty*, and inserting *thirty*, in the third clause of the second section of the first article.

continually sitting, joined with their being one complete branch of the legislature, will destroy any balance in the government, and enable them to accomplish what usurpations they please upon the rights and liberties of the people.

The judiciary of the United States is so constructed and extended as to absorb and destroy the judiciaries of the several states, thereby rendering laws as tedious, intricate, and expensive, and justice as unattainable, by a great part of the community, as in England; and enabling the rich to oppress and ruin the poor.

The President of the United States has no constitutional council (a thing unknown in any safe and regular government). He will therefore be unsupported by proper information and advice, and will generally be directed by minions and favorites, or he will become a tool to the Senate, or a council of state will grow out of the principal officers of the great departments, the worst and most dangerous of all ingredients for such a council, in a free country; they may be induced to join in any dangerous or oppressive measures, to shelter themselves, and prevent an inquiry into their own misconduct in office. Whereas, had a constitutional council been formed (as was proposed) of six members, *viz.*, two from the Eastern, two from the Middle, and two from the Southern States, to be appointed by vote of the states in the House of Representatives, with the same duration and rotation of office as the Senate, the executive would always have had safe and proper information and advice. The president of such a council might have acted as Vice-President of the United States, *pro tempore*, upon any vacancy or disability of the chief magistrate, and long-continued sessions of the Senate would in a great measure have been prevented. From this fatal defect of a constitutional council has arisen the improper power of the Senate in the appointment of the public officers, and the alarming dependence and connection between that branch of the legislature and the supreme executive. Hence also sprang that unnecessary officer the Vice-President, who, for want of other employment, is made president of the Senate, thereby dangerously blending the executive and legislative powers, besides always giving to some one of the states an unnecessary and unjust preeminence over the others.

The President of the United States has the unrestrained power of granting pardon for treason, which may be sometimes exercised to screen from punishment those whom he had secretly instigated to commit the crime, and thereby prevent a discovery of his own guilt. By declaring all treaties supreme laws of the land, the executive and the Senate have, in many cases, an exclusive power of legislation which might have been avoided by proper distinctions with respect to treaties, and requiring the assent of the House of Representatives where it could be done with safety.

By requiring only a majority to make all commercial and navigation laws, the five Southern States (whose produce and circumstances are totally different from those of the eight Northern and Eastern States) will be ruined; for such rigid and premature regulations may be made, as will enable the merchants of the Northern and Eastern States not only to demand an exorbitant freight, but to monopolize the purchase of the commodities, at their own price, for many years, to the great injury of the landed interest, and the impoverishment of the people. And the danger is the greater, as the gain on one side will be in proportion to the loss on the other; whereas, requiring two thirds of the members present in both houses would have produced mutual moderation, promoted the general interest, and removed an insuperable objection to the adoption of the government.

Under their own construction of the general clause at the end of the enumerated powers, the Congress may grant monopolies in trade and commerce, constitute new crimes, inflict unusual and severe punishments, and extend their power as far as they shall think proper; so that the state legislatures have no security for the powers now presumed to remain to them, or the people for their rights. There is no declaration of any kind for preserving the liberty of the press, the trial by jury in civil cases, nor against the danger of standing armies in time of peace.

The state legislatures are restrained from laying export duties on their own produce, the general legislature is restrained from prohibiting the further importation of slaves for twenty-odd years, though such importations render the United States weaker, more vulnerable, and less capable of defense. Both the general legislature and the state legislatures are expressly prohibited making *ex post facto* laws, though there never was, nor can be, a legislature but must and will make such laws when necessity and the public safety require them, which will hereafter be a breach of all the constitutions in the Union and afford precedents for other innovations.

This government will commence in a moderate aristocracy. It is at present impossible to foresee whether it will, in its operation, produce a monarchy or a corrupt oppressive aristocracy. It will most probably vibrate some years between the two, and then terminate in the one or the other.

Robert Yates and John Lansing
Reasons of Dissent
(A Letter to George Clinton, Governor of New York)
Albany, 21 December, 1787

Sir,

We do ourselves the honor to advise your excellency, that in pursuance of concurrent resolutions of the honorable senate and assembly, we have, together with Mr. Hamilton, attended the convention, appointed for revising the Articles of Confederation, and reporting amendments to the same.

It is with the sincerest concern we observe, that in the prosecution of the important objects of our mission, we have been reduced to the disagreeable alternative, of either exceeding the powers delegated to us, and giving our assent to measures which we conceived destructive of the political happiness of the citizens of the United States, or opposing our opinion to that of a body of respectable men, to whom those citizens had given the most unequivocal proofs of confidence. Thus circumstanced, under these impressions, to have hesitated, would have been to be culpable. We therefore gave the principles of the constitution, which has received the sanction of a majority of the convention, our decided and unreserved dissent; but we must candidly confess, that we should have been equally opposed to any system, however modified, which had in object the consolidation of the United States into one government.

We beg leave briefly to state some cogent reasons, which, among others, influenced us to decide against a consolidation of the states. These are reducible into two heads.

First. The limited and well-defined powers under which we acted, and which could not, on any posible construction, embrace an idea of such magnitude, as to assent to a general constitution, in subversion of that of the state.

Second. A conviction of the impracticability of establishing a general government, pervading every part of the United States, and extending essential benefits to all.

Our powers were explicit, and confined to the *sole and express purpose of revising the Articles of Confederation*, and reporting such alterations and provisions therein as should render the federal constitution adequate to the exigencies of government and the preservation of the Union.

From these expressions we were led to believe that a system of consolidated government could not, in the remotest degree, have been in contemplation of the legislature of this state; for that so important a trust as the adopting measures which tended to deprive the state government of its most essential rights of sovereignty, and to place it in a dependent situation, could not have been confided by implication; and the circumstance, that the acts of the convention were to receive a state approbation in the last resort, forcibly corroborated the opinion, that our powers could not involve the subversion of a constitution, which being immediately derived from the people, could only be abolished by their express consent, and not by a legislature, possessing authority vested in them for its preservation. Nor could we suppose that if it had been the intention of the legislature to abrogate the existing Confederation, they would, in such pointed terms, have directed the attention of their delegates to the revision and amendment of it, in total exclusion of every other idea.

Reasoning in this manner, we were of the opinion that the leading feature of every amendment ought to be the preservation of the individual states, in their uncontrolled constitutional rights, and that in reserving these, a mode might have been devised of granting to the Confederacy, the monies arising from a general system of revenue, the power of regulating commerce, and enforcing the observance of foreign treaties, and other necessary matters of less moment.

Exclusive of our objections, originating from the want of power, we entertained an opinion, that a general government, however guarded by declarations of rights, or cautionary provisions, must unavoidably, in a short time, be productive of the destruction of the civil liberty of such citizens who could be effectually coerced by it; by reason of the extensive territory of the United States, the dispersed situation of its inhabitants, and the insuperable difficulty of controlling or counteracting the views of a set of men (however unconstitutional and oppressive their acts might be) possessed of all the powers of government; and who, from their remoteness from their constituents, and necessary permanency of office, could not be supposed to be uniformly actuated by an attention to their welfare and happiness; that however wise and energetic the principles of the general government might be, the extremities of the United States could not be kept in due submission and obedience to its laws, at the distance of many hundred miles from the seat of government; that if the general legislature was composed of so numerous a body of men, as to represent the interests of all the inhabitants of the United States, in the usual and true ideas of representation, the expense of supporting it would become intolerably burdensome; and that, if a few only were vested with a power of legislation, the interests of a great majority of the inhabitants of the United States must necessarily be unknown; or, if known, even in the first stages of the operations of the new government, unattended to.

These reasons were, in our opinion, conclusive against any system of consolidated government. To that recommended by the convention, we suppose most of them very forcibly apply.

It is not our intention to pursue this subject further than merely to explain our conduct in the discharge of the trust which the honorable legislature reposed in us. Interested, however, as we are, in common with our fellow citizens, in the result, we cannot forbear to declare that we have the strongest apprehensions that a government so organized, as that recommended by the convention, cannot afford that security to equal and permanent liberty which we wished to make an invariable object of our pursuit.

We were not present at the completion of the new constitution; but before we left the convention, its principles were so well established as to convince us that no alteration was to be expected to conform it to our ideas of expediency and safety. A persuasion, that our further attendance would be fruitless, and unavailing, rendered us less solicitous to return.

We have thus explained our motives for opposing the adoption of the national constitution, which we conceived it our duty to communicate to your Excellency, to be submitted to the consideration of the honorable legislature.

Luther Martin
Objections
(from Yates' records of the Federal Convention)
27 and 28 June, 1787

(Mr. Martin, the attorney general from Maryland, spoke on this subject upwards of three hours. As his arguments were too diffuse, and in many instances desultory, it was not possible to trace him through the whole, or to methodize his ideas into a systematic or argumentative arrangement. I shall therefore only note such points as I conceive merit most particular notice.)

The question is important (said Mr. Martin), and I have already expressed my sentiments on the subject. My opinion is, that the general government ought to protect and secure the state governments; others, however, are of a different sentiment, and reverse the principle.

The present reported system is a perfect medley of confederated and national government, without example and without precedent. Many who wish the general government to protect the state governments, are anxious to have the line of jurisdiction well drawn and defined, so that they may not clash. This suggests the necessity of having this line well detailed; possibly this may be done. If we do this, the people will be convinced that we meant well to the state governments; and should there be any defects, they will trust a future convention with the power of making further amendments.

A general government may operate on individuals in cases of general concern, and still be federal. This distinction is with the states, as states, represented by the people of those states. States will take care of their internal police and local concerns. The general government has no interest, but the protection of the whole. Every other government must fail. We are proceeding in forming this government as if there were no state governments at all. The states must approve, or you will have none at all. I have never heard of a confederacy having two legislative branches. Even the celebrated Mr. Adams, who talks so much of checks and balances, does not suppose it necessary in a confederacy. Public and domestic debts are our great distress. The treaty between Virginia and Maryland about the navigation of the Chesapeake and Potomac, is no infraction of the confederacy. The cornerstone of a federal government is *equality* of votes. States may surrender this right; but if they do, their liberties are lost. If I err on this point, it is the error of the head, not of the heart.

The first principle of government is founded on the natural rights of individuals, and in perfect equality. Locke, Vattel, Lord Somers, and Dr. Priestly all confirm this principle. This principle of equality, when applied to individuals, is lost in some degree, when he becomes a member of a society, to which it is transferred; and this society, by the name of state or kingdom, is, with respect to others, again on a perfect footing of equality: a right to govern themselves as they please. Nor can any other state, of right, deprive them of this equality. If such a state confederates, it is intended for the good of the whole; and if it again confederates, those rights must be well guarded. Nor can any state demand a surrender of any of those rights; if it can, equality is already destroyed. We must treat as free states with each other upon the same terms of equality that men originally formed themselves into societies. Vattel, Rutherford, and Locke are united in support of the position, that states, as to each other, are in a state of nature.

Thus, says Mr. Martin, have I travelled with the most respectable authorities in support of principles, all tending to prove the equality of independent states. This is equally applicable to the smallest as well as the largest states on the true principles of reciprocity and political freedom.

Unequal confederacies can never produce good effects. Apply this to the Virginia Plan. Out of the number 90, Virginia has 16 votes, Massachusetts 14, Pennsylvania 12—in all 42. Add to this a state having four votes, and it gives a majority in the general legislature. Consequently a combination of these states will govern the remaining nine or ten states. Where is the safety and independency of those states? Pursue this subject farther. The executive is to be appointed by the legislature, and becomes the executive in consequence of this undue influence. And hence flows the appointment of all your officers, civil, military, and judicial. The executive is also to have a negative on all laws. Suppose the possibility of a combination of ten states; he negatives a law; it is totally lost, because those states cannot form two-thirds of the legislature. I am willing to give up private interest for the public good, but I must be satisfied first that it is the public interest. Who can decide this point? A majority only of the union.

The Lacedemonians insisted in the Amphictionic council to exclude some of the smaller states from a right to vote in order that they might tyrannize over them. If the plan now on the table be adopted, three states in the union have the control, and they may make use of their power when they please.

If there exists no separate interests, there is no danger of an equality of votes; and if there be danger, the smaller states cannot yield. If the foundation of the existing confederation is well laid, powers may be added. You may safely add a third story to a house where the foundation is good. Read then the votes and proceedings of Congress on forming the confederation: Virginia only was opposed to the principle of equality; the smaller states yielded rights, not the large states; they gave up their claim to the unappropriated lands with the tenderness of the mother recorded by Solomon; they sacrificed affection to the preservation of others. New Jersey and Maryland rendered more essential services during the war than many of the larger states. The partial representation in Congress is not the cause of its weakness, but the want of power. I would not trust a government organized upon the reported plan for all the slaves of Carolina or the horses and oxen of Massachusetts. Price says, that laws made by one man or a set of men, and not by common consent, is slavery. And it is so when applied to states, if you give them an unequal representation. What are called human feelings in this instance are only the feelings of ambition and the lust of power.

On federal grounds, it is said, that a minority will govern a majority; but on the Virginia plan a minority would tax a majority. In a federal government, a majority of states must and ought to tax. In the local government of states, counties may be unequal; still numbers, not property, govern. What is the government now forming, over states or persons? As to the latter, their rights cannot be the object of a general government. These are already secured by their guardians, the state governments. The general government is therefore intended only to protect and guard the rights of the states as states.

This general government, I believe, is the first upon earth which gives checks against democracies or aristocracies. The only necessary check in a general government ought to be a restraint to prevent its absorbing the powers of the state governments. Representation on federal principles can only flow from state societies. Representation and taxation are ever inseparable, not according to the quantum of property, but the quantum of freedom.

Will the representatives of a state forget state interests? The mode of election cannot change it. These prejudices cannot be eradicated. Your general government cannot be just or equal upon the Virginia Plan, unless you abolish state interests. If this cannot be done, you must go back to principles purely federal.

On this latter ground, the state legislatures and their constituents will have no interests to pursue different from the general government, and both will be interested to support each other. Under these ideas can it be expected that the people can approve the Virginia Plan? But it is said, the people, not the state legislatures, will be called upon for approbation, with an evident design to separate the interest of the governors from the governed. What must be the consequence? Anarchy and confusion. We lose the idea of the powers with which we are entrusted. The legislatures must approve. By them it must, on your own plan, be laid before the people. How will such a government, over so many great states, operate? Wherever new settlements have been formed in large states, they immediately want to shake off their independency. Why? Because the government is too remote for their good. The people want it nearer home.

The basis of all ancient and modern confederacies is the freedom and the independency of the states composing it. The states forming the Amphictionic council were equal, though Lacedemon, one of the greatest states, attempted the exclusion of three of the lesser states from this right. The plan reported, it is true, only intends to diminish those rights, not to annihilate them. It was the ambition and power of the great Grecian states which at last ruined this respectable council. The states as societies are ever respectful. Has Holland or Switzerland ever complained of the equality of the states which compose their respective confederacies? Bern and Zurich are larger than the remaining eleven cantons (so are many of the states of Germany); and yet their governments are not complained of. Bern alone might usurp the whole power of the Helvetic confederacy, but she is contented still with being equal.

The admission of the larger states into the confederation, on the principles of equality, is dangerous. But on the Virginia system, it is ruinous and destructive. Still it is the true interest of all the states to confederate. It is their joint efforts which must protect and secure us from foreign danger, and give us peace and harmony at home.

(Here Mr. Martin entered into a detail of the comparative powers of each state, and stated their probable weakness and strength.)

At the beginning of our troubles with Great Britain, the smaller states were attempted to be cajoled to submit to the views of that nation, lest the larger states should usurp their rights. We then answered them, your present plan is slavery, which, on the remote prospect of a distant evil, we will not submit to.

I would rather confederate with any single state, than submit to the Virginia Plan. But we are already confederated, and no power on earth can dissolve it but by the consent of *all* the contracting powers, and four states, on this floor, have already declared their opposition to annihilate it. Is the old confederation dissolved because some of the states wish a new confederation?

Elbridge Gerry
Objections
(A Letter to the Massachusetts State Legislature)
New York, 18 October, 1787

Gentlemen,

I have the honor to enclose, pursuant to my commission, the Constitution proposed by the Federal Convention.

To this system I gave my dissent, and shall submit my objections to the honorable Legislature.

It was painful for me, on a subject of such national importance, to differ from the respectable members who signed the constitution; but conceiving as I did, that the liberties of America were not secured by the system, it was my duty to oppose it.

My principal objections to the plan are, that there is no adequate provision for a representation of the people; that they have no security for the right of election; that some of the powers of the Legislature are ambiguous, and others indefinite and dangerous; that the Executive is blended with and will have an undue influence over the Legislature; that the judicial department will be oppressive; that treaties of the highest importance may be formed by the President with the advice of two thirds of a *quorum* of the Senate; and that the system is without the security of a bill of rights. These are objections which are not local, but apply equally to all the States.

As the Convention was called for "the *sole* and *express* purpose of revising the Articles of Confederation, and reporting to Congress and the several Legislatures such alterations and provisions as shall render the Federal Constitution adequate to the exigencies of government and the preservation of the union," I did not conceive that these powers extended to the formation of the plan proposed; but the Convention being of a different *opinion*, I acquiesced in *it*, being fully convinced that to preserve the union, an efficient government was indispensably necessary; and that it would be difficult to make proper amendments to the Articles of Confederation.

The Constitution proposed has few, if any *federal* features, but is rather a system of *national* government. Nevertheless, in many respects, I think it has great merit, and, by proper amendments, may be adapted to the "exigencies of government," and preservation of liberty.

The question on this plan involves others of the highest importance. First, whether there shall be a dissolution of the *federal* government? Second, whether the several State Governments shall be so altered as in effect to be dissolved? Third, whether in lieu of the *federal* and *State* Governments, the *national* Constitution now proposed shall be substituted without amendment? Never perhaps were a people called on to decide a question of greater magnitude. Should the citizens of America adopt the plan as it now stands, their liberties may be lost; or should they reject it altogether, Anarchy may ensue. It is evident, therefore, that they should not be precipitate in their decisions; that the subject should be well understood, lest they should refuse to *support* the government, after having *hastily* accepted it.

If those who are in favor of the Constitution, as well as those who are against it, should preserve moderation, their discussions may afford much information and finally direct to a happy issue.

It may be urged by some, that an *implicit* confidence should be placed in the Convention. But, however respectable the members may be who signed the Constitution, it must be admitted that a free people are the proper guardians of their rights and liberties, that the greatest men may err, and that their errors are sometimes of the greatest magnitude.

Others may suppose that the Constitution may be safely adopted, because therein provision is made to *amend* it. But cannot *this object* be better attained before a ratification than after it? And should a *free* people adopt a form of Government under conviction that it wants amendment?

And some may conceive, that, if the plan is not accepted by the people, they will not unite in another: But surely while they have the power to amend, they are not under the necessity of rejecting it.

I have been detained here longer than I expected, but shall leave this place in a day or two for Massachusetts, and on my arrival shall submit the reasons (if required by the Legislature) on which my objections are grounded.

I shall only add that, as the welfare of the union requires a better Constitution than the Confederation, I shall think it my duty as a citizen of Massachusetts, to support that which shall be finally adopted, sincerely hoping it will secure the liberty and happiness of America.

I have the honor to be, Gentlemen, with the highest respect for the honorable Legislature and yourselves, your most obedient, and very humble servant.

Richard Henry Lee
Objections
(A Letter to Edmund Randolph, Governor of Virginia)
New York, 16 October, 1787

I was duly honored with your favor of Sept. 17, from Philadelphia, which should have been acknowledged long before now, if the nature of the business that it related to had not required time.

The establishment of the new plan of government, in its present form, is a question that involves such immense consequences to the present times, and to posterity, that it calls for the deepest attention of the best and wisest friends of their country and of mankind; if it be found good after mature deliberation, adopt it; if wrong, amend it at all events, for to say (as many do) that a bad government must be established for fear of anarchy, is really saying, that we must kill ourselves for fear of dying. Experience and the actual state of things, show that there is no difficulty in procuring a general convention, the late one being collected without any obstruction. Nor does external war or internal discord prevent the most cool, collected, full, and fair discussion of this all-important subject. If with infinite ease a convention was obtained to prepare a system, why may not another with equal ease be procured to make proper and necessary amendments? Good government is not the work of a short time, or of sudden thought. From Moses to Montesquieu the greatest geniuses have been employed on this difficult subject, and yet experience has shown capital defects in the system produced for the government of mankind. But since it is neither prudent nor easy to make frequent changes in government, and as bad governments have been generally found the most fixed, so it becomes of the last consequence to frame the first establishment upon ground the most unexceptionable, and such as the best theories with experience justify; not trusting as our new constitution does, and as many approve of doing, to time and future events to correct evils, that both reason and experience in similar cases, point out in the new system. It has hitherto been supposed a fundamental maxim that in governments rightly balanced, the different branches of a legislature should be unconnected, and that the legislative and executive powers should be separate; in the new constitution, the president and senate have all the executive and two thirds of the legislative power. In some weighty instances (as making all kinds of treaties which are to be the laws of the land) they have the whole legislative and executive powers. They jointly appoint all officers civil and military, and they (the senate) try all impeachments either of their own members, or of the officers appointed by themselves.

Is there not a most formidable combination of power thus created in a few, and can the most critical eye, if a candid one, discover responsibility in this potent corps? Or will any sensible man say that great power without responsibility can be given to rulers with safety to liberty? It is most clear that the parade of impeachment is nothing to them, or any of them; as little restraint is to be found, I presume, from the fear of offending constituents. The president is for four years duration and Virginia (for example) has one vote of thirteen in the choice of him, and this thirteenth vote not of the people, but electors, two removes from the people. The senate is a body of six years duration, and as in choice of president, the largest state has but a thirteenth vote, so is it in the choice of senators. This latter statement is adduced to show that responsibility is as little to be apprehended from amenability to constituents, as from the terror of impeachment. You are therefore, sir, well warranted in saying, either a monarchy, or aristocracy will be generated, perhaps the most grievous system of government may arise. It cannot be denied with truth that this new constitution is, in its first principles, highly and dangerously oligarchic; and it is a point agreed that a government of the few, is, of all governments, the worst. The only check to be found in favor of the democratic principle in this system is the house of representatives, which I believe may justly be called a mere shred or rag of representation; it being obvious to the least examination that smallness of number and great comparative disparity of power, renders that house of little effect to promote good, or restrain bad government. But what is the power given to this ill-constructed body? To judge of what may be for the general welfare, and such judgments when made, the acts of congress become supreme laws of the land. This seems a power co-extensive with every possible object of human legislation. Yet there is no restraint in form of a bill of rights, to secure (what doctor Blackstone calls) that residuum of human rights, which is not intended to be given up to society, and which indeed is not necessary to be given for any good social purpose. The rights of conscience, the freedom of the press, and the trial by jury are at mercy. It is there stated that in criminal cases, the trial shall be by jury. But how? In the state. What then becomes of the jury of the vicinage or at least from the county in the first instance, the states being from 50 to 700 miles in extent? This mode of trial even in criminal cases may be greatly impaired, and in civil cases the inference is strong that it may be altogether omitted, as the constitution positively assumes it in criminal and is silent about it in civil causes. Nay, it is more strongly discountenanced in civil cases by giving the supreme court an appeals jurisdiction both as to law and fact.

Judge Blackstone in his learned commentaries says, this is the most transcendent privilege which any subject can enjoy or wish for, that he cannot be affected either in his property, his liberty, his person, but by the unanimous consent of twelve of his neighbors and equals. A constitution, that I may venture to affirm, has under providence, secured the just liberties of this nation for a long succession of ages. The impartial administration of justice, which secures both our persons and our properties, is the great end of civil society. But if that be entirely entrusted to the magistracy, a select body of men, and those generally selected by the prince, or such as enjoy the highest offices of the state, these decisions, in spite of their own natural integrity, will have frequently an involuntary bias towards those of their own rank and dignity. It is not to be expected from human nature, that the few should always be attentive to the good of the many. The learned judge further says, that every tribunal selected for the decision of facts is a step towards establishing aristocracy, the most oppressive of all governments. The answer to these objections is, that the new legislature may provide remedies! But as they may, so they may not, and if they did, a succeeding assembly may repeal the provisions. The evil is found resting upon constitutional bottom, and the remedy upon the mutable ground of legislation, revocable at any annual meeting. It is the more unfortunate that this great security of human rights, the trial by jury, should be weakened in this system, as power is unnecessarily given in the second section of the third article, to call people from their own country in all cases of controversy about property between citizens of different states and foreigners, with citizens of the United States, to be tried in a distant court where the congress meets. For although inferior congressional courts may for the above parties be instituted in the different states, yet this is a matter altogether in the pleasure of the new legislature, so that if they please not to institute them, or if they do not regulate the right of appeal reasonably, the people will be exposed to endless oppression, and the necessity of submitting in multitudes of cases, to pay unjust demands, rather than follow suitors, through great expense, to far distant tribunals, and to be determined upon there, as it may be, without a jury. In this congressional legislature a bare majority of votes, can enact commercial laws, so that the representatives of the seven northern states, as they will have a majority, can by law create the most oppressive monopoly upon the five southern states, whose circumstances and productions are essentially different from theirs, although not a single man of these voters are the representatives of, or amenable to the people of, the southern states. Can such a set of men be, with the least color of truth, called a representative of those they make laws for? It is supposed that the policy of the northern states, will prevent such abuses. . . .

It having been found from universal experience, that the most expressed declarations and reservations are necessary to protect the just rights and liberty of mankind from the silent powerful and ever active conspiracy of those who govern; and it appearing to be the sense of the good people of America, by the various bills or declarations of rights whereon the government of the greater number of states are founded: that such precautions are necessary to restrain and regulate the exercise of the great powers given to rulers. In conformity with these principles, and from respect for the public sentiment on this subject, it is submitted, that the new constitution proposed for the government of the United States be bottomed upon a declaration or bill of rights, clearly and precisely stating the principles upon which this social compact is founded, to wit: that the rights of conscience in matters of religion ought not to be violated, that the freedom of the press shall be secured, that the trial by jury in criminal and civil cases, and the modes prescribed by the common law for the safety of life in criminal prosecutions shall be held sacred, that standing armies in times of peace are dangerous to liberty, and ought not to be permitted unless assented to by two-thirds of the members composing each house of the legislature under the new constitution, that the elections should be free and frequent, that the right administration of justice should be secured by the independence of the judges, that excessive bail, excessive fines, or cruel and unusual punishments should not be demanded or inflicted, that the right of the people to assemble peaceably for the purpose of petitioning the legislature shall not be prevented, that the citizens shall not be exposed to unreasonable searches, seizure of their persons, houses, papers or property; and it is necessary for the good of society, that the administration of government be conducted with all possible maturity of judgment, for which reason it has been the practice of civilized nations and so determined by every state in the Union, that a council of state or privy council should be appointed to advise and assist in the arduous business assigned to the executive power. Therefore let the new constitution be so amended as to admit the appointment of a privy council to consist of eleven members chosen by the president, but responsible for the advice they may give. For which purpose the advice given shall be entered in a council book, and signed by the giver in all affairs of great moment, and that the counselors act under an oath of office. In order to prevent the dangerous blending of the legislative and executive powers, and to secure responsibility, the privy, and not the senate, shall be joined with the president in the appointment of all officers civil and military under the new constitution, that the constitution be so altered as not to admit the creation of a vice president, when duties as assigned may be discharged by the privy council, except in the instance of proceedings in the senate, which may be supplied by a speaker chosen from the body of senators by themselves as usual, that so may be avoided the establishment of a great officer of state, who is sometimes to be joined with the legislature, and sometimes administer the government, rendering responsibility difficult, besides giving unjust and needless pre-eminence to that state from whence this officer may have come, that such parts of the new constitution be amended as provide imperfectly for the trial of criminals by a jury of the vicinage, and so supply the omission of a jury trial in civil causes or disputes about property between individuals, whereby the common law is directed, and as generally it is secured by the several state constitutions. That such parts of the new constitution be amended as permit the vexatious and oppressive callings of citizens from their own country, and all controversies between citizens of different states and between citizens and foreigners, to be tried in a far distant court, and as it may be without a jury, whereby in a multitude of cases, the circumstances of distance and expense, may compel numbers to submit to the most unjust and ill founded demand. That in order to secure the rights of the people more effectually from violation, the power and respectability of the house of representatives be increased, by increasing the number of delegates to that house where the popular interest must chiefly depend for protection, that the constitution be so amended as to increase the number of votes necessary to determine questions in cases where a bare majority may be seduced by strong motives of interest to injure and oppress the minority of the community as in commercial regulations, where advantage may be taken of circumstances to ordain rigid and premature laws that will in effect amount to monopolies, to the great impoverishment of those states whose peculiar situation expose them to such injuries.

An Old Whig
Essay VII
(Philadelphia) Independent Gazette
28 November, 1787

Many people seem to be convinced that the proposed Constitution is liable to a number of important objections; that there are defects in it which ought to be supplied, and errors which ought to be amended, but they apprehend that we must either receive this Constitution in its present form, or be left without any continental government whatsoever. To be sure, if this were the case, it would be most prudent for us, like a man who is wedded to a bad wife, to submit to our misfortune with patience, and make the best of a bad bargain. But if we will summon up resolution sufficient to examine into our true circumstances, we shall find that we are not in so deplorable a situation as people have been taught to believe, from the suggestions of interested men, who wish to force down the proposed plan of government without delay, for the purpose of providing offices for themselves and their friends. We shall find that, with a little wisdom and patience, we have it yet in our power not only to establish a federal constitution, but to establish a good one.

It is true that the continental convention has directed their proposed Constitution to be laid before a convention of delegates to be chosen in each state, "for their assent and ratification," which seems to preclude the idea of any power in the several conventions, of proposing any alterations, or indeed of even rejecting the plan proposed if they should disapprove of it. Still, however, the question recurs, what authority the late convention had to bind the people of the United States to any particular form of government, or to forbid them to adopt such form of government as they should think fit. I know it is a language frequent in the mouths of some heaven-born PHAETONS amongst us, who like the son of Apollo, think themselves entitled to guide the chariot of the sun, that common people have no right to judge of the affairs of government, that they are not fit for it, that they should leave these matters to their superiors. This, however, is not the language of men of real understanding, even among the advocates for the proposed Constitution; but these still recognize the authority of the people, and will admit, at least in words, that the people have a right to be consulted. Then I ask, if the people in the different states have a right to be consulted, in the new form of continental government, what authority could the late convention have to preclude them from proposing amendments to the plan they should offer? Had the convention any right to bind the people to the form of government they should propose? Let us consider this matter.

The late convention were chosen by the general assembly of each state. They had the sanction of Congress. For what? to consider what alterations were necessary to be made in the Articles of Confederation. What have they done? They have made a new constitution for the United States. I will not say, that in doing so, they have exceeded their authority; but on the other hand, I trust that no man of understanding among them will pretend to say that anything they did or could do was of the least avail to lessen the rights of the people to judge for themselves in the last resort. This right is perhaps unalienable, but at all events there is no pretense for saying that this right was ever meant to be surrendered up into the hands of the late continental convention.

The people have an undoubted right to judge of every part of the government which is offered to them: No power on earth has a right to preclude them, and they may exercise this choice either by themselves or their delegates legally chosen to represent them in the state convention. I venture to say that no man, reasoning upon *revolution* principles, can possibly controvert this right.

Indeed very few go so far as to controvert the right of the people to propose amendments. But we are told that the thing is impracticable, that if we begin to propose amendments there will be no end to them, that the several states will never agree in their amendments, that we shall never unite in any plan; that if we reject this we shall either have a worse or none at all, that we ought therefore to adopt this *at once*, without alteration or amendment. Now these are very kind gentlemen, who insist upon doing so much good for us, whether we will or not. Idiots and maniacs ought certainly to be restrained from doing themselves mischief, and should be compelled to that which is for their own good. Whether the people of America are to be considered in this light and treated accordingly is a question which deserves, perhaps, more consideration than it has yet received. A contest between the patients and their doctors, which are mad or which are fools, might possibly be a very unhappy one. I hope at least that we shall be able to settle this important business without so preposterous a dispute. What then would you have us do, it may be asked? Would you have us adopt the proposed Constitution or reject it? I answer that I would neither wish the one nor the other. Though I would be far from pretending to dictate to the representatives of the people what steps ought to be pursued, yet a method seems to present itself so simple, so perfectly calculated to obviate all difficulties, to reconcile us with one another, and establish unanimity and harmony among the people of this country, that I cannot forbear to suggest it. I hope that most of my readers have already anticipated me in what I am about to propose. Whether they have or not, I shall venture to state it, in the humble expectations that it may have some tendency to reconcile honest men of all parties with one another.

The method I would propose is this:

First, let the Conventions of each state, as they meet, after considering the proposed Constitution, state their objections and propose their amendments.

So far from these objections and amendments clashing with each other in irreconcilable discord, as it has been too often suggested they would do, it appears that from what has been hitherto published in the different states in opposition to the proposed Constitution, we have a right to expect that they will harmonize in a very great degree. The reason I say so is that about the same time, in very different parts of the continent, the very same objections have been made, and the very same alterations proposed by different writers, who I verily believe, know nothing at all of each other, and were very far from acting a premeditated concert, and that others who have not appeared as writers in the newspapers, in the different states, have appeared to act and speak in perfect unison with those objections and amendments, particularly in the article of a Bill of Rights. That in short, the very same sentiments seem to have been echoed from the different parts of the continent by the opposers of the proposed Constitution; and these sentiments have been very little contradicted by its friends, otherwise than by suggesting their fears, that by opposing the Constitution at present proposed, we might be disappointed of any federal government or receive a worse one than the present. It would be a most delightful surprise to find ourselves all of one opinion at last; and I cannot forbear hoping that when we come fairly to compare our sentiments, we shall find ourselves much more nearly agreed than in the hurry and surprise in which we have been involved on this subject, we ever suffered ourselves to imagine.

Second, when the conventions have stated these objections and amendments, let them transmit them to Congress and adjourn, praying that Congress will direct another convention to be called from the different states, to consider of these objections and amendments, and pledging themselves to abide by whatever decision shall be made by such future Convention on the subject, whether it be to amend the proposed Constitution or to reject any alteration and ratify it as it stands.

Third, if a new convention of the United States should meet, and revise the proposed Constitution, let us agree to abide by their decision. It is past a doubt that every good citizen of America pants for an efficient federal government. I have no doubt we shall concur at last in some plan of continental government, even if many people could imagine exceptions to it; but if the exceptions which are made at present, shall be maturely considered and even be pronounced by our future representatives as of no importance, (which I trust they will not) even in that case, I have no doubt that almost every man will give up his own private opinion and concur in that decision.

Fourth, if by any means another Continental Convention should fail to meet, then let the conventions of the several states again assemble and at last decide the great solemn question whether we shall adopt the Constitution now proposed, or reject it. And, whenever it becomes necessary to decide upon this point, one at least who from the beginning has been invariably anxious for the liberty and independence of his country, will concur in adopting and supporting this Constitution, rather than none; though I confess I could easily imagine, some other form of confederation, which I should think better entitled to my hearty approbation, and indeed I am not afraid of a worse.

Address by A Plebian
New York, 1788

Friends and Fellow Citizens:

The advocates for the proposed new constitution, having been beaten off the field of argument, on its merits, have now taken new ground. They admit it is liable to well-founded objections; that a number of its articles ought to be amended; that if alterations do not take place, a door will be left open for an undue administration, and encroachments on the liberties of the people; and many of them go so far as to say, if it should continue for any considerable period, in its present form, it will lead to a subversion of our equal republican forms of government. But still, although they admit this, they urge that it ought to be adopted, and that we should confide in procuring the necessary alterations after we have received it. Most of the leading characters, who advocate its reception, now profess their readiness to concur with those who oppose it, in bringing about the most material amendments contended for, provided they will first agree to accept the proffered system as it is. These concessions afford strong evidence, that the opposers of the constitution have reason on their side, and that they have not been influenced, in the part they have taken, by the mean and unworthy motives of selfish and private interests with which they have been illiberally charged. As the favorers of the constitution seem, if their professions are sincere, to be in a situation similiar to that of Agrippa, when he cried out upon Paul's preaching, "almost thou persuadest me to be a Christian," I cannot help indulging myself in expressing the same wish which St. Paul uttered on that occasion, "Would to God you were not only almost, but altogether such an one as I am." But alas, as we hear no more of Agrippa's Christianity after this interview with Paul, so it is much to be feared that we shall hear nothing of amendments from most of the warm advocates for adopting the new government after it gets into operation. When the government is once organized, and all the offices under it filled, the inducements which our great men will have to support it, will be much stronger than they are now to urge its reception. Many of them will then hold places of great honor and emolument, and others will be candidates for such places. It is much harder to relinquish honor or emoluments, which we have in possession, than to abandon the pursuit of them, while the attainment is held in a state of uncertainty. The amendments contended for as necessary to be made are of such a nature as will tend to limit and abridge a number of the powers of the government. And is it probable, that those who enjoy these powers will be so likely to surrender them after they have them in possession as to consent to have them restricted in the act of granting them? Common sense says—they will not.

When we consider the nature and operation of government, the idea of receiving a form radically defective under the notion of making the necessary amendments is evidently absurd.

Government is a compact entered into by mankind in a state of society for the promotion of their happiness. In forming this compact, common sense dictates that no articles should be admitted that tend to defeat the end of its institution. If any such are proposed, they should be rejected. When the compact is once formed and put into operation, it is too late for individuals to object. The deed is executed, the conveyance is made, and the power of reassuming the right is gone, without the consent of the parties. Besides, when a government is once in operation, it acquires strength by habit and stability by exercise. If it is tolerably mild in its administration, the people sit down easy under it, be its principles and forms ever so repugnant to the maxims of liberty. It steals, by insensible degrees, one right from the people after another, until it rivets its powers so as to put it beyond the ability of the community to restrict or limit it. The history of the world furnishes many instances of a people's increasing the powers of their rulers by persuasion, but I believe it would be difficult to produce one in which the rulers have been persuaded to relinquish their powers to the people. Wherever this has taken place, it has always been the effect of compulsion. These observations are so well-founded, that they have become a kind of axiom in politics; and the inference to be drawn from them is equally evident, which is this: that, in forming a government, care should be taken not to confer powers which it will be necessary to take back. But if you err at all, let it be on the contrary side, because it is much easier, as well as safer, to enlarge the powers of your rulers, if they should prove not sufficiently extensive, than it is to abridge them if they should be too great.

It is agreed the plan is defective, that some of the powers granted are dangerous and others not well defined, and amendments are necessary. Why then not amend it? Why not remove the cause of danger and, if possible, even the apprehension of it? The instrument is yet in the hands of the people; it is not signed, sealed, and delivered, and they have power to give it any form they please.

But it is contended to adopt it first, and then amend it. I ask, why not amend, and then adopt it? Most certainly the latter mode of proceeding is more consistent with our ideas of prudence in the ordinary concerns of life. If men were about entering into a contract respecting their private concerns, it would be highly absurd in them to sign and seal an instrument containing stipulations which are contrary to their interests and wishes, under the expectation that the parties, after its execution, would agree to make alterations agreeable to their desires. They would insist upon the exceptionable clauses being altered before they would ratify the contract. And is a compact for the government of ourselves and our posterity of less moment than contracts between individuals? Certainly not. But to this reasoning, which at first view would appear to admit of no reply, a variety of objections are made, and a number of reasons urged for adopting the system, and afterwards proposing amendments. Such as have come under my observation, I shall state, and remark upon.

It is insisted that the present situation of our country is such as not to admit of a delay in forming a new government, or of time sufficient to deliberate and agree upon the amendments which are proper, without involving ourselves in a state of anarchy and confusion.

On this head, all the powers of rhetoric, and arts of deception, are employed to paint the condition of this country in the most hideous and frightful colors. We are told that agriculture is without encouragement, trade is languishing, private faith and credit are disregarded, and public credit is prostrate, that the laws and magistrates are condemned and set at nought, that a spirit of licentiousness is rampant, and ready to break over every bound set to it by the government, that private embarrassments and distresses invade the house of every man of middling property, and insecurity threatens every man in affluent circumstances; in short, that we are in a state of the most grievous calamity at home, and that we are contemptible abroad, the scorn of foreign nations, and the ridicule of the world. From this high-wrought picture, one would suppose that we were in a condition the most deplorable of any people upon earth. But suffer me, my countrymen, to call your attention to a serious and sober estimate of the situation in which you are placed, while I trace the embarrassments under which you labor, to their true sources. What is your condition? Does not every man sit under his own vine and under his own fig tree, having none to make him afraid? Does not every one follow his calling without impediments and receive the reward of his well-earned industry? The farmer cultivates his land, and reaps the fruit which the bounty of heaven bestows on his honest toil. The mechanic is exercised in his art, and receives the reward of his labors. The merchant drives his commerce, and none can deprive him of the gain he honestly acquires. All classes and callings of men among us are protected in their various pursuits, and secured by the laws in the possession and enjoyment of the property obtained in those pursuits. The laws are as well executed as they ever were, in this or any other country. Neither the hand of private violence, nor the more to be dreaded hand of legal oppression, are reached out to distress us.

It is true, many individuals labor under embarrassments, but these are to be imputed to the unavoidable circumstances of things, rather than to any defect in our governments. We have just emerged from a long and expensive war. During its existence few people were in a situation to increase their fortunes, but many to diminish them. Debts contracted before the war were left unpaid while it existed, and these were left a burden too heavy to be borne at the commencement of peace. Add to these, that when the war was over, too many of us, instead of reassuming our old habits of frugality and industry, by which alone every country must be placed in a prosperous condition, took up the profuse use of foreign commodities. The country was deluged with articles imported from abroad, and the cash of the country has been sent out to pay for them, and still left us laboring under the weight of a huge debt to persons abroad. These are the true sources to which we are to trace all the private difficulties of individuals. But will a new government relieve you from these? The advocates for it have not yet told you how it will do it. And I will venture to pronounce, that there is but one way in which it can be effected, and that is by industry and economy. Limit your expenses within your earnings, sell more than you buy, and everything will be well on this score. Your present condition is such as is common to take place after the conclusion of a war. Those who can remember our situation after the termination of the war preceding the last, will recollect that our condition was similar to the present, but time and industry soon recovered us from it. Money was scarce, the produce of the country much lower than it has been since the peace, and many individuals were extremely embarrassed with debts; and this happened, although we did not experience the ravages, desolations, and loss of property that were suffered during the late war.

With regard to our public and national concerns, what is there in our condition that threatens us with any immediate danger? We are at peace with all the world, no nation menaces us with war, nor are we called upon by any cause of sufficient importance to attack any nation. The state governments answer the purposes of preserving the peace, and providing for present exigencies. Our condition as a nation is in no respect worse than it has been for several years past. Our public debt has been lessened in various ways, and the western territory, which has always been relied upon as a productive fund to discharge the national debt, has at length been brought to market, and a considerable part actually applied to its reduction. I mention these things to show that there is nothing special, in our present situation, as it respects our national affairs, that should induce us to accept the proffered system without taking sufficient time to consider and amend it. I do not mean by this to insinuate that our government does not stand in need of a reform. It is admitted by all parties that alterations are necessary in our federal constitution, but the circumstances of our case do by no means oblige us to precipitate this business, or require that we should adopt a system materially defective. We may safely take time to deliberate and amend without in the mean time hazarding a condition in any considerable degree worse than the present.

But it is said that if we postpone the ratification of this system until the necessary amendments are first incorporated, the consequence will be a civil war among the states. On this head weak minds are alarmed with being told that the militia of Connecticut and Massachusetts on the one side, and of New Jersey and Pennsylvania on the other, will attack us with hostile fury, and either destroy us from off the face of the earth, or at best divide us between the two states adjoining us on either side. The apprehension of danger is one of the most powerful incentives to human action, and is therefore generally excited on political questions. But still, a prudent man, though he foresees the evil and avoids it, yet he will not be terrified by imaginary dangers. We ought therefore to inquire what ground there is to fear such an event? There can be no reason to apprehend that the other states will make war with us for not receiving the constitution proposed until it is amended, but from one of the following causes; either that they will have just cause to do it, or that they have a disposition to do it. We will examine each of these. That they will have no just cause to quarrel with us for not acceding is evident, because we are under no obligation to do it arising from any existing compact or previous stipulation. The confederation is the only compact now existing between the states. By the terms of it, it cannot be changed without the consent of every one of the parties to it. Nothing therefore can be more unreasonable than for part of the states to claim of the others, as matter of right, an accession to a system to which they have material objections. No war can therefore arise from this principle, but on the contrary, it is to be presumed, it will operate strongly the opposite way. The states will reason on the subject in the following manner. On this momentuous question, every state has an indubitable right to judge for itself. This is secured to it by solemn compact, and if any of our sister states disagree with us upon the question, we ought to attend to their objections, and accommodate ourselves as far as possible to the amendments they propose.

As to the inclination of the states to make war with us, for declining to accede, until it is amended, this is highly improbable, not only because such a procedure would be most unjust and unreasonable in itself, but for various other reasons.

The idea of a civil war among the states is abhorrent to the principles and feelings of almost every man of every rank in the union. It is so obvious to every one of the least reflection, that in such an event we should hazard the loss of all things, without the hope of gaining anything, that the man who should entertain a thought of this kind would be justly deemed more fit to be shut up in Bedlam than to be reasoned with. But the idea of one or more states attacking another for insisting upon alterations in this system before it is adopted is more extravagant still; it is contradicting every principle of liberty which has been entertained by the states, violating the most solemn compact, and taking from the state the right of deliberation. Indeed to suppose that a people, entertaining such refined ideas of the rights of human nature as to be induced to wage war with the most powerful nation on earth, upon a speculative point, and from the mere apprehension of danger only, should so far be lost to their own feelings and principles, as to deny to their brethren, who were associated with them in the arduous conflict, the right of free deliberation on a question of the first importance to their political happiness and safety, is equally an insult to the character of the people of America and to common sense and could only be suggested by a vicious heart and a corrupt mind.

The reasonings made use of to persuade us that no alterations can be agreed upon previous to the adoption of the system are as curious as they are futile. It is alleged that there was great diversity of sentiments in forming the proposed constitution, that it was the effect of mutual concessions and a spirit of accommodation, and from hence it is inferred, that further changes cannot be hoped for. I should suppose that the contrary inference was the fair one. If the convention, who framed this plan, were possessed of such a spirit of moderation and condescension as to be induced to yield to each other certain points, and to accommodate themselves to each other's opinions, and even prejudices, there is reason to expect that this same spirit will continue and prevail in a future convention, and produce an union of sentiments on the points objected to. There is the more reason to hope for this because the subject has received a full discussion, and the minds of the people much better known than they were when the convention sat. Previous to the meeting of the convention, the subject of a new form of government had been little thought of and scarcely written upon at all. It is true it was the general opinion that some alterations were requisite in the federal system. This subject had been contemplated by almost every thinking man in the union. It had been the subject of many well written essays, and was the anxious wish of every true friend to America. But it never was in the contemplation of one in a thousand of those who had reflected on the matter, to have an entire change in the nature of our federal government, to alter it from a confederation of states to that of one entire government which will swallow up that of the individual states. I will venture to say that the idea of a government similar to the one proposed never entered the mind of the legislatures who appointed the convention, and of but very few of the members who composed it, until they had assembled and heard it proposed in that body; much less had the people any conception of such a plan until after it was promulgated. While it was agitated, the debates of the convention were kept an impenetrable secret, and no opportunity was given for well informed men to offer their sentiments upon the subject. The system was therefore never publicly discussed, nor indeed could be, because it was not known to the people until after it was proposed. Since then, it has been the object of universal attention; it has been thought of by every reflecting man, been discussed in a public and private manner, in conversation and in print. Its defects have been pointed out, and every objection to it stated. Able advocates have written in its favor, and able opponents have written against it. And what is the result? It cannot be denied but that the general opinion is that it contains material errors and requires important amendments. This then being the general sentiment, both of the friends and foes of the system, can it be doubted, that another convention would concur in such amendments as would quiet the fears of the opposers, and effect a great degree of union on the subject: an event most devoutly to be wished. But it is further said that there can be no prospect of procuring alterations before it is acceded to, because those who oppose it do not agree among themselves with respect to the amendments that are necessary. To this I reply that this may be urged against attempting alterations after it is received with as much force as before; and, therefore, if it concludes anything, it is that we must receive any system of government proposed to us because those who object to it do not entirely concur in their objections. But the assertion is not true to any considerable extent. There is a remarkable uniformity in the objections made to the constitution on the most important points. It is also worthy of notice that very few of the matters found fault with in it are of a local nature or such as affect any particular state; on the contrary, they are such as concern the principles of general liberty, in which the people of New Hampshire, New York, and Georgia are equally interested.

It would be easy to show that in the leading and most important objections that have been made to the plan, there has been and is an entire concurrence of opinion among writers and in public bodies throughout the United States.

I have not time fully to illustrate this by a minute narration of particulars, but to prove that this is the case, I shall adduce a number of important instances.

It has been objected to the new system that it is calculated to and will effect such a consolidation of the States as to supplant and overturn the state governments. In this the minority of Pennsylvania, the opposition in Massachusetts, and all the writers of any ability or note in Philadelphia, New York, and Boston concur. It may be added that this appears to have been the opinion of the Massachusetts convention, and gave rise to that article in the amendments proposed which confines the general government to the exercise only of powers expressly given.

It has been said that the representation in the general legislature is too small to secure liberty or to answer the intention of representation. In this there is an union of sentiments in the opposers.

The constitution has been opposed, because it gives to the legislature an unlimited power of taxation, both with respect to direct and indirect taxes, a right to lay and collect taxes, duties, imposts, and excises of every kind and description, and to any amount. In this, there has been as general a concurrence of opinion as in the former.

The opposers to the constitution have said that it is dangerous because the judicial power may extend to many cases which ought to be reserved to the decision of the State courts, and because the right of trial by jury is not secured in the judicial courts of the general government in civil cases. All the opposers are agreed in this objection.

The power of the general legislature to alter and regulate the time, place, and manner of holding elections has been stated as an argument against the adoption of the system. It has been urged that this power will place in the hands of the general government the authority whenever they shall be disposed, and a favorable opportunity offers, to deprive the body of the people, in effect, of all share in the government. The opposers to the constitution universally agree in this objection, and of such force is it that most of its ardent advocates admit its validity, and those who have made attempts to vindicate it have been reduced to the necessity of using the most trifling arguments to justify it.

The mixture of legislative, judicial, and executive powers in the senate, the little degree of responsibility under which the great officers of government will be held, and the liberty granted by the system to establish and maintain a standing army, without any limitation or restriction, are also objected to the constitution; and in these, there is a great degree of unanimity of sentiment in the opposers.

From these remarks it appears that the opponents to the system accord in the great and material points on which they wish amendments. For the truth of the assertion, I appeal to the protest of the minority of the convention of Pennsylvania, to all the publications against the constitution, and to the debates of the convention of Massachusetts.

The present is the most important crisis at which you ever have arrived. You have before you a question big with consequences, unutterably important to yourselves, to your children, to generations yet unborn, to the cause of liberty and of mankind. Every motive of religion and virtue, of private happiness and public good, of honor and dignity, should urge you to consider cooly and determine wisely.

Almost all the governments that have arisen among mankind have sprung from force and violence. The records of history inform us of none that have been the result of cool and dispassionate reason and reflection. It is reserved for this favored country to exhibit to mankind the first example. This opportunity is now given us, and we are to exercise our rights in the choice of persons to represent us in convention, to deliberate and determine upon the constitution proposed. It will be to our everlasting disgrace to be indifferent on such a subject, for it is impossible we can contemplate anything that relates to the affairs of this life of half the importance.

You have heard that both sides on this great question agree that there are in it great defects; yet the one side tell you, choose such men as will adopt it, and then amend it; while the other say, amend previous to its adoption. I have stated to you my reasons for the latter, and I think they are unanswerable. Consider you the common people, the yeomanry of the country, for to such I principally address myself, you are to be the principal losers if the constitution should prove oppressive. When a tyranny is established, there are always masters as well as slaves; the great and the well born are generally the former, and the middling class the latter. Attempts have been made, and will be

repeated, to alarm you with the fear of consequences; but reflect, there
are consequences on both sides, and none can be apprehended more
dreadful than entailing on ourselves and posterity a government which
will raise a few to the height of human greatness and wealth, while it
will depress the many to the extreme of poverty and wretchedness.
Consequences are under the control of that all-wise and all-powerful
being, whose providence directs the affairs of men. Our part is to act
right, and we may then have confidence that the consequences will be
favorable. The path in which you should walk is plain and open before
you; be united as one man, and direct your choice to such men as have
been uniform in their opposition to the proposed system in its present
form, or without proper alterations. In men of this description you
have reason to place confidence, while on the other hand, you have
just cause to distrust those who urge the adoption of a bad constitution under the delusive expectation of making amendments after it is
acceded to. Your jealousy of such characters should be the more
excited when you consider that the advocates for the constitution have
shifted their ground. When men are uniform in their opinions, it
affords evidence that they are sincere. When they are shifting, it gives
reason to believe they do not change from conviction. It must be
recollected, that when this plan was first announced to the public, its
supporters cried it up as the most perfect production of human wisdom. It was represented either as having no defects or, if it had, they
were so trifling and inconsiderable that they served only as the shades
in a fine picture, to set off the piece to the greater advantage. One
gentleman in Philadelphia went so far in the ardor of his enthusiasm in
its favor as to pronounce that the men who formed it were as really
under the guidance of Divine Revelation as was Moses, the Jewish
lawgiver. Their language is now changed. The question has been
discussed, the objections to the plan ably stated, and they are admitted
to be unanswerable. The same men who held it almost perfect, now
admit it is very imperfect; that it is necessary it should be amended.
The only question between us is simply this: Shall we accede to a bad
constitution, under the uncertain prospect of getting it amended after
we have received it, or shall we amend it before we adopt it? Common
sense will point out which is the most rational, which is the most
secure line of conduct. May heaven inspire you with wisdom, union,
moderation and firmness, and give you hearts to make a proper
estimate of your invaluable privileges, and preserve them to you, to be
transmitted to your posterity unimpaired, and may they be maintained
in this our country, while Sun and Moon endure.

Agrippa
Letters XV and XVI
(Boston) Massachusetts Gazette
29 January, 5 February, 1788

To the Massachusetts Convention:

Gentlemen.

As it is essentially necessary to the happiness of a free people that the constitution of government should be established in principles of truth, I have endeavored, in a series of papers, to discuss the proposed form, with that degree of freedom which becomes a faithful citizen of the commonwealth. It must be obvious to the most careless observer, that the friends of the new plan appear to have nothing more in view than to establish it by a popular current, without any regard to the truth of its principles. Propositions, novel, erroneous and dangerous, are boldly advanced to support a system, which does not appear to be founded in, but in every instance to contradict, the experience of mankind. We are told that a constitution is in itself a bill of rights, that all power not expressly given is reserved, that no powers are given to the new government which are not already vested in the state governments, and that it is for the security of liberty that the persons elected should have the absolute control over the time, manner and place of election. These, and an hundred other things of the like kind, though they have gained the hasty assent of men, respectable for learning and ability, are false in themselves, and invented merely to serve a present purpose. This will, I trust, clearly appear from the following considerations.

It is common to consider man at first as in a state of nature, separate from all society. The only historical evidence that the human species ever actually existed in this state is derived from the book of Genesis. There it is said that Adam remained a while alone. While the whole species was comprehended in his person was the only instance in which this supposed state of nature really existed. Ever since the completion of the first pair, mankind appear as natural to associate with their own species as animals of any other kind herd together. Wherever we meet with their settlements, they are found in clans. We are therefore justified in saying that a state of society is the natural state of man. Wherever we find a settlement of men, we find also some appearance of government. The state of government is therefore as natural to mankind as a state of society. Government and society appear to be co-eval. The most rude and artless form of government is probably the most ancient. This we find to be practiced among the Indian tribes in America. With them the whole authority of government is vested in the whole tribe. Individuals depend upon their reputation of valor and wisdom to give them influence. Their government is genuinely democratic. This was probably the first kind of government among mankind, as we meet with no mention of any other kind, till royalty was introduced in the person of Nimrod. Immediately after that time, the Asiatic nations seem to have departed from the simple democracy, which is still retained by their American brethren, and universally adopted the kingly form. We do indeed meet with some vague rumors of an aristocracy in India so late as the time of Alexander the great. But such stories are altogether uncertain and improbable. For in the time of Abraham, who lived about sixteen hundred years before Alexander, all the little nations mentioned in the Mosaic history appear to be governed by kings. It does not appear from any accounts of the Asiatic kingdoms that they have practiced at all upon the idea of a limited monarchy. The whole power of society has been delegated to the kings; and though they may be said to have constitutions of government because the succession to the crown is limited by certain rules, yet the people are not benefited by their constitutions, and enjoy no share of civil liberty. The first attempt to reduce republicanism to a system, appears to be made by Moses when he led the Israelites out of Egypt. This government stood a considerable time, about five centuries, till in a frenzy the people demanded a king that they might resemble the nations about them. They were dissatisfied with their judges, and instead of changing the administration, they madly changed their constitution. However they might flatter themselves with the idea that an high spirited people could get the power back again when they pleased, they never did get it back, and they fared like the nations about them. Their kings tyrannized over them for some centuries, till they fell under a foreign yoke. This is the history of that nation. With a change of names, it describes the progress of political changes in other countries. The people are dazzled with the splendor of distant monarchies, and a desire to share their glory induces them to sacrifice their domestic happiness.

From this general view of the state of mankind it appears that all the power of government originally reside in the body of the people; and that when they appoint certain persons to administer the government, they delegate all the powers of government not expressly reserved. Hence, it appears that a constitution does not in itself imply any more than a declaration of the relation which the different parts of the government bear to each other, but does not in any degree imply security to the rights of individuals. This has been the uniform practice. In all doubtful cases the decision is in favor of the government. It is therefore impertinent to ask by what right government exercises powers not expressly delegated. Mr. Wilson, the great oracle of federalism, acknowledges in his speech to the Philadelphians the truth of these remarks as they respect the state governments, but attempts to set up a distinction between them and the continental government. To anybody who will be at the trouble to read the new system, it is evidently in the same situation as the state constitutions now possess. It is a compact among the *people* for the purposes of government, and not a compact between states. It begins in the name of the people and not of the states.

It has been shown in the course of this paper that when people institute government, they of course delegate all rights not expressly reserved. In our state constitution the bill of rights consists of thirty articles. It is evident therefore that the new constitution proposes to delegate greater powers than are granted to our own government, sanguine as the person was who denied it. The complaints against the separate governments, even by the friends of the new plan, are not that they have not power enough, but that they are disposed to make a bad use of what power they have. Surely then they reason badly when they purpose to set up a government possessed of much more extensive powers than the present and subject to much smaller checks.

Bills of rights, reserved by authority of the people, are, I believe, peculiar to America. A careful observance of the abuse practiced in other countries has had its just effect by inducing our people to guard against them. We find the happiest consequences to flow from it. The separate governments know their powers, their objects, and operations. We are therefore not perpetually tormented with new experiments. For a single instance of abuse among us there are thousands in other countries. On the other hand, the people know their rights and feel happy in the possession of their freedom, both civil and political. Active industry is the consequence of their security; and within one year the circumstances of the state and of individuals have improved to a degree never before known in this commonwealth. Though our bill of rights does not, perhaps, contain all the cases in which power might be safely reserved, yet it affords a protection to the persons and possessions of individuals not known in any foreign country. In some respects the power of government is a little too confined. In many other countries we find the people resisting their governors for exercising their power in an unaccustomed mode. But for want of a bill of rights the resistance is always by the principles of their government, a rebellion which nothing but success can justify. In our constitution we have aimed at delegating the necessary powers of government and confining their operation to beneficial purposes. At present we appear to have come very near the truth. Let us therefore have wisdom and virtue enough to preserve it inviolate. It is a stale contrivance to get the people into a passion, in order to make them sacrifice their liberty. Repentance always comes, but it comes too late. Let us not flatter ourselves that we shall always have good men to govern us. If we endeavor to be like other nations we shall have more bad men than good ones to exercise extensive powers. That circumstance alone will corrupt them. While they fancy themselves the viceregents of God, they will resemble him only in power, but will always depart from his wisdom and goodness.

In my last address I ascertained from historical records the following principles that, in the original state of government, the whole power resides in the whole body of the nation, that when a people appoint certain persons to govern them, they delegate their whole power, that a constitution is not itself a bill of rights, and that, whatever is the form of government, a bill of rights is essential to the security of the persons and property of the people. It is an idea favorable to the interest of mankind at large that government is founded in compact. Several instances may be produced of it, but none is more remarkable than our own. In general I have chosen to apply to such facts as are in the reach of my readers. For this purpose I have chiefly confined myself to examples drawn from the history of our own country and to the old testament. It is in the power of every reader to verify examples thus substantiated. Even in the remarkable argument on the fourth section, relative to the power over election, I was far from stating the worst of it, as it respects the adverse party. A gentleman, respectable in many points, but more especially for his systematic and perspicuous reasoning in his profession, has repeatedly stated to the Convention among his reasons in favor of that section, that *the Rhode Island assembly have for a considerable time past had a bill lying on their table for altering the manner of elections for representatives in that state.* He has stated it with all the zeal of a person who believed his argument to be a good one. But surely a *bill lying on a table* can never be considered as any more than an intention to pass it, and nobody pretends that it ever actually did pass. It is in strictness only the intention of a part of the assembly, for nobody can aver that it ever will pass.* I write not with an intention to deceive, but that the whole argument may be stated fairly. Much eloquence and ingenuity have been employed in showing that side of the argument in favor of the proposed constitution; but it ought to be considered that if we accept it upon mere verbal explanations, we shall find ourselves deceived. I appeal to the knowledge of everyone, if it does not frequently happen, that a law is interpreted in practice very differently from the intention of the legislature. Hence arises the necessity of acts to amend and explain former acts. This is not an inconvenience in the common and ordinary business of legislation, but is a great one in a constitution. A constitution is a legislative act of the whole people. It is an excellence that it should be permanent, otherwise we are exposed to perpetual insecurity from the fluctuation of government. We should be in the same situation as under absolute government, sometimes exposed to the pressure of greater, and sometimes unprotected by the weaker power in the sovereign.

It is now generally understood that it is for the security of the people that the powers of the government should be lodged in different branches. By this means public business will go on when they all agree, and stop when they disagree. The advantage of checks in government is thus manifested, where the concurrence of different branches is necessary to the same act, but the advantage of a division of business is advantageous in other respects. As in every extensive empire, local laws are necessary to suit the different interests; no single legislature is adequate to the business. All human capacities are limited to a narrow space; and as no individual is capable of practicing a great variety of trades, no single legislature is capable of managing all the variety of national and state concerns. Even if a legislature was capable of it, the business of the judicial department must, from the same cause, be slovenly done. Hence arises the necessity of a division of the business into national and local. Each department ought to have all the powers necessary for executing its own business, under such limitations as tend to secure us from any inequality in the operations of government. I know it is often asked against whom in a government by representation is a bill of rights to secure us? I answer, that such a government is indeed a government by ourselves; but as a just government protects

---

*A writer in the Gazette of 29th January, under the signature of Captain McDaniel having with civility and apparent candor, called for an explanation of what was said in one of my former papers. I have chosen to mention him with respect, as the only one of my reviewers who deserves an answer.

all alike, it is necessary that the sober and industrious part of the community should be defended from the rapacity and violence of the vicious and idle. A bill of rights, therefore, ought to set forth the purposes for which the compact is made, and serves to secure the minority against the usurpation and tyranny of the majority. It is a just observation of his excellency, Doctor Adams, in his learned defense of the American constitutions, that unbridled passions produce the same effect whether in a king, nobility, or a mob. The experience of all mankind has proved the prevalence of a disposition to use power wantonly. It is therefore as necessary to defend an individual against the majority in a republic as against the king in a monarchy. Our state constitution has wisely guarded this point. The present confederation has also done it.

I confess that I have yet seen no sufficient reason for not amending the confederation, though I have weighed the argument with candor. I think it would be much easier to amend it than the new constitution. But this is a point on which men of very respectable character differ. There is another point in which nearly all agree, and that is that the new constitution would be better in many respects if it had been differently framed. Here the question is not so much what the amendments ought to be, as in what manner they shall be made; whether they shall be made as conditions of our accepting the constitution, or whether we shall first accept it, and then try to amend it. I can hardly conceive that it should seriously be made a question. If the first question, whether we will receive it as it stands be negatived, as it undoubtedly ought to be, while the conviction remains that amendments are necessary, the next question will be, what amendments shall be made? Here permit an individual, who glories in being a citizen of Massachusetts, and who is anxious that the character may remain undiminished, to propose such articles as appear to him necessary for preserving the rights of the state. He means not to retract anything with regard to the expediency of amending the old confederation, and rejecting the new one totally; but only to make a proposition which he thinks comprehends the general idea of all parties. If the new constitution means no more than the friends of it acknowledge, they certainly can have no objection to affixing a declaration in favor of the rights of states and of citizens, especially as a majority of the states have not yet voted upon it.

"Resolved, that the constitution lately proposed for the United States be received only upon the following conditions:

1. Congress shall have no power to alter the time, place or manner of elections, nor any authority over elections, otherwise than by fining

such state as shall neglect to send its representatives or senators, a sum not exceeding the expense of supporting its representatives or senators one year.

2. Congress shall not have the power of regulating the intercourse between the states, nor to levy any direct tax on polls or estates, or any excise.

3. Congress shall not have power to try causes between a state and citizens of another state, nor between citizens of different states; nor to make any laws relative to the transfer of property between those parties, nor any other matter which shall originate in the body of any state.

4. It shall be left to every state to make and execute its own laws, except laws impairing contracts, which shall not be made at all.

5. Congress shall not incorporate any trading companies, nor alienate the territory of any state. And no treaty, ordinance or law of the United States shall be valid for these purposes.

6. Each state shall have the command of its own militia.

7. No continental army shall come within the limits of any state, other than garrison to guard the public stores, without the consent of such states in time of peace.

8. The president shall be chosen annually and shall serve but one year, and shall be chosen successively from the different states, changing every year.

9. The judicial department shall be confined to cases in which ambassadors are concerned, to cases depending upon treaties, to offenses committed upon the high seas, to the capture of prizes, and to cases in which a foreigner residing in some foreign country shall be a party, and an American state or citizen shall be the other party, provided no suit shall be brought upon a state note.

10. Every state may emit bills of credit without making them a tender, and may coin money, of silver, gold, or copper, according to the continental standard.

11. No powers shall be exercised by Congress or the president but such as are expressly given by this constitution and not excepted against by this declaration. And any officer of the United States offending against an individual state shall be held accountable to such state as any other citizen would be.

12. No officer of Congress shall be free from arrest for debt by authority of the state in which the debt shall be due.

13. Nothing in this constitution shall deprive a citizen of any state of the benefit of the bill of rights established by the constitution of the

state in which he shall reside, and such bills of rights shall be considered as valid in any court of the United States where they shall be pleaded.

14. In all those causes which are triable before the continental courts, the trial by jury shall be held sacred."

These at present appear to me the most important points to be guarded. I have mentioned a reservation of excise to the separate states because it is necessary that they should have some way to discharge their own debts, and because it is placing them in an humiliating and disgraceful situation to depute them to transact the business of internal government without the means to carry it on. It is necessary also as a check on the national government, for it has hardly been known that any government having the powers of war, peace, and revenue, has failed to engage in needless and wanton expense. A reservation of this kind is therefore necessary to preserve the importance of the state governments; without this the extremes of the empire will in a very short time sink into the same degradation and contempt with respect to the middle state as Ireland, Scotland, and Wales, are in with regard to England. All the men of genius and wealth will resort to the seat of government, that will be center of revenue, and of business, which the extremes will be drained to supply.

This is not mere vision, it is justified by the whole course of things. We shall therefore, if we neglect the present opportunity to secure ourselves, only increase the number of proofs, already too many, that mankind are incapable of enjoying their liberty. I have been the more particular in stating the amendments to be made, because many gentlemen think it would be preferable to receive the new system with corrections. I have by this means brought the corrections into one view, and shown several of the principal points in which it is unguarded. As it is agreed, at least professedly, on all sides, that those rights should be guarded, it is among the inferior questions in what manner it is done, provided it is absolutely and effectually done. For my own part, I am fully of the opinion that it would be best to reject this plan and pass an explicit resolve defining the powers of Congress to regulate the intercourse between us and foreign nations, under such restrictions as shall render their regulations equal in all parts of the empire. The impost, if well collected, would be fully equal to the interest of the foreign debt, and the current charges of the national government. It is evidently for our interest that the charges should be as small as possible. It is also for our interest that the western lands should, as fast as possible, be applied to the purpose of paying the home debt.

Internal taxation and that fund have already paid two thirds of the whole debt, notwithstanding the embarrassments usual at the end of a war.

We are now rising fast above our difficulties, everything at home has the appearance of improvement, government is well established, manufactures increasing rapidly, and trade expanding. Till since the peace we never sent a ship to India, and the present year, it is said, sends above a dozen vessels from this state only, to the countries round the Indian ocean. Vast quantities of our produce are exported to those countries. It has been so much the practice of European nations to farm out this branch of trade that we ought to be exceedingly jealous of our right. The manufactures of the state probably exceed in value one million pounds for the last year. Most of the useful and some ornamental fabrics are established. There is great danger of these improvements being injured unless we practice extreme caution at setting out. It will always be for the interest of the southern states to raise a revenue from the more commercial ones. It is said that the consumer pays it; but does not a commercial state consume more foreign goods than a landed one? The people are more crowded, and of consequence the land is less able to support them. We know it to be a favorite system to raise the money where it is. But the money is to be expended at another place, and is therefore so much withdrawn annually from our stock. This is a single instance of the difference of interest; it would be very easy to produce others. Innumerable are the differences of manners, and these produce differences in the laws. Uniformity in legislation is of no more importance than in religion; yet the framers of this new constitution did not even think it necessary that the president should believe that there is a God, although they require an oath of him. It would be easy to show the propriety of a general declaration upon that subject. But this paper is already extended too far.

Another reason which I had in stating the amendments to be made was to show how nearly those who are for admitting the system with the necessary alterations agree with those who are for rejecting this system and amending the confederation. In point of convenience, the confederation amended would be infinitely preferable to the proposed constitution. In amending the former, we know the powers granted, and are subject to no perplexity; but in reforming the latter, the business is excessively intricate, and great part of the checks on Congress are lost. It is to be remembered too, that if you are so far charmed with eloquence, and misled by fair representations and charitable constructions, as to adopt an undefined system, there will be no saying afterwards that you were mistaken, and wish to correct it. *It will then be the constitution of our country, and entitled to defense.* If Congress should choose to avail themselves of a popular commotion to continue in being, as the fourth section justifies, and as the British parliament has repeatedly done, the only answer will be that it is the constitution of our country and the people chose it. It is therefore necessary to be exceedingly critical. Whatsoever way shall be chosen to secure our rights, the same resolve ought to contain the whole system of amendment. If it is rejected, the resolve should contain the emendations of the old system; and if accepted, it should contain the corrections of the new one.

Sidney
Essay II
(Poughkeepsie) Country Journal
21 February, 1788

"Let Cicero then live in submission and servitude, since he is capable of it; and neither his age nor his honors nor his past actions, make him ashamed to suffer it. For my own part, no condition of slavery, how honorable soever it may appear, shall hinder me from declaring war against tyranny, against decrees irregularly made, against unjust dominion, and every power that would set itself above the laws."

Brutus.

The dangers of adopting the new Constitution having been pointed out, I shall now proceed to consider, whether it would be necessary and proper, and, whether Americans have any good reason to put more confidence in their rulers than Europeans.

It is admitted that it has been matter of dispute at all times, whether a monarchical, aristocratic or democratic government is the best. It was the case in the time of Samuel, and in the council of the seven princes of Persia. This was also the case with the Dutch upon their revolt from Philip the second, with the English after the death of Charles the first, and the Americans during the late revolution.

It is, however, established by the experience of all ages that in the two first, there is no security for the rights of the people, in the last, no dispatch. "That the two first are too strong, encroach too much upon liberty, and incline too much to tyranny; the last too weak, delivers people too much to themselves, and tends to confusion and licentiousness."

These were the rocks we had to avoid when, in 1777, we agreed to a republican government.

"In political arithmetic, it is necessary to substitute a calculation of probabilities to mathematical exactness. That force which continually impels us to our own private interests, like gravity, acts incessantly, unless it meets an obstacle to oppose it."

"A perfect government (says Rollin) would be that which should unite in itself, all the advantages of the three former, and avoid the dangers and inconveniences they include", and then it is called a republican or mixed government. Such, even in their present state, are the English and the Dutch.

But a difficulty remained: what proportion of ingredients should be taken out of each; or, in the words of Montesquieu, "to combine the several powers, to regulate, temper and set them in motion to give as it were ballast to the one, in order to enable it to resist the other." (The English and the Dutch have missed it in their compound, by adopting, the first, too great a proportion of the monarchical, the Dutch, too much of the aristocratic ingredient.). Even then, all the difficulties would not be removed as the fundamental principles they act upon are so different.

In a monarchy, the king* rules in duplicity and partiality, and makes himself *respectable* among the *nations* of the earth, by *luxury, extravagance*† and *dissipation;* when, on the contrary, in a republic there is no king except the LORD OF HOSTS, the pillars of whose government are righteousness‡ and truth; and to them and them only, ought all nations upon earth to look for respecticability. In considering the rules of propriety, the principal object with the one is, how to be generous, the other how to be just. And in respect to the public burdens, the former considers how much he can spend, the

---

*"Kings hate virtuous men who oppose their unjust designs, but caress the wicked who favor them." 2 Burlamaqui 67. Montague 276.

"In monarchies, the actions of men are judged not as *virtuous* but as shining—not as *just* but as great—not as *reasonable* but as extraordinary." 1 Montesquieu 36.

"In monarchies, policy effects great things by as little virtue as possible, if there should chance to be some unlucky, honest man, Cardinal Richlieu, in his political testament, seems to hint, that a prince should take care not to employ him: so true it is that virtue is not the mainspring of this Government." 3 Montesquieu 28, 30.

†"Luxury is absolutely necessary in monarchies; hence arises a very natural reflection. Republics end with luxury, monarchy with poverty." Ibid. 124.

‡"There is no great share of probity necessary to the support of monarchical or despotic government; but in a popular state one spring more is necessary, namely virtue. When virtue is banished, ambition invades the hearts of those that are disposed to receive it, and avarice possesses the whole community." 1 Montesquieu, 24, 25.

latter, how much they can save; that, how much the people can bear, this how little may do. The Congress at Philadelphia (a body of men, in the words of Mr. Pitt, "that for solidity of reasoning, force of sagacity, and wisdom of conclusion, no nation or body of men stand in preference to"), upon the greatest deliberation and circumspection, unanimously agreed to a republican form; wherein, they have united all the advantages of the three former, and, as much as possible, avoided the dangers and inconveniencies of each (the objection of Maryland was not to the form of government, but to the soil and jurisdiction of all the western lands, not foreseeing, as they now do or soon will, the dangerous tendency it would have to the liberty and property of the old states) not that I suppose it perfect. For I hold, that there never was nor ever will be a government perfect, so as not to be open to corruption (unless at Millenium) but I am persuaded, that every person who has considered the difference between the condition of the people in Europe, compared with those of the United States of America, will agree with Doctor Franklin, who says, "whoever has traveled through the various parts of Europe, and observed how small is the proportion of people in affluence or easy circumstances there, compared to those in poverty and misery, the few haughty landlords, with the multitude of poor, abject, rack-rented, to the paying tenants and half paid, and half-starved ragged laborers, and views here the happy mediocrity, that so generally prevails throughout these states, where the cultivator works for himself, and supports his family with decent plenty, will see abundant reason to bless Providence for the evident and great difference in our favor, and be convinced that no nation known to us enjoys a greater share of human felicity."

The good opinion I have of the frame and composition as well of the Confederation as the several state Constitutions; and that they are, if administered upon republican principles, the greatest blessings we enjoy; the danger I apprehend of the one proposed, that it will become the greatest curse and be the means of destroying ours, as the like measures ever have destroyed the liberties of every people that have attempted to do so, has led me into the following discussions, conceiving it not only the duty of a patriot to inquire, like Daniel, *Whose footsteps are these?* but to call out like Paul, *Stand fast in the liberty, be not entangled with the yoke of bondage.* "What, in a quarrel (says Vattel) that is going to decide forever their most valuable interests and their very safety, are the people to stand by as tranquil spectators, as a flock of sheep is, to wait till it be determined whether they are to be delivered to the butcher or restored to the shepherd's care."

For my own part, I adopt the sentiments of Sidney: "While I live I shall endeavor to preserve my liberty, or at least not consent to the destroying of it. I hope I shall die in the same principle in which I lived, and will no longer live than they can preserve me."

In my discussions on this subject, I do not mean to ascribe every bad consequence that may appear to flow necessarily from certain measures to the evil intentions of ALL those that advocate the measure, nor to every member of Congress; for I am well assured, that there have been at all times members in that honorable body, and even among the wealthy, that have disapproved of the measures and acted the worthy patriots, and others, that deserve no more blame than those who in their innocence accompanied Absalom in his treasonable practices, it being even a hard fate that the burden of the proof was turned upon them, without an evil intent. And as it will require to point out the reprehensible conduct of the public officers, which will sometimes also apply to their superiors, I shall endeavor to do it with as much delicacy as I am able, consistent with truth; and "truth (says Montague) will never offend the honest and well meaning, for the plain dealing remonstrances of a friend differ as widely from the rancor of an enemy, as the friendly probe of a physician from the dagger of an assassin." Yet, in sentiment with Hardwick, "that there is a decency required in tracing the faults of past times, we may look for information and warning, and even reproof, but not invective."

The Address and Reasons of Dissent of the Minority of the Convention of Pennsylvania
Pennsylvania Packet and Daily Advertiser
18 December, 1787

The convention met, and the same disposition was soon manifested in considering the proposed constitution that had been exhibited in every other stage of the business. We were prohibited by an express vote of the convention from taking any question on the separate articles of the plan, and reduced to the necessity of adopting or rejecting *in toto*. It is true the majority permitted us to debate on each article, but restrained us from proposing amendments. They also determined not to permit us to enter on the minutes our reasons of dissent against any of the articles, nor even on the final question our reasons of dissent against the whole. Thus situated we entered on the examination of the proposed system of government, and found it to be such as we could not adopt without, as we conceived, surrendering up your dearest rights. We offered our objections to the convention, and opposed those parts of the plan, which, in our opinion, would be injurious to you, in the best manner we were able; and closed our arguments by offering the following propositions to the convention.

1. The right of conscience shall be held inviolable, and neither the legislative, executive nor judicial powers of the United States shall have authority to alter, abrogate, or infringe any part of the constitution of the several states which provide for the preservation of liberty in matters of religion.

2. That in controversies respecting property, and in suits between man and man, trial by jury shall remain as heretofore, as well in the federal courts, as in those of the several states.

3. That in all capital and criminal prosecutions, a man has a right to demand the cause and nature of his accusation, as well in the federal courts, as in those of the several states; to be heard by himself and his counsel; to be confronted with the accusers and witnesses; to call for evidence in his favor, and a speedy trial by an impartial jury of his vicinage, without whose unanimous consent, he cannot be found guilty, nor can he be compelled to give evidence against himself; and that no man be deprived of his liberty, except by the law of the land or the judgment of his peers.

4. That excessive bail ought not to be required, nor excessive fines imposed, nor cruel nor unusual punishments inflicted.

5. That warrants unsupported by evidence, whereby any officer or messenger may be commanded or required to search suspected places, or to seize any person or persons, his or their property, not particularly described, are grievous and oppressive, and shall not be granted either by the magistrates of the federal government or others.

6. That the people have a right to the freedom of speech, of writing and publishing their sentiments. Therefore, the freedom of the press shall not be restrained by any law of the United States.

7. That the people have a right to bear arms for the defense of themselves and their own state, or the United States, or for the purpose of killing game; and no law shall be passed for disarming the people or any of them, unless for crimes committed, or real danger of public injury from individuals; and as standing armies in the time of peace are dangerous to liberty, they ought not to be kept up; and that the military shall be kept under strict subordination to and be governed by the civil powers.

8. The inhabitants of the several states shall have liberty to fowl

and hunt in seasonable times, on the lands they hold, and on all other lands in the United States not enclosed, and in like manner to fish in all navigable waters, and others not private property, without being restrained therein by any laws to be passed by the legislature of the United States.

9. That no law shall be passed to restrain the legislatures of the several states from enacting laws for imposing taxes, except imposts and duties on goods imported or exported, and that no taxes, except imposts and duties upon goods imported and exported, and postage on letters shall be levied by the authority of Congress.

10. That the house of representatives be properly increased in number; that elections shall remain free; that the several states shall have power to regulate the elections for senators and representatives, without being controlled either directly or indirectly by any interference on the part of the Congress; and that elections of representatives be annual.

11. That the power of organizing, arming, and disciplining the militia (the manner of disciplining the militia to be prescribed by Congress) remain with the individual states, and that Congress shall not have authority to call or march any of the militia out of their own state, without the consent of such state, and for such length of time only as such state shall agree.

That the sovereignty, freedom and independency of the several states shall be retained, and every power, jurisdiction and right which is not by this constitution expressly delegated to the United States in Congress assembled.

12. That the legislative, executive, and judicial powers be kept separate; and to this end that a constitutional council be appointed, to advise and assist the president, who shall be responsible for the advice they give, thereby the senators would be relieved from almost constant attendance; and also that the judges be made completely independent.

13. That no treaty which shall be directly opposed to the existing laws of the United States in Congress assembled, shall be valid until such laws shall be repealed, or made conformable to such treaty; neither shall any treaties be valid which are in contradiction to the constitution of the United States, or the constitutions of the several states.

14. That the judiciary power of the United States shall be confined to cases affecting ambassadors, other public ministers and consuls; to cases of admiralty and maritime jurisdiction; to controversies to which the United States shall be a party; to controversies between two or more states; between a state and citizens of different states; between

citizens claiming lands under grants of different states; and between a
state or the citizen thereof and foreign states, and in criminal cases, to
such only as are expressly enumerated in the constitution, and that the
United States in Congress assembled, shall not have power to enact
laws, which shall alter the laws of descents and distribution of the
effects of deceased persons, the titles of lands or goods, or the regulation of contracts in the individual states.

After reading these propositions, we declared our willingness to
agree to the plan, provided it was so amended as to meet these
propositions, or something similar to them; and finally moved the
convention to adjourn to give the people of Pennsylvania time to
consider the subject and determine for themselves; but these were all
rejected, and the final vote was taken, when our duty to you induced
us to vote against the proposed plan and to decline signing the ratification of the same.

During the discussion we met with many insults, and some personal
abuse. We were not even treated with decency, during the sitting of the
convention, by the persons in the gallery of the house. However, we
flatter ourselves that in contending for the preservation of those invaluable rights you have thought proper to commit to our charge, we acted
with a spirit becoming freemen, and being desirous that you might
know the principles which actuated our conduct, and being prohibited
from inserting our reasons of dissent on the minutes of the convention,
we have subjoined them for your consideration, as to you alone we are
accountable. It remains with you whether you will think those inestimable privileges, which you have so ably contended for, should be
sacrificed at the shrine of despotism, or whether you mean to contend
for them with the same spirit that has so often baffled the attempts of
an aristocratic faction, to rivet the shackles of slavery on you and your
unborn posterity.

Our objections are comprised under three general heads of dissent.

We dissent, first, because it is the opinion of the most celebrated
writers on government, and confirmed by uniform experience, that a
very extensive territory cannot be governed on the principles of freedom, otherwise than by a confederation of republics, possessing all the
powers of internal government, but united in the management of their
general, and foreign concerns.

If any doubt could have been entertained of the truth of the foregoing principle, it has been fully removed by the concession of *Mr.
Wilson*, one of the majority on this question, and who was one of the
deputies in the late general convention. In justice to him, we will give

his own words. They are as follows. "The extent of country for which the new constitution was required produced another difficulty in the business of the federal convention. It is the opinion of some celebrated writers, that to a small territory, the democratic; to a middling territory (as Montesquieu has termed it) the monarchical; and to an extensive territory, the despotic form of government is best adapted. Regarding then the wide and almost unbounded jurisdiction of the United States, at first view, the hand of despotism seemed necessary to control, connect, and protect it; and hence the chief embarrassment rose. For we know that, although our constituents would cheerfully submit to the legislative restraints of a free government, they would spurn at every attempt to shackle them with despotic power." And again in another part of his speech he continues. "Is it probable that the dissolution of the state governments, and the establishment of one *consolidated empire* would be eligible in its nature, and satisfactory to the people in its administration? I think not, as I have given reasons to show that so extensive a territory could not be governed, connected, and preserved, but by the *supremacy of despotic power.* All the exertions of the most potent emperors of Rome were not capable of keeping that empire together, which in extent was far inferior to the dominion of America."

We dissent, secondly, because the powers vested in Congress by this constitution, must necessarily annihilate and absorb the legislative, executive, and judicial powers of the several states, and produce from their ruins one consolidated government, which from the nature of things will be *an iron-handed despotism,* as nothing short of the supremacy of despotic sway could connect and govern these United States under one government.

As the truth of this position is of such decisive importance, it ought to be fully investigated and, if it is founded, to be clearly ascertained; for, should it be demonstrated that the powers vested by this constitution in Congress will have such an effect as necessarily to produce one consolidated government, the question then will be reduced to this short issue, *viz.,* whether satiated with the blessings of liberty, whether repenting of the folly of so recently asserting their unalienable rights against foreign despots at the expense of so much blood and treasure and such painful and arduous struggles, the people of America are now willing to resign every privilege of freemen and submit to the dominion of an absolute government that will embrace all America in one chain of despotism; or whether they will with virtuous indignation, spurn at the shackles prepared for them, and confirm their liberties by a conduct becoming freemen.

That the new government will not be a confederacy of states as it ought, but one consolidated government, founded upon the destruction of the several governments of the states we shall now show.

The powers of Congress under the new constitution are complete and unlimited over the *purse* and the *sword*, and are perfectly independent of, and supreme over, the state governments, whose intervention in these great points is entirely destroyed. By virtue of their power of taxation, Congress may command the whole, or any part of the property of the people. They may impose what imposts upon commerce; they may impose what land taxes, poll taxes, excises, duties on all written instruments, and duties on every other article that they may judge proper. In short, every species of taxation, whether of an external or internal nature is comprised in section eight of article one, *viz.*, "The Congress shall have power to lay and collect taxes, duties, imposts, and excises, to pay the debts, and provide for the common defense and general welfare of the United States."

As there is no one article of taxation reserved to the state governments, the Congress may monopolize every source of revenue, and thus indirectly demolish the state governments; for without funds they could not exist. The taxes, duties and excises imposed by Congress may be so high as to render it impracticable to levy further sums on the same articles; but whether this should be the case or not, if the state governments should presume to impose taxes, duties or excises, on the same articles with Congress, the latter may abrogate and repeal the laws whereby they are imposed, upon the allegation that they interfere with the due collection of their taxes, duties or excises, by virtue of the following clause, part of section eight article one *viz.*, "To make all laws which shall be necessary and proper for carrying into execution the foregoing powers, and all other powers vested by this constitution in the government of the United States, or in any department or officer thereof."

The Congress might gloss over this conduct by construing every purpose for which the state legislatures now lay taxes, to be for the *"general welfare,"* and therefore as of their jurisdiction.

And the supremacy of the laws of the United States is established by article six, *viz.*, "That this constitution and the laws of the United States, which shall be made in pursuance thereof, and *all treaties* made, or which shall be made, under the authority of the United States, shall be the *supreme law* of the *land; and the judges in every state shall be bound thereby; anything in the constitution or laws of any state to the contrary notwithstanding.*" It has been alleged that the words "pursuant to the constitution," are a restriction upon the authority of Congress. But when it is considered that by other sections they are invested with every efficient power of government, and which may be exercised to the absolute destruction of the state governments, without any violation of even the forms of the constitution, this seeming restriction, as well as every other restriction in it, appears to us to be nugatory and delusive, and only introduced as a blind upon the real nature of the government. In our opinion, "pursuant to the constitution," will be co-extensive with the *will* and *pleasure* of Congress, which indeed will be the only limitation of their powers.

We apprehend that two co-ordinate sovereignties would be a solecism in politics. That therefore as there is no line of distinction drawn between the general and state governments; as the sphere of their jurisdiction is undefined, it would be contrary to the nature of things that both should exist together, one or the other would necessarily triumph in the fullness of dominion. However the contest could not be of long continuance, as the state governments are divested of every means of defense and will be obliged by "the supreme law of the land" *to yield at discretion.*

It has been objected to this total destruction of the state governments, that the existence of their legislatures is made essential to the organization of Congress; that they must assemble for the appointment of the senators and president general of the United States. True, the state legislatures may be continued for some years, as boards of appointment, merely after they are divested of every other function. But the framers of the constitution, foreseeing that the people will soon be disgusted with this solemn mockery of a government without power and usefulness, have made a provision for relieving them from the imposition, in section four, of article one, *viz.,* "The times, places, and manner of holding elections for senators and representatives, shall be prescribed in each state by the legislature thereof; *but the Congress may at any time, by law make or alter such regulations, except as to the place of choosing senators.*"

As Congress have the control over the time of the appointment of the president general, of the senators and of the representatives of the United States, they may prolong their existence in office for life by postponing the time of their election and appointment from period to period under various pretences, such as an apprehension of invasion, the factious disposition of the people, or any other plausible pretence that the occasion may suggest.

Having thus obtained life-estates in the government, they may fill up the vacancies themselves, by their control over the mode of appointment; with this exception in regard to the senators, that as the place of appointment for them must, by the constitution, be in the particular state, they may depute somebody in the respective states to fill up the vacancies in the senate, occasioned by death, until they can venture to assume it themselves. In this manner, may the only restriction in this clause be evaded. By virtue of the foregoing section, when the spirit of the people shall be gradually broken, when the general government shall be firmly established, and when a numerous standing army shall render opposition vain, the Congress may complete the system of despotism, in renouncing all dependence on the people by continuing themselves and children in the government.

The celebrated *Montesquieu*, in his Spirit of Laws, volume 1, page 12, says, "That in a democracy there can be no exercise of sovereignty, but by the suffrages of the people, which are their will; now the sovereign's will is the sovereign himself; the laws therefore, which establish the right of suffrage, are fundamental to this government. In fact, it is as important to regulate in a republic in what manner, by whom, and concerning what suffrages are to be given, as it is in a monarchy to know who is the prince, and after what manner he ought to govern." The *time, mode* and *place* of the election of representatives, senators and president general of the United States ought not to be under the control of Congress, but fundamentally ascertained and established.

The new constitution, consistently with the plan of consolidation, contains no reservation of the rights and privileges of the state governments, which was made in the confederation of the year 1778, by article two, *viz.*, "That each state retains its sovereignty, freedom and independence, and every power, jurisdiction and right, which is not by this confederation expressly delegated to the United States in Congress assembled."

The legislative power vested in Congress by the foregoing recited sections is so unlimited in its nature, may be so comprehensive and boundless in its exercise, that this alone would be amply sufficient to annihilate the state governments, and swallow them up in the grand vortex of general empire.

The judicial powers vested in Congress are also so various and extensive, that by legal ingenuity they may be extended to every case, and thus absorb the state judiciaries; and when we consider the decisive influence that a general judiciary would have over the civil polity of the several states, we do not hesitate to pronounce that this power, unaided by the legislative, would effect a consolidation of the states under one government.

The powers of a court of equity vested by this constitution in the tribunals of Congress, powers which do not exist in Pennsylvania, unless so far as they can be incorporated with jury trial, would, in this state, greatly contribute to this event. The rich and wealthy suitors would eagerly lay hold of the infinite mazes, perplexities, and delays which a court of chancery, with the appellate powers of the supreme court in fact as well as law would furnish him with, and thus the poor man being plunged in the bottomless pit of legal discussion would drop his demand in despair.

In short, consolidation pervades the whole constitution. It begins with an annunciation that such was the intention. The main pillars of the fabric correspond with it, and the concluding paragraph is a confirmation of it. The preamble begins with the words, "We the people of the United States," which is the style of a compact between individuals entering into a state of society, and not that of a confederation of states. The other features of consolidation we have before noticed.

Thus we have fully established the position that the powers vested by this constitution in Congress will effect a consolidation of the states under one government, which even the advocates of this constitution admit could not be done without the sacrifice of all liberty.

3. We dissent, thirdly, because if it were practicable to govern so extensive a territory as these United States includes, on the plan of a consolidated government, consistent with the principles of liberty and the happiness of the people, yet the construction of this constitution is not calculated to attain the object for, independent of the nature of the case, it would of itself necessarily produce a despotism, and that not by the usual gradations, but with the celerity that has hitherto only attended revolutions effected by the sword.

To establish the truth of this position, a cursory investigation of the principles and form of this constitution will suffice.

The first consideration that this review suggests is the omission of a BILL OF RIGHTS, ascertaining and fundamentally establishing those unalienable and personal rights of men without the full, free, and secure enjoyment of which there can be no liberty, and over which it is not necessary for a good government to have the control. The principal of which are the rights of conscience, personal liberty by the clear and unequivocal establishment of the writ of *habeas corpus*, jury trial in criminal and civil cases by an impartial jury of the vicinage or county with the common-law proceedings, for the safety of the accused in criminal prosecutions, and the liberty of the press, that scourge of tyrants, and the grand bulwark of every other liberty and privilege. The stipulations heretofore made in favor of them in the state constitutions are entirely superceded by this constitution.

The legislature of a free country should be so formed as to have a competent knowledge of its constituents and enjoy their confidence. To produce these essential requisites the representation ought to be fair, equal, and sufficiently numerous, to possess the same interests, feelings, opinions, and views, which the people themselves would possess, were they all assembled; and so numerous as to prevent bribery and undue influence and so responsible to the people, by frequent and fair elections, as to prevent their neglecting or sacrificing the views and interests of their constituents to their own pursuits.

We will now bring the legislature under this constitution to the test of the foregoing principles, which will demonstrate that it is deficient in every essential quality of a just and safe representation.

The house of representatives is to consist of 65 members, that is one for about every 50,000 inhabitants, to be chosen every two years. Thirty-three members will form a quorum for doing business; and 17 of these, being the majority determine the sense of the house.

The senate, the other constituent branch of the legislature, consists of 26 members being *two* from each state, appointed by their legislatures every six years. Fourteen senators make a quorum, the majority of whom, eight, determines the sense of that body, except in judging on impeachments, or in making treaties, or in expelling a member, when two thirds of the senators present, must concur.

The president is to have the control over the enacting of laws, so far as to make the concurrence of *two* thirds of the representatives and senators present necessary, if he should object to the laws.

Thus it appears that the liberties, happiness, interests, and great concerns of the whole United States may be dependent upon the integrity, virtue, wisdom, and knowledge of 25 or 26 men. How inadequate and unsafe a representation! Inadequate, because the sense and views of 3 or 4 million people diffused over so extensive a territory comprising such various climates, products, habits, interests, and opinions, cannot be collected in so small a body; and besides, it is not a fair and equal representation of the people even in proportion to its number, for the smallest state has as much weight in the senate as the largest. From the smallness of the number to be chosen for both branches of the legislature, from the mode of election and appointment, which is under the control of Congress, and from the nature of the thing, men of the most elevated rank in life will alone be chosen. The other orders in the society, such as farmers, traders, and mechanics, who all ought to have a competent number of their best informed men in the legislature, will be totally unrepresented.

The representation is unsafe, because in the exercise of such great powers and trusts it is so exposed to corruption and undue influence, by the gift of the numerous places of honor and emoluments at the disposal of the executive, by the arts and address of the great and designing, and by direct bribery.

The representation is moreover inadequate and unsafe because of the long terms for which it is appointed, and the mode of its appointment; by which Congress may not only control the choice of the people, but may so manage as to divest the people of this fundamental right and become self-elected.

The number of members in the house of representatives *may* be increased to one for every 30,000 inhabitants. But when we consider that this cannot be done without the consent of the senate, who from their share in the legislative, in the executive, and judicial departments, and permanency of appointment, will be the great efficient body in this government, and whose weight and predominance would be abridged by an increase of the representatives, we are persuaded that this is a circumstance that cannot be expected. On the contrary, the number of representatives will probably be continued at 65, although the population of the country may swell to treble what it now is, unless a revolution should effect a change.

We have before noticed the judicial power as it would effect a consolidation of the states into one government; we will now examine it as it would affect the liberties and welfare of the people, supposing such a government were practicable and proper.

The judicial power under the proposed constitution is founded on the well known principles of the *civil law*, by which the judge determines both on law and fact, and appeals are allowed from the inferior tribunals to the superior upon the whole question; so that *facts* as well as *law* would be re-examined, and even new facts brought forward in the court of appeals; and to use the words of a very eminent civilian, "The cause is many times another thing before the court of appeals, than what it was at the time of the first sentence."

That this mode of proceeding is the one which must be adopted under this constitution is evident from the following circumstances. First, that the trial by jury, which is the grand characteristic of the common law, is secured by the constitution, only in criminal cases. Second, that the appeal from both *law* and *fact* is expressly established, which is utterly inconsistent with the principles of the common law and trials by jury. The only mode in which an appeal from law and fact can be established is by adopting the principles and practice of the civil law, unless the United States should be drawn into the absurdity of calling and swearing juries merely for the purpose of contradicting their verdicts, which would render juries contemptible and worse than useless. Third, that the courts to be established would decide on all cases *of law and equity*, which is a well known character- istic of the civil law, and these courts would have cognizance not only of the laws of the United States and of treaties, and of cases affecting ambassadors, but of all cases of *admiralty and maritime jurisdiction*, which last are matters belonging exclusively to the civil law, in every nation in Christendom.

Not to enlarge upon the loss of the invaluable right of trial by an unbiased jury, so dear to every friend of liberty, the monstrous expense and inconveniences of the mode of proceedings to be adopted are such as will prove intolerable to the people of this country. The lengthy proceedings of the civil law courts in the chancery of England, and in the courts of Scotland and France, are such that few men of moderate fortune can endure the expense of; the poor man must therefore submit to the wealthy. Length of purse will too often prevail against right and justice. For instance, we are told by the learned judge *Blackstone* that a question only on the property of an ox, of the value of *three* guineas, originating under the civil law proceedings in Scotland, after many interlocutory orders and sentences below, was carried at length from the court of sessions, the highest court in that part of Great Britain, by way of *appeal* to the house of lords *where* the question of law and fact was finally determined. He adds that no pique or spirit could in the court of king's bench or common pleas at Westminster have given continuance to such a cause for a tenth part of the time, nor have cost a twentieth part of the expense. Yet the costs in the courts of king's bench and common please in England are infinitely greater than those which the people of this country have ever experi- enced. We abhor the idea of losing the transcendant privilege of trial by jury, with the loss of which, it is remarked by the same learned author, that in Sweden, the liberties of the commons were extinguished by an aristocratic senate, and that *trial by jury* and the liberty of the people went out together. At the same time we regret the intolerable delay, the enormous expenses, and infinite vexation to which the people of this country will be exposed from the voluminous proceed- ings of the courts of civil law, and especially from the appellate jurisdiction, by means of which a man may be drawn from the utmost boundaries of this extensive country to the seat of the supreme court of the nation to contend, perhaps with a wealthy and powerful adver- sary. The consequence of this establishment will be an absolute confir- mation of the power of aristocratic influence in the courts of justice;

for the common people will not be able to contend or struggle against it.

Trial by jury in criminal cases may also be excluded by declaring that the libeler, for instance, shall be liable to an action of debt for a specified sum, thus evading the common law prosecution by indictment and trial by jury. And the common course of proceeding against a ship for breach of revenue laws by information (which will be classed among civil causes) will at the civil law be within the resort of a court, where no jury intervenes. Besides, the benefit of jury trial in cases of a criminal nature, which cannot be evaded, will be rendered of little value, by calling the accused to answer far from home, there being no provision that the trial be by a jury of the neighborhood or country. Thus an inhabitant of Pittsburgh, on a charge of crime committed on the banks of the Ohio, may be obliged to defend himself at the side of the Delaware, and so *vice versa*. To conclude this head, we observe that the judges of the courts of Congress would not be independent, as they are not debarred from holding other offices during the pleasure of the president and senate, and as they may derive their support in part from fees alterable by the legislature.

The next consideration that the constitution presents is the undue and dangerous mixture of the powers of government: the same body possessing legislative, executive, and judicial powers. The senate is a constituent branch of the legislature, it has judicial power in judging on impeachments, and in this case unites in some measure the characters of judge and party, as all the principal officers are appointed by the president-general, with the concurrence of the senate and therefore they derive their offices in part from the senate. This may bias the judgments of the senators and tend to screen great delinquents from punishment. And the senate has, moreover, various and great executive powers, *viz.*, in concurrence with the president-general, they form treaties with foreign nations that may control and abrogate the constitutions and laws of the several states. Indeed, there is no power, privilege, or liberty of the state governments, or of the people, but what may be affected by virtue of this power. For all treaties made by them are to be the "supreme law of the land, anything in the constitution or laws of any state, to the contrary notwithstanding."

And this great power may be exercised by the president and 10 senators (being two-thirds of 14, which is a quorum of that body). What an inducement would this offer to the ministers of foreign powers to compass by bribery *such concessions* as could not otherwise be obtained. It is the unvaried usage of all free states, whenever treaties interfere with the positive laws of the land, to make the intervention of the legislature necessary to give them operation. This became necessary, and was afforded by the parliament of Great Britain, in consequence of the late commercial treaty between that kingdom and France. As the senate judges on impeachments, who is to try the members of the senate for the abuse of this power? And none of the great appointments to office can be made without the consent of the senate.

Such various, extensive, and important powers combined in one body of men are inconsistent with all freedom. The celebrated Montesquieu tells us that "when the legislative and executive powers are united in the same person, or in the same body of magistrates, there can be no liberty because apprehensions may arise, lest the same monarch or *senate* should enact tyrannical laws, to execute them in a tyrannical manner."

"Again, there is no liberty, if the power of judging be not separated from the legislative and executive powers. Were it joined with the legislative, the life and liberty of the subject would be exposed to arbitrary control, for the judge would then be legislator. Were it joined to the executive power, the judge might behave with all the violence of an oppressor. There would be an end of everything, were the same man, or the same body of the nobles, or of the people, to exercise those three powers: that of enacting laws, that of executing the public resolutions, and that of judging the crimes or differences of individuals."

The president-general is dangerously connected with the senate; his coincidence with the views of the ruling junto in that body is made essential to his weight and importance in the government, which will destroy all independence and purity in the executive department. And, having the power of pardoning without the concurrence of a council, he may screen from punishment the most treasonable attempts that may be made on the liberties of the people when instigated by his coadjutors in the senate. Instead of this dangerous and improper mixture of the executive with the legislative and judicial, the supreme executive powers ought to have been placed in the president, with a small independent council, made personally responsible for every appointment to office or other act by having their opinions recorded; and that without the concurrence of the majority of the quorum of this council, the president should not be capable of taking any step.

We have before considered internal taxation, as it would effect the destruction of the state governments, and produce one consolidated government. We will now consider that subject as it affects the personal concerns of the people.

The power of direct taxation applies to every individual as congress, under this government, is expressly vested with the authority of laying a capitation or poll tax upon every person to any amount. This is a tax that, however oppressive in its nature, and unequal in its operation, is certain as to its produce and simple in its collection; it cannot be evaded like the objects of imposts or excise and will be paid because all that a man hath will he give for his head. This tax is so congenial to the nature of despotism, that it has ever been a favorite under such governments. Some of those who were in the late general convention from this state have long labored to introduce a poll tax among us.

The power of direct taxation will further apply to every individual, as congress may tax land, cattle, trades, occupations, etc. in any amount, and every object of internal taxation is of that nature. However oppressive, the people will have but this alternative, except to pay the tax, or let their property be taken, for all resistance will be in vain. The standing army and select militia would enforce the collection.

For the moderate exercise of this power, there is no control left in the state governments whose intervention is destroyed. No relief, or redress of grievances can be extended, as heretofore by them. There is not even a declaration of RIGHTS to which the people may appeal for the vindication of their wrongs in the court of justice. They must, therefore, implicitly obey the most arbitrary laws, as the worst of them will be pursuant to the principles and form of the constitution, and that strongest of all checks upon the conduct of administration, *responsibility to the people*, will not exist in this government. The permanency of the appointments of senators and representatives, and the control the congress have over their election, will place them independent of the sentiments and resentment of the people; and the administration having a greater interest in the government than in the community, there will be no consideration to restrain them from oppression and tyranny. In the government of this state, under the old confederation, the members of the legislature are taken from among the people, and their interests and welfare are so inseparably connected with those of their constituents that they can derive no advantage from oppressive laws and taxes, for they would suffer in common with their fellow citizens. They would participate in the burdens they impose on the community as they must return to the common level after a short period, and notwithstanding every exertion of influence, every means of corruption, a necessary rotation excludes them from permanency in the legislature.

This large state is to have but ten members in that Congress which is to have the liberty, property and dearest concerns of every individual in this vast country at absolute command and even these ten persons, who are to be our only guardians, who are to supercede the legislature of Pennsylvania, will not be of the choice of the people, nor amenable to them. From the mode of their election and appointment they will consist of the lordly and high minded; of men who will have no congenial feelings with the people, but a perfect indifference for, and contempt of them. They will consist of those harpies of power that prey upon the very vitals, that riot on the miseries of the community. But we will suppose, although in all probability it may never be realized in fact, that our deputies in Congress have the welfare of their constituents at heart, and will exert themselves in their behalf. What security could even this afford? What relief could they extend to their oppressed constituents? To attain this, the majority of the deputies of the twelve other states in Congress must be alike well disposed, must alike forego the sweets of power, and relinquish the pursuits of ambition, which from the nature of things is not to be expected. If the people part with a responsible representation in the legislature, founded upon fair, certain and frequent elections, they have nothing left they can call their own. Miserable is the lot of that people whose every concern depends on the WILL and PLEASURE of their rulers. Our soldiers will become Janissaries, and our officers of government Bashaws; in short, the system of despotism will soon be completed.

From the foregoing investigation it appears that the Congress under this constitution will not possess the confidence of the people, which is an essential requisite in a good government. Unless the laws command the confidence and respect of the great body of the people, so as to induce them to support them, when called on by the civil magistrate, they must be executed by the aid of a numerous standing army, which would be inconsistent with every idea of liberty. The same force that may be employed to compel obedience to good laws, might and probably would be used to wrest from the people their constitutional liberties. The framers of this constitution appear to have been aware of this great deficiency, to have been sensible that no dependence could be placed on the people for their support but, on the contrary, that the government must be executed by force. They have therefore made a provision for this purpose in a permanent STANDING ARMY, and a MILITIA that may be subjected to as strict discipline and government.

A standing army in the hands of a government placed so independent of the people, may be made a fatal instrument to overturn the public liberties; it may be employed to enforce the collection of the most oppressive taxes, and to carry into execution the most arbitrary measures. An ambitious man who may have the army at his devotion may step up into the throne and seize upon absolute power.

The absolute unqualified command that Congress have over the militia may be made instrumental to the destruction of all liberty, both public and private, whether of a personal, civil or religious nature.

First, the personal liberty of every man probably from sixteen to sixty years of age may be destroyed by the power Congress have in organizing and governing of the militia. As militia they may be subjected to fines to any amount, levied in a military manner, they may be subjected to corporal punishments of the most disgraceful and humiliating kind, and to death itself, by the sentence of a court martial. To this our young men will be more immediately subjected, as a select militia, composed of them, will best answer the purposes of government.

Second, the rights of conscience may be violated as there is no exemption of those persons who are conscientiously scrupulous of bearing arms. These compose a respectable proportion of the community in the state. This is the more remarkable because even when the distresses of the late war and the evident disaffection of many citizens of that description inflamed our passions, and when every person who was obliged to risk his own life must have been exasperated against such as on any account kept back from the common danger; yet even then, when outrage and violence might have been expected, the rights of conscience were held sacred.

At this momentous crisis, the framers of our state constitution made the most express and decided declaration and stipulations in favor of the rights of conscience; but now, when no necessity exists, those dearest rights of men are left insecure.

Third, the absolute command of Congress over the militia may be destructive of public liberty, for under the guidance of an arbitrary government they may be made the unwilling instruments of tyranny. The militia of Pennsylvania may be marched to New England or Virginia to quell an insurrection occasioned by the most galling oppression, and aided by the standing army, they will no doubt be successful in subduing their liberty and independence. But in so doing, although the magnanimity of their minds will be extinguished, yet the meaner passions of resentment and revenge will be increased, and these in turn will be the ready and obedient instruments of despotism to enslave the others, and that with an irritated vengeance. Thus may the militia be made the instruments of crushing the last efforts of expiring liberty, of riveting the chains of despotism on their fellow citizens, and on one another. This power can be exercised not only without violating the constitution, but in strict conformity with it; it is calculated for this express purpose, and will doubtless be executed accordingly.

As this government will not enjoy the confidence of the people, but be executed by force, it will be a very expensive and burdensome government. The standing army must be numerous, and as a further support, it will be the policy of this government to multiply officers in every department; judges, collectors, tax gatherers, excisemen and the whole host of revenue officers will swarm over the land, devouring the hard earnings of the industrious. Like the locusts of old, impoverishing and desolating all before them.

We have not noticed the smaller, nor many of the considerable blemishes, but have confined our objections to the great and essential defects, the main pillars of the constitution, which we have shown to be inconsistent with the liberty and happiness of the people, as its establishment will annihilate the state governments, and produce one consolidated government that will eventually and speedily issue in the supremacy of despotism.

In this investigation, we have not confined our views to the interests or welfare of this state in preference to the others. We have overlooked all local circumstances. We have considered this subject on the broad scale of the general good, we have asserted the cause of the present and future ages, the cause of liberty and mankind.

Nathaniel Breading	John Ludwig
John Smilie	Abraham Lincoln
Richard Baird	John Bishop
Adam Orth	Joseph Heister
John A. Hanna	Joseph Powel
John Whitehill	James Martin
John Harris	William Findley
Robert Whitehill	John Baird
John Reynolds	James Edgar
Jonathan Hoge	William Todd
Nicholas Lutz	

Thomas Jefferson
Letter to Alexander Donald
Paris, 7 February, 1788

I wish with all my soul that the nine first Conventions may accept the new Constitution, because this will secure to us the good it contains, which I think great and important. But I equally wish that the four latest conventions, whichever they be, may refuse to accede to it till a declaration of rights be annexed. This would probably command the offer of such a declaration, and thus give to the whole fabric perhaps as much perfection as any one of that kind ever had. By a declaration of rights I mean one which shall stipulate freedom of religion, freedom of the press, freedom of commerce against monopolies, trial by juries in all cases, no suspensions of the habeas corpus, no standing armies. These are fetters against doing evil which no honest government should decline. There is another strong feature in the new constitution which I as strongly dislike. That is the perpetual re-eligibility of the President. Of this I expect no amendment at present because I do not see that anybody has objected to it on your side the water. But it will be productive of cruel distress to our country even in your day and mine. The importance to France and England to have our government in the hands of a Friend or a foe, will occasion their interference by money, and even by arms. Our President will be of much more consequence to them than a king of Poland. We must take care, however, that neither this nor any other objection to the new form produce a schism in our union. That would be an incurable evil, because near friends falling out never reunite cordially; whereas, all of us going together, we shall be sure to cure the evils of our new constitution before they do great harm.

Chapter II

The Antifederalist Views of Federalism

The Antifederalists argued that the proposed Constitution was insufficiently federal. Despite the obfuscation of the meaning of federalism by both sides in the debate, there was a common agreement that the status of the state governments was central to understanding the character of a federal arrangement.

For example, there was no dispute that the Articles of Confederation conformed to five principles of federalism. First, the articles of union were created by the states and second, could only be amended by the unanimous consent of the states. Only the states, in contrast to the people, were represented in a unicameral legislature with each state receiving equal representation regardless of population size. A fourth and essential principle was that the government operated on and through the states and not on and over individuals. Finally, the governmental powers of the union were limited to those expressly delegated. The Articles announced clearly that we were a federation of states and not a nation of people.

During the ratification controversy, the Antifederalists focused their critique of the Constitution on the unwarranted departure from the fourth and fifth principles stated above. The powers bestowed on the new government were far greater than were legitimate. The Antifederalists surmised that the "general welfare," "common defense," "interstate commerce," "necessary and proper" clauses of Article I and the "supremacy" clause of Article V constituted a dangerous temptation to consolidate the essential power of government in the new union, thereby undermining the ability of the state governments to play their proper role in the system.

It is interesting to note that in *Federalist* 39, Publius conceded that, when measured against the five principles of federalism, the new plan was "neither a national nor a federal constitution, but a composition of both." He admitted flatly that with regard to the operation of powers, "it is national not federal." He denied that the government was wholly national in extent of powers because "its jurisdiction extends to certain enumerated objects only, and leaves to the several states a residuary and inviolable sovereignty over all other objects." To be sure, jurisdictional disputes were to be decided by courts established under the general government, but "the decision is to be impartially made, according to the rules of the Constitution." The Antifederalists believed that Congress would interpret the enumerated powers of Article I very broadly and that this loose construction would be supported by courts established by Congress. The Antifederalists did not believe that a more perfect union required the consolidation of the states. Rather, geographical diversity and individual liberty were better provided through state governments acting as intermediaries between the union and the people. Antifederalists wrestled thoughtfully with the dilemma of how they could retain what they liked from the Articles, its emphasis on preserving several distinct republics, and nonetheless pursue what "Federal Farmer" described as their object, namely, "to reform our federal system, and to strengthen our governments." They were willing to amend the Articles in order to procure national advantages, but they were unwilling to consolidate all the states into one entire government to accomplish that goal. To them, the determining factor was that the American people were not situated so as "to enjoy equal happiness and advantages under one government."

The clearest articulation of these dilemmas is found in "Federal Farmer I." He outlined three possibilities for the United States, namely, to exist as distinct republics under a federal head, to consolidate all the states in one general government, and, finally, to consolidate the states regarding certain functions of government but to leave them as distinct republics otherwise. Calling the last form a complex or mixed consolidation, we see that it contrasts with the first form by being more than a league or alliance, and with the second form by retaining the distinct republics. Is this complex consolidation the equivalent of Publius's "partly federal, partly national" Constitution?

Antifederalists answered this question negatively. While there are superficial resemblances between Federal Farmer's outline and that of Publius, they saw substantive differences beneath the surface. The differences arose from their anticipation of the operation of the proposed Constitution. They thought that in the process of amending the Articles it had compromised the liberty of the people and the essential republicanism of the states as well as the nation. Their design sought to amend the Articles without raising the question of republicanism. By providing a guarantee for republicanism in the states, they hoped to confine the discussion of a central governing body to its workability.

The Constitution did not retain integral, sovereign units. Even for its adoption it relied upon the "great body politic" rather than the body of sovereign states. But, "states are the characteristic and the soul of a confederation." For the government to be confederal the states must be agents to establish it. "The people have no right to enter into leagues, alliances, or confederations . . . " From this first principle depends the conclusion: the system was not confederal despite some federal features.

What Antifederalists would have added to the Constitution for the sake of creating a workable federalism were an equitable division of responsibilities, the limitation of powers, and the installation of adequate balances and checks. The last would assure the existence of intergovernmental barriers, arming multiple levels with power to limit the excesses of others. In the case of revenue, for example, unless absolute access to it were prescribed both for the states and the confederation, the one which did not have it would be at the mercy of the one which did.

Federalists argued that all the states must be republican in order to confederate and that, accordingly, this necessity excused the degree of consolidation in the Constitution. But Antifederalists rejected this line, appealing to history to sustain their view "of how much less importance it is, that the constituent parts be rightly framed, than it is that the confederacy itself be rightly organized." Thus, the Antifederalist notion of federalism emphasized that a "rightly organized" union would attain national purposes without endangering liberty.

Federal Farmer
Letters I and XVII
(Poughkeepsie) Country Journal
8 October, 1787, 23 January, 1788

My letters to you last winter, on the subject of a well balanced national government for the United States were the result of free inquiry. When I passed from that subject to inquiries relative to our commerce, revenues, past administration, *etc.*, I anticipated the anxieties I feel on carefully examining the plan of government proposed by the convention. It appears to be a plan retaining some federal features, but to be the first important step, and to aim strongly, to one consolidated government of the United States. It leaves the powers of government and the representation of the people so unnaturally divided between the general and state governments, that the operations of our system must be very uncertain. My uniform federal attachments, and the interest I have in the protection of property, and a steady execution of the laws, will convince you that, if I am under any bias at all, it is in favor of any general system which shall promise those advantages. The instability of our laws increases my wishes for firm and steady government; but then I can consent to no government which, in my opinion, is not calculated equally to preserve the rights of all orders of men in the community. My object has been to join with those who have endeavored to supply the defects in the forms of our governments by a steady and proper administration of them. Though I have long apprehended that fraudulent debtors and embarrassed men on the one hand, and men on the other unfriendly to republican equality, would produce an uneasiness among the people and prepare the way, not for cool and deliberate reforms in the governments, but for changes calculated to promote the interests of particular orders of men. Acquit me, sir, of any agency in the formation of the new system; I shall be satisfied with seeing, if it shall be adopted, a prudent administration. Indeed I am so much convinced of the truth of Pope's maxim, that "That which is best administered is best," that I am much inclined to subscribe to it from experience. I am not disposed to unreasonably contend about forms. I know our situation is critical, and it behooves us to make the best of it. A federal government of some sort is necessary. We have suffered the present to languish; and whether the confederation was capable or not originally of answering any valuable purposes, it is now but of little importance. I will pass by the men and states who have been particularly instrumental in preparing the way for a change and perhaps for governments not very favorable to the people at large. A constitution is now presented which we may reject, or which we may accept, with or without amendments, and to which point we ought to direct our exertions is the question. To determine this question with propriety we must attentively examine the system itself and the probable consequences of either step. This I shall endeavor to do, so far as I am able, with candor and fairness, and leave you to decide upon the propriety of my opinions, the weight of my reasons, and how far my conclusions are well drawn. Whatever may be the conduct of others on the present occasion, I do not mean hastily and positively to decide on the merits of the constitution proposed. I shall be open to conviction, and always disposed to adopt that which, all things considered, shall appear to me to be most for the happiness of the community. It must be granted that if men hastily and blindly adopt a system of government, they will as hastily and as blindly be led to alter or abolish it; and changes must ensue, one after another, till the peaceable and better part of the community will grow weary with changes, tumults, and disorders, and be disposed to accept any government, however despotic, that shall promise stability and firmness.

The first principal question that occurs is whether, considering our situation, we ought to precipitate the adoption of the proposed constitution? If we remain cool and temperate, we are in no immediate danger of any commotions. We are in a state of perfect peace, and in no danger of invasions. The state governments are in the full exercise of their powers, and our governments answer all present exigencies, except the regulation of trade, securing credit, in some cases, and providing for the interest, in some instances, of the public debts. Whether we adopt a change, three or nine months hence, can make but little odds with the private circumstances of individuals; their happiness and prosperity, after all, depend principally upon their own exertions. We are hardly recovered from a long and distressing war; the farmers, fishmen, *etc.*, have not yet fully repaired the waste made by it. Industry and frugality are again assuming their proper station. Private debts are lessened, and public debts incurred by the war have been, by various ways, diminished; and the public lands have now become a productive source for diminishing them much more. I know uneasy men, who wish very much to precipitate, do not admit all these facts, but they are facts well known to all men who are thoroughly informed in the affairs of this country. It must, however, be admitted, that our federal system is defective, and that some of the state governments are not well administered; but, then, we impute to the defects in our governments many evils and embarrassments which are most clearly the result of the late war. We must allow men to conduct on the present occasion, as on all similar ones. They will urge a thousand pretences to answer their purposes on both sides. When we want a man to change his condition, we describe it as miserable, wretched, and despised, and draw a pleasing picture of that which we would have him assume. And when we wish the contrary, we reverse our descriptions. Whenever a clamor is raised, and idle men get to work, it is highly necessary to examine facts carefully, and without unreasonably suspecting men of falsehood, to examine, and inquire attentively, under what impressions they act. It is too often the case in political concerns, that men state facts not as they are, but as they wish them to be, and almost every man, by calling to mind past scenes, will find this to be true.

Nothing but the passions of ambitious, impatient, or disorderly men, I conceive, will plunge us into commotions, if time should be taken fully to examine and consider the system proposed. Men who feel easy in their circumstances, and such as are not sanguine in their expectations relative to the consequences of the proposed change, will remain quiet under the existing governments. Many commercial and monied men, who are uneasy, not without just cause, ought to be respected; and, by no means, unreasonably disappointed in their expectations and hopes. But as to those who expect employments under the new constitution, as to those weak and ardent men who always expect to be gainers by revolutions, and whose lot it generally is to get out of one difficulty into another, they are very little to be regarded; and as to those who designedly avail themselves of this weakness and ardor, they are to be despised. It is natural for men who wish to hasten the adoption of a measure to tell us now is the crisis, now is the critical moment which must be seized, or all will be lost: and to shut the door against free inquiry, whenever conscious the thing presented has defects in it, which time and investigation will probably discover. This has been the custom of tyrants and their dependents in all ages. If it is true, what has been so often said, that the people of this country cannot change their condition for the worse, I presume it still behooves them to endeavor deliberately to change it for the better. The fickle and ardent in any community are the proper tools for establishing despotic government. But it is deliberate and thinking men who must establish and secure governments on free principles. Before they decide on the plan proposed, they will inquire whether it will probably be a blessing or a curse to this people.

The present moment discovers a new face in our affairs. Our object has been all along to reform our federal system and to strengthen our governments, to establish peace, order and justice in the community; but a new object now presents. The plan of government now proposed is evidently calculated totally to change, in time, our condition as a people. Instead of being thirteen republics under a federal head, it is clearly designed to make us one consolidated government. Of this, I think, I shall fully convince you, in my following letters on this subject. This consolidation of the states has been the object of several men in this country for some time past. Whether such a change can ever be effected in any manner, whether it can be effected without convulsions and civil wars, whether such a change will not totally destroy the liberties of this country, time only can determine.

To have a just idea of the government before us and to show that a consolidated one is the object in view, it is necessary not only to examine the plan, but also its history, and the politics of its particular friends.

The confederation was formed when great confidence was placed in the voluntary exertions of individuals, and of the respective states; and the framers of it, to guard against usurpation, so limited and checked the powers, that, in many respects, they are inadequate to the exigencies of the union. We find, therefore, members of congress urging alterations in the federal system almost as soon as it was adopted. It was early proposed to vest congress with powers to levy an impost, to regulate trade, *etc.*, but such was known to be the caution of the states in parting with power, that the vestment, even of these, was proposed to be under several checks and limitations. During the war, the general confusion, and the introduction of paper money, infused in the minds of people vague ideas respecting government and credit. We expected too much from the return of peace, and of course we have been disappointed. Our governments have been new and unsettled; and several legislatures, by making tender, suspension, and paper money laws, have given just cause of uneasiness to creditors. By these and other causes, several orders of men in the community have been prepared, by degrees, for a change of government; and this very abuse of power in the legislatures, which, in some cases, has been charged upon the democratic part of the community, has furnished aristocratical men with those very weapons, and those very means, with which, in great measure, they are rapidly effecting their favorite object. And should an oppressive government be the consequence of the proposed change, posterity may reproach not only a few overbearing unprincipled men, but those parties in the states which have misused their powers.

The conduct of several legislatures, touching paper money, and tender laws, has prepared many honest men for changes in government, which otherwise they would not have thought of. When by the evils on the one hand, and by the secret instigations of artful men on the other, the minds of men were become sufficiently uneasy, a bold step was taken, which is usually followed by a revolution or a civil war. A general convention for mere commercial purposes was moved for; the authors of this measure saw that the people's attention was turned solely to the amendment of the federal system; and that, had the idea of a total change been started, probably no state would have appointed members to the convention. The idea of destroying ultimately the state government, and forming one consolidated system could not have been admitted; a convention, therefore, merely for vesting in congress power to regulate trade was proposed. This was pleasing to the commercial towns, and the landed people had little or no concern about it. September, 1786 a few men from the middle states met at Annapolis, and hastily proposed a convention to be held in May, 1787 for the purpose, generally, of amending the confederation. This was done before the delegates of Massachusetts, and of the other states arrived. Still not a word was said about destroying the old constitution, and making a new one. The states still unsuspecting and not aware that they were passing the Rubicon, appointed members to the new convention for the sole and express purpose of revising and amending the confederation and probably not one man in ten thousand in the United States, till within these ten or twelve days, had an idea that the old ship was to be destroyed, and he put to the alternative of embarking in the new ship presented, or of being left in danger of sinking. The States, I believe, universally supposed the convention would report alterations in the confederation, which would pass an examination in congress, and after being agreed to there, would be confirmed by all the legislatures, or be rejected. Virginia made a very respectable appointment, and placed at the head of it the first man in America. In this appointment there was a mixture of political characters, but Pennsylvania appointed principally those men who are esteemed aristocratic. Here the favorite moment for changing the government was evidently discerned by a few men, who seized it with address. Ten other states appointed, and though they chose men principally connected with commerce and the judicial department yet they appointed many good republican characters; had they all attended we should now see, I am persuaded a better system presented. The nonattendance of eight or nine men, who were appointed members of the convention, I shall ever consider as a very unfortunate event to the United States. Had they attended, I am pretty clear the result of the convention would not have had that strong tendency to aristocracy now discernible in every part of the plan. There would not have been so great an accumulation of powers, especially as to the internal police of the country, in a few hands, as the constitution reported proposes to vest in them; the young visionary men and the consolidating aristocracy would have been more restrained than they have been. Eleven states met in the convention, and after four months close attention presented the new constitution, to be adopted or rejected by the people. The uneasy and fickle part of the community may be prepared to receive any form of government; but I presume the enlightened and substantial part will give any constitution presented for their adoption a candid and thorough examination; and silence those designing or empty men, who weakly and rashly attempt to precipitate the adoption of a system of so much importance. We shall view the convention with proper respect and, at the same time that we reflect there were men of abilities and integrity in it, we must recollect how disproportionably the democratic and aristocratic parts of the community were represented. Perhaps the judicious friends and opposers of the new constitution will agree that it is best to let it rest solely on its own merits, or be condemned for its own defects.

In the first place, I shall premise, that the plan proposed is a plan of accommodation; and that it is in this way only, and by giving up a part of our opinions, that we can ever expect to obtain a government founded in freedom and compact. This circumstance candid men will always keep in view in the discussion of this subject.

The plan proposed appears to be partly federal, but principally however, calculated ultimately to make the states one consolidated government.

The first interesting question, therefore, is how far the states can be consolidated into one entire government on free principles. In considering this question extensive objects are to be taken into view, and important changes in the forms of government to be carefully attended to in all their consequences. The happiness of the people at large must be the great object with every honest statesman, and he will direct every movement to this point. If we are so situated as a people, as not to be able to enjoy equal happiness and advantages under one government, the consolidation of the states cannot be admitted.

There are three different forms of free government under which the United States may exist as one nation; and now is, perhaps, the time to determine to which we will direct our views. 1. Distinct republics connected under a federal head. In this case the respective state governments must be the principal guardians of the people's rights, and exclusively regulate their internal police; in them must rest the balance of government. The congress of the states, or federal head, must consist of delegates amenable to, and removable by the respective states. This congress must have general directing powers, powers to require men and monies of the states, to make treaties, peace and war, to direct the operations of armies, etc. Under this federal modification of government, the powers of congress would be rather advisory or recommendatory than coercive. 2. We may do away the several state governments, and form or consolidate all the states into one entire government, with one executive, one judiciary, and one legislature, consisting of senators and representatives collected from all parts of the union. In this case there would be a complete consolidation of the states. 3. We may consolidate the states as to certain national objects, and leave them severally distinct independent republics, as to internal police generally. Let the general government consist of an executive, a judiciary, and balanced legislature, and its powers extend exclusively to all foreign concerns, causes arising on the seas, to commerce, imports, armies, navies, Indian affairs, peace and war, and to a few internal concerns of the community; to the coin, post offices, weights and measures, a general plan for the militia, to naturalization, *and, perhaps to bankruptcies,* leaving the internal police of the community, in other respects, exclusively to the state governments. As the adminis- tration of justice in all causes arising internally, the laying and collecting of internal taxes, and the forming of the militia according to a general plan prescribed. In this case there would be a complete consolidation, *quoad* certain objects only.

Touching the first, or federal plan, I do not think much can be said in its favor. The sovereignty of the nation, without coercive and efficient powers to collect the strength of it, cannot always be depended on to answer the purposes of government; and in a congress of representatives of sovereign states, there must necessarily be an unrea- sonable mixture of powers in the same hands.

As to the second, or complete consolidating plan, it deserves to be carefully considered at this time by every American. If it be impracti- cable, it is a fatal error to model our governments, directing our views ultimately to it.

The third plan, or partial consolidation is, in my opinion, the only one that can secure the freedom and happiness of this people. I once had some general ideas that the second plan was practicable, but from long attention, and the proceedings of the convention, I am fully satisfied that this third plan is the only one we can with safety and propriety proceed upon. Making this the standard, to point out with candor and fairness the parts of the new constitution which appear to be improper is my object. The convention appears to have proposed the partial consolidation evidently with a view to collect all powers ultimately in the United States into one entire government; and from its views in this respect, and from the tenacity of the small states to have an equal vote in the senate, probably originated the greatest defects in the proposed plan.

Independent of the opinions of many great authors that a free elective government cannot be extended over large territories, a few reflections must evince, that one government and general legislation alone, never can extend equal benefits to all parts of the United States. Different laws, customs, and opinions exist in the different states, which by a uniform system of laws would be unreasonably invaded. The United States contain about a million of square miles, and in half a century will, probably, contain ten millions of people; and from the center to the extremes is about 800 miles.

Before we do away the state governments, or adopt measures that will tend to abolish them, and to consolidate the states into one entire government, several principles should be considered and facts ascertained. These, and my examination into the essential parts of the proposed plan, I shall pursue in my next.

*   *   *

I believe the people of the United States are full in the opinion, that a free and mild government can be preserved in their extensive territories, only under the substantial forms of a federal republic. As several of the ablest advocates for the system proposed have acknowledged this (and I hope the confessions they have published will be preserved and remembered), I shall not take up time to establish this point. A question then arises: how far that system partakes of a federal republic? I observed in a former letter that it appears to be the first important step to a consolidation of the states, that its strong tendency is to that point.

But what do we mean by a federal republic? And what by a consolidated government? To erect a federal republic, we must first make a number of states on republican principles; each state with a government organized for the internal management of its affairs. The states, as such, must unite under a federal head, and delegate to it powers to make and execute laws in certain enumerated cases, under certain restrictions. This head may be a single assembly, like the present congress, or the Amphictionic council, or it may consist of a legislature, with one or more branches, of an executive, and of a judiciary. To form a consolidated, or one entire government, there must be no state or local governments, but all things, persons and property, must be subject to the laws of one legislature alone, to one executive, and one judiciary. Each state government, as the government of New Jersey, *etc.*, is a consolidated, or one entire government, as it respects the counties, towns, citizens and property within the limits of the state. The state governments are the basis, the pillar on which the federal head is placed, and the whole together, when formed on elective principles, constitute a federal republic. A federal republic in itself supposes state or local governments to exist, as the body or props, on which the federal head rests, and that it cannot remain a moment after they cease. In erecting the federal government, and always in its councils, each state must be known as a sovereign body; but in erecting this government, I conceive, the legislature of the state, by the expressed or implied assent of the people, or the people of the state, under the direction of the government of it, may accede to the federal compact. Nor do I conceive it to be necessarily a part of a confederacy of states, that each have an equal voice in the general councils. A confederated republic being organized, each state must retain powers for managing its internal police, and all delegate to the union power to manage general concerns. The quantity of power the union must possess is one thing, the mode of exercising the powers given is quite a different consideration. It is the mode of exercising them, that makes one of the essential distinctions between one entire or consolidated government, and a federal republic; that is, however the government may be organized, if the laws of the union, in most important concerns, as in levying and collecting taxes, raising troops, *etc.*, operate immediately upon the persons and property of individuals, and not on states, extend to organizing the militia, *etc.*, the government, as to its administration, as to making and executing laws, is not federal, but consolidated. To illustrate my idea, the union makes a requisition and assigns to each state its quota of men or monies wanted; each state, by its own laws and officers, in its own way, furnishes its quota. Here the state governments stand between the union and individuals; the laws of the union operate only on states, as such, and federally. Here nothing can be done without the meetings of the state legislatures. But in the other case the union, though the state legislatures should not meet for years together, proceeds immediately, by its own laws and officers, to levy and collect monies of individuals, to enlist men, form armies, *etc.* Here the laws of the union operate immediately on the body of the people, on persons and property, in the same manner the laws of one entire consolidated government operate. These two modes are very distinct, and in their operation and consequences have directly opposite tendencies. The first makes the existence of the state governments indispensable, and throws all the detail business of levying and collecting the taxes, *etc.*, into the hands of those governments, and into the hands, of course, of many thousand officers solely created by, and dependent on the state. The last entirely excludes the agency of the respective states, and throws the whole business of levying and collecting taxes, *etc.*, into the hands of many thousand officers solely created by, and dependent upon the union, and makes the existence of the state government of no consequence in the case. It is true, congress in raising any given sum in direct taxes, must by the constitution, raise so much of it in one state, and so much in another, by a fixed rule, which most of the states some time since agreed to. But this does not effect the principle in question, it only secures each state against any arbitrary proportions. The federal mode is perfectly safe and eligible, founded in the true spirit of a confederated republic; there could be no possible exception to it, did we not find by experience, that the states will sometimes neglect to comply with the reasonable requisitions of the union. It being according to the fundamental principles of federal republics, to raise men and monies by requisitions, and for the states individually to organize and train the militia. I conceive, there can be no reason whatever for departing from them, except this; that the states sometimes neglect to comply with reasonable requisitions, and that it is dangerous to attempt to compel a delinquent state by force, as it may often produce a war. We ought, therefore, to inquire attentively how extensive the evils to be guarded against are, and cautiously limit the remedies to the extent of the evils. I am not about to defend the confederation, or to charge the proposed constitution with imperfections not in it; but we ought to examine facts, and strip them of the false coloring often given them by incautious observations, by unthinking or designing men. We ought to premise that laws for raising men and monies, even in consolidated governments, are not often punctually complied with. Historians, except in extraordinary cases, but very seldom take notice of the detail collection of taxes; but these facts we have fully proved and well attested that the most energetic governments have relinqushed taxes frequently, which were of many years standing. These facts amply prove that taxes assessed have remained many years uncollected. I agree there have been instances in the republics of Greece, Holland *etc.*, in the course of several centuries, of states neglecting to pay their quotas of requisitions; but it is a circumstance certainly deserving of attention, whether these nations which have depended on requisitions principally for their defense, have not raised men and monies nearly as punctually as entire governments, which have taxed directly; whether we have not found the latter as often distressed for the want of troops and monies as the former. It has been said that the Amphictionic council and the Germanic head have not possessed sufficient powers to control the members of the republic in a proper manner. Is this, if true, to be imputed to requisitions? Is it not principally to be imputed to the unequal powers of those members connected with this important circumstance that each member possessed power to league itself with foreign powers and powerful neighbors without the consent of the head? After all, has not the Germanic body a government as good as its neighbors in general? And did not the Grecian republic remain united several centuries, and form the theater of human greatness? No government in Europe has commanded monies more plentifully than the government of Holland. As to the United States, the separate states lay taxes directly, and the union calls for taxes by way of requisitions; and is it a fact, that more monies are due in proportion on requisitions in the United States, than on the state taxes directly laid? It is but about ten years since congress began to make requisitions, and in that time, the monies, *etc.*, required and the bounties given for men required of the states have amounted, specie value, to about 36 million dollars, about 24 million dollars of which have been actually paid; and a very considerable part of the 12 million not paid, remains so not so much from the neglect of the states, as from the sudden changes in paper money, *etc.*, which in a great measure rendered payments of no service, and which often induced the union indirectly to relinquish one demand, by making another in a different form. Before we totally condemn requisitions, we ought to consider what immense bounties the states gave, and what prodigious exertions they made in the war, in order to comply with the requisitions of congress; and if since the peace they have been delinquent, ought we not carefully to inquire, whether that delinquency is to be imputed solely to the nature of requisitions? Ought it not in part to be imputed to two other causes? I mean first, an opinion that has extensively prevailed that the requisitions for domestic interest have not been founded on just principles; and second, the circumstance that the government itself by proposing imposts, *etc.*, has departed virtually from the constitutional system, which proposed changes, like all changes proposed in government, produce an inattention and negligence in the execution of the government in being.

I am not for depending wholly on requisitions; but I mention these few facts to show they are not so totally futile as many pretend. For the truth of many of these facts I appeal to the public records; and for the truth of the others, I appeal to many republican characters, who are best informed in the affairs of the United States. Since the peace and till the convention reported, the wisest men in the United States generally supposed that certain limited funds would answer the purposes of the union; and though the states are by no means in so good a condition as I wish they were, yet, I think I may very safely affirm, they are in a better condition than they would be had congress always possessed the powers of taxation now contended for. The fact is admitted that our federal government does not possess sufficient powers to give life and vigor to the political system, and that we experience disappointments and several inconveniencies. But we ought carefully to distinguish those which are merely the consequences of a severe and tedious war from those which arise from defects in the federal system. There has been an entire revolution in the United States within thirteen years, and the least we can compute the waste of labor and property at, during that period, by the war, is three hundred million dollars.

Our people are like a man just recovering from a severe fit of sickness. It was the war that disturbed the course of commerce, introduced floods of paper money, the stagnation of credit, and threw many valuable men out of steady business. From these sources our greatest evils arise; men of knowledge and reflection must perceive it. But then, have we not done more in three or four years past, in repairing the injuries of the war, by repairing houses and estates, restoring industry, frugality, the fisheries, manufactures, *etc.*, and thereby laying the foundation of good government, and of individual and political happiness, than any people ever did in a like time? We must judge from a view of the country and facts, and not from foreign newspapers, or our own, which are printed chiefly in the commercial towns, where imprudent living, imprudent importations, and many unexpected disappointments have produced a despondency and a disposition to view every thing on the dark side. Some of the evils we feel, all will agree, ought to be imputed to the defective administration of the governments. From these and various considerations, I am very clearly of opinion that the evils we sustain merely on account of the defects of the confederation are but as a feather in the balance against a mountain, compared with those which would infallibly be the result of the loss of general liberty and that happiness men enjoy under a frugal, free, and mild government.

Heretofore we do not seem to have seen danger any where, but in giving power to congress, and now nowhere but in congress wanting powers; and, without examining the extent of the evils to be remedied, by one step, we are for giving up to congress almost all powers of any importance without limitation. The defects of the confederation are extravagantly magnified, and every species of pain we feel imputed to them. Hence it is inferred there must be a total change of the principles, as well as forms of government; and in the main point, touching the federal powers, we rest all on a logical inference, totally inconsistent with experience and sound political reasoning.

It is said that as the federal head must make peace and war and provide for the common defense, it ought to possess all powers necessary to that end; that powers unlimited as to the purse and sword, to raise men and monies, and form the militia, are necessary to that end, and, therefore, the federal head ought to possess them. This reasoning is far more specious than solid; it is necessary that these powers so exist in the body politic, as to be called into exercise whenever necessary for the public safety. But it is by no means true that the man or congress of men whose duty it more immediately is to provide for the common defense ought to possess them without limitation. But clear it

is that if such men or congress be not in a situation to hold them
without danger to liberty, he or they ought not to possess them. It has
long been thought to be a well founded position that the purse and
sword ought not to be placed in the same hands in a free government.
Our wise ancestors have carefully separated them, placed the sword in
the hands of their king, even under considerable limitations, and the
purse in the hands of the commons alone; yet the king makes peace
and war, and it is his duty to provide for the common defense of the
nation. This authority at least goes thus far that a nation well versed in
the science of government does not conceive it to be necessary or
expedient for the man entrusted with the common defense and general
tranquility, to possess unlimitedly the powers in question, or even in
any considerable degree. Could he, whose duty it is to defend the
public, possess in himself independently all the means of doing it
consistent with the public good, it might be convenient. But the people
of England know that their liberties and happiness would be in infinitely greater danger from the king's unlimited possession of these
powers than from all external enemies and internal commotions to
which they might be exposed. Therefore, though they have made it his
duty to guard the empire, yet they have wisely placed in other hands,
the hands of their representatives, the power to deal out and control
the means. In Holland their high mightinesses must provide for the
common defense, but for the means they depend, in a considerable
degree, upon requisitions made on the state or local assemblies. Reason and facts evince, that however convenient it might be for an
executive magistrate, or federal head, more immediately charged with
the national defense and safety, solely, directly, and independently to
possess all the means; yet such magistrate, or head, never ought to
possess them if thereby the public liberties shall be endangered. The
powers in question never have been by nations wise and free deposited,
nor can they ever be, with safety, anywhere, but in the principal
members of the national system; where these form one entire government, as in Great Britain, they are separated and lodged in the principal members of it. But in a federal republic, there is quite a different
organization; the people form this kind of government, generally,
because their territories are too extensive to admit of their assembling
in one legislature, or of executing the laws on free principles under one
entire government. They convene in their local assemblies for local
purposes, and for managing their internal concerns, and unite their
states under a federal head for general purposes. It is the essential
characteristic of a confederated republic that this head be dependent
on, and kept within limited bounds by the local governments; and it is

because in these alone, in fact, the people can be substantially assembled or represented. Therefore, we very universally see in this kind of government the congressional powers placed in a few hands, and accordingly limited, and specifically enumerated; and the local assemblies strong and well guarded, and composed of numerous members. Wise men will always place the controlling power where the people are substantially collected by their representatives. By the proposed system, the federal head will possess without limitation almost every species of power that can in its exercise tend to change the government, or to endanger liberty; while in it, I think it has been fully shown, the people will have but the shadow of representation, and but the shadow of security for their rights and liberties. In a confederated republic, the division of representation, *etc.*, in its nature requires a correspondent division and deposit of powers relative to taxes and military concerns. I think the plan offered stands quite alone in confounding the principles of governments in themselves totally distinct. I wish not to exculpate the states for their improper neglect in not paying their quotas of requisitions, but in applying the remedy we must be governed by reason and facts. It will not be denied that the people have a right to change the government when the majority choose it, if not restrained by some existing compact; that they have a right to displace their rulers, and consequently to determine when their measures are reasonable or not; and that they have a right, at any time, to put a stop to those measures they may deem prejudicial to them by such forms and negatives as they may see fit to provide. From all these and many other well founded considerations I need not mention, a question arises: what powers shall there be delegated to the federal head, to insure safety as well as energy, in the government? I think there is a safe and proper medium pointed out by experience, by reason, and facts. When we have organized the government we ought to give power to the union so far only as experience and present circumstances shall direct, with a reasonable regard to time to come. Should future circumstances, contrary to our expectations, require that further powers be transferred to the union, we can do it far more easily than get back those we may now imprudently give. The system proposed is untried; candid advocates and opposers admit, that it is, in a degree, a mere experiment, and that its organization is weak and imperfect. Surely then, the safe ground is cautiously to vest power in it, and when we are sure we have given enough for ordinary exigencies, to be extremely careful how we delegate powers, which, in common cases, must necessarily be useless or abused, and of very uncertain effect in uncommon ones.

By giving the union power to regulate commerce and to levy and collect taxes by imposts, we give it an extensive authority and permanent productive funds, I believe quite as adequate to the present demands of the union as excises and direct taxes can be made to the present demands of the separate states. The state governments are now about four times as expensive as that of the union; and their several state debts added together are nearly as large as that of the union. Our impost duties since the peace have been almost as productive as the other sources of taxation, and when under one general system of regulations, the probability is that those duties will be very considerably increased. Indeed the representation proposed will hardly justify giving to congress unlimited powers to raise taxes by imposts, in addition to the other powers the union must necessarily have. It is said that if congress possess only authority to raise taxes by imposts, trade probably will be overburdened with taxes, and the taxes of the union be found inadequate to any uncommon exigencies. To this we may observe that trade generally finds its own level, and will naturally and necessarily leave off any undue burdens laid upon it. Further, if congress alone possess the impost, and also unlimited power to raise monies by excises and direct taxes, there must be much more danger that two taxing powers, the union and states, will carry excises and direct taxes to an unreasonable extent, especially as these have not the natural boundaries taxes on trade have. However, it is not my object to propose to exclude congress from raising monies by internal taxes, as by duties, excises, and direct taxes, but my opinion is that congress, especially in its proposed organization, ought not to raise monies by internal taxes, except in strict conformity to the federal plan; that is, by the agency of the state governments in all cases, except where a state shall neglect for an unreasonable time to pay its quota of a requisition, but never where so many of the state legislatures as represent a majority of the people shall formally determine an excise law or requisition is improper in their next session after the same be laid before them. We ought always to recollect that the evil to be guarded against is found by our own experience, and the experience of others, to be mere neglect in the states to pay their quotas; and power in the union to levy and collect the neglecting states' quotas with interest is fully adequate to the evil. By this federal plan, with this exception mentioned, we secure the means of collecting the taxes by the usual process of law, and avoid the evil of attempting to compel or coerce a state; and we avoid also a circumstance, which never yet could be, and I am fully confident never can be, admitted in a free federal republic. I mean a permanent and continued system of tax laws of the union, executed in the bowels of the states by many thousand officers, dependent as to the assessing and collecting federal taxes, solely upon the union. On every principle then, we ought to provide that the union render an exact account of all monies raised by imposts and other taxes; and that whenever monies shall be wanted for the purposes of the union, beyond the proceeds of the impost duties, requisitions shall be made on the states for the monies so wanted; and that the power of laying and collecting shall never be exercised, except in cases where a state shall neglect a given time to pay its quota. This mode seems to be strongly pointed out by the reason of the case and spirit of the government; and I believe there is no instance to be found in a federal republic where the congressional powers ever extended generally to collecting monies by direct taxes or excises. Creating all these restrictions, still the powers of the union in matters of taxation will be too unlimited; further checks, in my mind, are indispensably necessary. Nor do I conceive that as full a representation as is practicable in the federal government will afford sufficient security; the strength of the government, and the confidence of the people must be collected principally in the local assemblies. Every part or branch of the federal head must be feeble, and unsafely trusted with large powers. A government possessed of more power than its constituent parts will justify will not only probably abuse it, but be unequal to bear its own burden; it may as soon be destroyed by the pressure of power as languish and perish for want of it.

There are two ways further of raising checks, and guarding against undue combinations and influence in a federal system. The first is in levying taxes, raising and keeping up armies, in building navies, in forming plans for the militia, and in appropriating monies for the support of the military, to require the attendance of a large proportion of the federal representatives as two-thirds or three-fourths of them; and in passing laws, in these important cases, to require the consent of two-thirds or three-fourths of the members present. The second is by requiring that certain important laws of the federal head, as a requisition or a law for raising monies by excise shall be laid before the state legislatures, and if disapproved of by a given number of them (say by as many of them as represent a majority of the people), the law shall have no effect. Whether it would be advisable to adopt both or either of these checks, I will not undertake to determine. We have seen them both exist in confederated republics. The first exists substantially in the confederation and will exist in some measure in the plan proposed, as in choosing a president by the house, and in expelling members; in the senate, in making treaties, and in deciding on impeachments, and in the whole in altering the constitution. The last exists in the United Netherlands, but in a much greater extent. The first is founded on this principle that these important measures may sometimes be adopted by a bare quorum of members, perhaps from a few states, and that a bare majority of the federal representatives may frequently be of the aristocracy, or some particular interests, connections, or parties in the community, and governed by motives, views, and inclinations not compatible with the general interest. The last is founded on this principle, that the people will be substantially represented only in their state or local assemblies; that their principal security must be found in them; and that therefore, they ought to have ultimately a constitutional control over such interesting measures.

I have often heard it observed, that our people are well informed, and will not submit to oppressive governments; that the state governments will be their ready advocates, and possess their confidence, mix with them, and enter into all their wants and feelings. This is all true. But of what avail will these circumstances be if the state governments, thus allowed to be the guardians of the people, possess no kind of power by the forms of the social compact to stop in their passage the laws of congress injurious to the people? State governments must stand and see the law take place; they may complain and petition; so may individuals; the members of them, in extreme cases may resist on the principles of self-defense; so may the people and individuals.

It has been observed that the people in extensive territories have more power, compared with that of their rulers, than in small states. Is not directly the opposite true? The people in a small state can unite and act in concert and with vigor, but in large territories, the men who govern find it more easy to unite, while people cannot; while they cannot collect the opinions of each part, while they move to different points, and one part is often played off against the other.

It has been asserted that the confederate head of a republic at best is in general weak and dependent, that the people will attach themselves to and support their local governments in all disputes with the union. Admit the fact: is it any way to remove the inconvenience by accumulating powers upon a weak organization? The fact is that the detail administration of affairs in this mixed republics depends principally on the local governments, and the people would be wretched without them. A great proportion of social happiness depends on the internal administration of justice and on internal police. The splendor of the monarch, and the power of the government are one thing. The happiness of the subject depends on very different causes, but it is to the latter that the best men, the greatest ornaments of human nature, have most carefully attended. It is to the former tyrants and oppressors have always aimed.

Centinel
Letter I
(Philadelphia) Independent Journal
5 October, 1787

To the Freemen of Pennsylvania:

Friends, Countrymen and Fellow Citizens,

Permit one of yourselves to put you in mind of certain *liberties* and *privileges* secured to you by the constitution of this commonwealth, and to beg your serious attention to his uninterested opinion upon the plan of federal government submitted to your consideration before you surrender these great and valuable privileges up forever. Your present frame of government secures to you a right to hold yourselves, houses, papers and possessions free from search and seizure, and therefore warrants granted without oaths or affirmations first made, affording sufficient foundation for them, whereby any officer or messenger may be commanded or required to search your houses or seize your persons or property, not particularly described in such warrant, shall not be granted. Your constitution further provides "that in controversies respecting property, and in suits between man and man, the parties have a right *to trial by jury, which ought to be held sacred.*" It also provides and declares, "*that the people have a right of* FREEDOM OF SPEECH, *and of* WRITING *and* PUBLISHING *their sentiments, therefore* THE FREEDOM OF THE PRESS OUGHT NOT TO BE RESTRAINED." The constitution of Pennsylvania is *yet* in existence, *as yet* you have the right to *freedom of speech*, and of *publishing your sentiments.* How long those rights will appertain to you, you yourselves are called upon to say. Whether your *houses* shall continue to be your *castles*, whether your *papers*, your *persons* and your *property*, are to be held sacred and free from *general warrants*, you are now to determine. Whether the *trial by jury* is to continue as your birthright, the freemen of Pennsylvania, nay, of all America, are now called upon to declare.

Without presuming upon my own judgment, I cannot think it an unwarrantable presumption to offer my private opinion, and call upon others for theirs, and if I use my pen with the boldness of a freeman, it is because I know that *the liberty of the press yet remains unviolated,* and *juries yet are judges.*

The late Convention have submitted to your consideration a plan of a new federal government. The subject is highly interesting to your future welfare. Whether it be calculated to promote the great ends of civil society, *viz.,* the happiness and prosperity of the community, it behooves you well to consider, uninfluenced by the authority of names, instead of that frenzy of enthusiasm that has actuated the citizens of Philadelphia in their approbation of the proposed plan. Before it was possible that it could be the result of a rational investigation into its principles, it ought to be dispassionately and deliberately examined, and its own intrinsic merit the only criterion of your patronage. If ever free and unbiased discussion was proper or necessary, it is on such an occasion. All the blessings of liberty and the dearest privileges of freemen are now at stake and dependent on your present conduct. Those who are competent to the task of developing the principles of government ought to be encouraged to come forward, and thereby the better enable the people to make a proper judgment; for the science of government is so abstruse that few are able to judge for themselves. Without such assistance the people are too apt to yield an implicit assent to the opinions of those characters, whose abilities are held in the highest esteem, and to those in whose integrity and patriotism they can confide, not considering that the love of domination is generally in proportion to talents, abilities, and superior acquirements, and that the men of the greatest purity of intention may be made instruments of despotism in the hands of the *artful and designing.* If it were not for the stability and attachment which time and habit gives to forms of government, it would be in the power of the enlightened and aspiring few if they should combine at any time to destroy the best establishments, and even make the people the instruments of their own subjugation.

The late revolution having effaced in a great measure all former habits and the present institutions are so recent that there exists not that great reluctance to innovation, so remarkable in old communities, and which accords with reason, for the most comprehensive mind cannot foresee the full operation of material changes on civil polity; it is the genius of the common law to resist innovation.

The wealthy and ambitious, who in every community think they have a right to lord it over their fellow creatures, have availed themselves very successfully of this favorable disposition; for the people thus unsettled in their sentiments have been prepared to accede to any extreme of government. All the distresses and difficulties they experience, proceeding from various causes, have been ascribed to the impotency of the present confederation, and thence they have been led to expect full relief from the adoption of the proposed system of government, and in the other event, immediately ruin and annihilation as a nation. These characters flatter themselves that they have lulled all distrust and jealousy of their new plan by gaining the concurrence of the two men in whom America has the highest confidence [George Washington and Benjamin Franklin], and now triumphantly exult in the completion of their long meditated schemes of power and aggrandisement. I would be very far from insinuating that the two illustrious personages alluded to have not the welfare of their country at heart, but that the unsuspecting goodness and zeal of the one has been imposed on in a subject of which he must be necessarily inexperienced from his other arduous engagements; and that the weakness and indecision attendant on old age, has been practiced on in the other.

I am fearful that the principles of government inculcated in Mr. Adams' treatise, and enforced in the numerous essays and paragraphs in the newspapers have misled some well designing members of the late Convention. But it will appear in the sequel that the construction of the proposed plan of government is infinitely more extravagant.

I have been anxiously expecting that some enlightened patriot would, ere this, have taken up the pen to expose the futility and counteract the baneful tendency of such principles. Mr. Adams' *sine qua non* of a good government is three balancing powers, whose repelling qualities are to produce an equilibrium of interests, and thereby promote the happiness of the whole community. He asserts that the administrators of every government will ever be actuated by views of private interest and ambition to the prejudice of the public good; that therefore the only effectual method to secure the rights of the people and promote their welfare is to create an opposition of interests between the members of two distinct bodies in the exercise of the powers of government and balanced by those of a third. This hypothesis supposes human wisdom competent to the task of instituting three co-equal orders in government, and a corresponding weight in the community to enable them respectively to exercise their several parts, and whose views and interests should be so distinct as to prevent a coalition of any two of them for the destruction of the third. Mr. Adams, although he has traced the constitution of every form of government that ever existed as far as history affords materials, has not been able to adduce a single instance of such a government; he indeed says that the British constitution is such in theory, but this is rather a confirmation that his principles are chimerical and not to be reduced to practice. If such an organization of power were practicable, how long would it continue? Not a day, for there is so great a disparity in the talents, wisdom and industry of mankind, that the scale would presently preponderate to one or the other body and with every accession of power the means of further increase would be greatly extended. The state of society in England is much more favorable to such a scheme of government than that of America. There they have a powerful hereditary nobility, and real distinctions of rank and interests, but even there, for want of that perfect equality of power and distinction of interests in the three orders of government they exist but in name; the only operative and efficient check upon the conduct of administration is the sense of the people at large.

Suppose a government could be formed and supported on such principles, would it answer the great purposes of civil society? If the administrators of every government are actuated by views of private interest and ambition, how is the welfare and happiness of the community to be the result of such jarring adverse interests?

Therefore, as different orders in government will not produce the good of the whole, we must recur to other principles. I believe it will be found that the form of government which holds those entrusted with power in the greatest responsibility to their constitutents the best calculated for freemen. A republican or free government can only exist where the body of the people are virtuous and where property is pretty equally divided; in such a government the people are the sovereign and their sense or opinion is the criterion of every public measure. When this ceases to be the case, the nature of the government is changed, and an aristocracy, monarchy or despotism will rise on its ruin. The highest responsibility is to be attained in a simple structure of government, for the great body of the people never steadily attend to the operations of government and for want of due information are liable to be imposed on. If you complicate the plan by various orders, the people will be perplexed and divided in their sentiments about the source of abuses or misconduct; some will impute it to the senate, others to the house of representatives, and so on, that the interposition of the people may be rendered imperfect or perhaps wholly abortive. But if imitating the constitution of Pennsylvania, you vest all the legislative power in one body of men (separating the executive and judicial) elected for a short period, and necessarily excluded by rotation from permanency, and guarded from precipitancy and surprise by delays imposed on its proceedings, you will create the most perfect responsibility, for then whenever the people feel a grievance they cannot mistake the authors and will apply the remedy with certainty and effect, discarding them at the next election. This tie of responsibility will obviate all the dangers apprehended from a single legislature, and will the best secure the rights of the people.

Having premised this much, I shall now proceed to the examination of the proposed plan of government, and I trust, shall make it appear to the meanest capacity, that it has none of the essential requisites of a free government; that it is neither founded on those balancing restraining powers recommended by Mr. Adams and attempted in the British constitution, nor possessed of that responsibility to its constituents which, in my opinion, is the only effectual security for the liberties and happiness of the people, but, on the contrary, that it is a most daring attempt to establish a despotic aristocracy among freemen, that the world has ever witnessed.

I shall previously consider the extent of the powers intended to be vested in Congress, before I examine the construction of the general government.

It will not be controverted that the legislative is the highest delegated power in government, and that all others are subordinate to it. The celebrated *Montesquieu* establishes it as a maxim that legislation necessarily follows the power of taxation. By section eight of the first article of the proposed plan of government, "the Congress are to have power to lay and collect taxes, duties, imposts and excises, to pay the debts and provide for the common defense and *general welfare* of the United States; but all duties, imposts and excises, shall be uniform throughout the United States." Now what can be more comprehensive than these words. Not content by other sections of this plan, to grant all the great executive powers of a confederation and a STANDING ARMY IN TIME OF PEACE, that grand engine of oppression, and moreover the absolute control over the commerce of the United States and all external objects of revenue, such as unlimited imposts upon imports, *etc.*, they are to be vested with every species of *internal* taxation. Whatever taxes, duties and excises that they may deem requisite for the *general welfare* may be imposed on the citizens of these states, levied by the officers of Congress, distributed through every district in America, and the collection would be enforced by the standing army, however grievous or improper they may be. The Congress may construe every purpose for which the state legislatures now lay taxes to be for the *general welfare* and thereby seize upon every object of revenue.

The judicial power by section one of article three shall extend "to all cases, in law and equity, arising under this constitution, the laws of the United States, and treaties made or which shall be made under their authority; to all cases affecting ambassadors, other public ministers and consuls; to all cases of admirality and maritime jurisdiction, to controversies to which the United States shall be a party, to controversies between two or more states, between a state and citizens of another state, between citizens of different states, between citizens of the same state claiming lands under grants of different states, and between a state, or the citizens thereof, and foreign states, citizens or subjects."

The judicial power is to be vested in one Supreme Court, and in such Inferior Courts as the Congress may from time to time ordain and establish.

The objects of jurisdiction recited above are so numerous and the shades of distinction between civil causes are oftentimes so slight that it is more than probable that the state judicatories would be wholly superceded; for in contests about jurisdiction, the federal court as the most powerful, would ever prevail. Every person acquainted with the history of the courts in England knows by what ingenious sophisms they have, at different periods, extended the sphere of their jurisdiction over objects out of the line of their institution, and contrary to their very nature courts of a criminal jurisdiction obtaining cognizance in civil causes.

To put the omnipotence of Congress over the state government and judicatories out of all doubt, the sixth article ordains that "this constitution and the laws of the United States which shall be made in pursuance thereof, and all treaties made, or which shall be made under the authority of the United States, shall be the *supreme law of the land*, and the judges in every state shall be bound thereby, anything in the constitution or laws of any state to the contrary notwithstanding."

By these sections the all prevailing power of taxation, and such extensive legislative and judicial powers are vested in the general government, as must in their operation, necessarily absorb the state legislatures and judicatories; and that such was in the contemplation of the framers of it will appear from the provision made for such event in another part of it; (but that, fearful of alarming the people by so great an innovation, they have suffered the forms of the separate governments to remain as a blind.) By section four of article one, "the times, places and manner of holding elections for senators and representatives shall be prescribed in each state by the legislature thereof; *but the Congress may at any time, by law, make or alter such regulations, except as to the place of choosing senators.*" The plain construction of which is that, when the state legislatures drop out of sight from the necessary operation of this government, then Congress are to provide for the election and appointment of representatives and senators.

If the foregoing be a just comment, if the United States are to be melted down into one empire, it becomes you to consider whether such a government, however constructed, would be eligible in so extended a territory; and whether it would be practicable, consistent with freedom? It is the opinion of the greatest writers that a very extensive country cannot be governed on democratic principles, on any other plan, than a confederation of a number of small republics possessing all the powers of internal government but united in the management of their foreign and general concerns.

It would not be difficult to prove, that anything short of despotism could not bind so great a country under one government; and that whatever plan you might at the first setting out establish, it would issue in a depotism.

If one general government could be instituted and maintained on principles of freedom, it would not be so competent to attend to the various local concerns and wants of every particular district as well as the peculiar governments, who are nearer the scene, and possessed of superior means of information; besides, if the business of the *whole* union is to be managed by one government, there would not be time. Do we not already see that the inhabitants in a number of larger states, who are remote from the seat of government are loudly complaining of the inconveniences and disadvantages they are subjected to on this account, and that to enjoy the comforts of local government they are separating into smaller divisions.

Having taken a review of the powers, I shall now examine the construction of the proposed general government.

Article one, section one. "All legislative powers herein granted shall be vested in a Congress of the United States which shall consist of a senate and house of representatives." By another section, the president (the principal executive officer) has a conditional control over their proceedings.

Section two. "The house of representatives shall be composed of members chosen every second year by the people of the several states. The number of representatives shall not exceed one for every 30,000 inhabitants."

The senate, the other constituent branch of the legislature, is formed by the legislature of each state appointing two senators for the term of six years.

The executive power by article two, section one is to be vested in a president of the United States of America elected for four years. Section two gives him "power, by and with the consent of the senate to make treaties, provided two-thirds of the senators present concur; and he shall nominate, and by and with the advice and consent of the senate, shall appoint ambassadors, other public ministers and consuls, judges of the Supreme Court, and all other officers of the United States, whose appointments are not herein otherwise provided for, and which shall be established by law, *etc."* And by another section he has the absolute power of granting reprieves and pardons for treason and all other high crimes and misdemeanors, except in case of impeachment.

The foregoing are the outlines of the plan.

Thus we see the house of representatives are on the part of the people to balance the senate, who I suppose will be composed of the *better sort,* the *well born, etc.* The number of the representatives (being only one for every 30,000 inhabitants) appears to be too few, either to communicate the requisite information of the wants, local circumstances, and sentiments of so extensive an empire, or to prevent corruption and undue influence in the exercise of such great powers. The term for which they are to be chosen is too long to preserve a due dependence and accountability to their constituents, and the mode and places of their election are not sufficiently ascertained; for as Congress have the control over both, they may govern the choice by ordering the *representatives* of a *whole* state to be *elected* in *one* place and that too may be the most *inconvenient.*

The senate, the great efficient body in this plan of government, is constituted on the most unequal principles. The smallest state in the union has equal weight with the great states of Virginia, Massachusetts, or Pennsylvania. The Senate, besides its legislative functions, has a very considerable share in the Executive; none of the principal appointments to office can be made without its advice and consent. The term and mode of its appointment will lead to permanency; the members are chosen for six years, the mode is under the control of Congress, and as there is no exclusion by rotation, they may be continued for life, which, from their extensive means of influence, would follow of course. The President, who would be a mere pageant of state, unless he coincides with the views of the Senate, would either become the head of the aristocratic junto in that body or its minion; besides, their influence being the most predominant could the best secure his re-election to office. And from his power of granting pardons, he might screen from punishment the most treasonable attempts on the liberties of the people when instigated by the Senate.

From this investigation into the organization of this government, it appears that it is devoid of all responsibility or accountability to the great body of the people, and that so far from being a regular balanced government, it would be in practice a *permanent* ARISTOCRACY.

The framers of it, actuated by the true spirit of such a government, which ever abominates and suppresses all free inquiry and discussion, have made no provision for the *liberty of the press*, that grand *palladium of freedom* and *scourge of tyrants;* but observed a total silence on that head. It is the opinion of some great writers that if the liberty of the press, by an institution of religion or otherwise, could be rendered *sacred*, even in *Turkey*, that despotism would fly before it. And it is worthy of remark, that there is no declaration of personal rights, premised in most free constitutions; and that trial by *jury* in *civil* cases is taken away. For what other construction can be put on the following, *viz.*, article three, section two: "In all cases affecting ambassadors, other public ministers and consuls, and those in which a State shall be party, the Supreme Court shall have *original* jurisdiction. In all the other cases above mentioned, the Supreme Court shall have *appellate* jurisdiction, both as to *law and fact?*" It would be a novelty in jurisprudence, as well as evidently improper to allow an appeal from the verdict of a jury on the matter of fact; therefore, it implies and allows of a dismission of the jury in civil cases, and especially when it is considered, that jury trial in criminal cases is expressly stipulated for, but not in civil cases.

But our situation is represented to be so *critically* dreadful that, however reprehensible and exceptionable the proposed plan of government may be, there is no alternative between the adoption of it and absolute ruin. My fellow citizens, things are not at that crisis. It is the argument of tyrants. The present distracted state of Europe secures us from injury on that quarter, and as to domestic dissensions, we have not so much to fear from them, as to precipitate us into this form of government, without it is a safe and a proper one. For remember, of all *possible* evils, that of *despotism* is the *worst* and the most to be *dreaded*.

Besides, it cannot be supposed that the first essay on so difficult a subject is so well digested as it ought to be. If the proposed plan, after a mature deliberation, should meet the approbation of the respective States, the matter will end; but if it should be found to be fraught with dangers and inconveniences, a future general Convention being in possession of the objections, will be the better enabled to plan a suitable government.

> *Who's here so base, that would a bondman be?*
> *If any, speak; for him have I offended.*
> *Who's here so vile, that will not love his country?*
> *If any, speak; for him have I offended.*

Brutus
Letters I and V
New York Journal
18 October, 13 December, 1787

To the Citizens of the State of New-York:

When the public is called to investigate and decide upon a question in which not only the present members of the community are deeply interested, but upon which the happiness and misery of generations yet unborn is in great measure suspended, the benevolent mind cannot help feeling itself peculiarly interested in the result.

In this situation I trust the feeble efforts of an individual to lead the minds of the people to a wise and prudent determination, cannot fail of being acceptable to the candid and dispassionate part of the community. Encouraged by this consideration, I have been induced to offer my thoughts upon the present important crisis of our public affairs.

Perhaps this country never saw so critical a period in their political concerns. We have felt the feebleness of the ties by which these United States are held together, and the want of sufficient energy in our present confederation to manage, in some instances, our general concerns. Various expedients have been proposed to remedy these evils, but none have succeeded. At length a convention of the states has been assembled; they have formed a constitution which will now, probably, be submitted to the people to ratify or reject, who are the fountain of all power, to whom alone it of right belongs to make or unmake constitutions or forms of government at their pleasure. The most important question that was ever proposed to your decision, or to the decision of any people under heaven, is before you, and you are to decide upon it by men of your own election, chosen specially for this purpose. If the constitution, offered to your acceptance, be a wise one, calculated to preserve the invaluable blessings of liberty, to secure the inestimable rights of mankind, and promote human happiness, then if you accept it, you will lay a lasting foundation of happiness for millions yet unborn; generations to come will rise up and call you blessed. You may rejoice in the prospects of this vast extended continent becoming filled with freemen who will assert the dignity of human nature. You may solace yourselves with the idea that society, in this favored land, will fast advance to the highest point of perfection; the human mind will expand in knowledge and virtue, and the golden age be, in some measure, realized. But if, on the other hand, this form of government contains principles that will lead to the subversion of liberty; if it tends to establish a despotism, or what is worse, a tyrannic aristocracy, then, if you adopt it, this only remaining asylum for liberty will be shut up, and posterity will execrate your memory.

Momentous then is the question you have to determine, and you are called upon by every motive which should influence a noble and virtuous mind to examine it well and to make a wise judgment. It is insisted indeed, that this constitution must be received, be it ever so imperfect. If it has its defects, it is said, they can be best amended when they are experienced. But remember, when the people once part with power, they can seldom or never resume it again but by force. Many instances can be produced in which the people have voluntarily increased the powers of their rulers; but few, if any, in which rulers have willingly abridged their authority. This is a sufficient reason to induce you to be careful in the first instance how you deposit the powers of government.

With these few introductory remarks, I shall proceed to a consideration of this constitution.

The first question that presents itself on the subject is, whether a confederated government be the best for the United States or not? Or in other words, whether the thirteen United States should be reduced to one great republic, governed by one legislature, and under the direction of one executive and judicial; or whether they should continue thirteen confederated republics, under the direction and control of a supreme federal head for certain defined national purposes only?

This inquiry is important, because although the government reported by the convention does not go to a perfect and entire consolidation, yet it approaches so near to it that it must, if executed, certainly and infallibly terminate in it.

This government is to possess absolute and uncontrollable power, legislative, executive and judicial, with respect to every object to which it extends, for by the last clause of section eight, article one it is declared "that the Congress shall have power to make all laws which shall be necessary and proper for carrying into execution the foregoing powers, and all other powers vested by this constitution, in the government of the United States; or in any department or office thereof." And by the sixth article it is declared "that this constitution, and the laws of the United States, which shall be made in pursuance thereof, and the treaties made, or which shall be made, under the authority of the United States, shall be the supreme law of the land; and the judges in every state shall be bound thereby, any thing in the constitution, or law of any state to the contrary notwithstanding." It appears from these articles that there is no need of any intervention of the state governments between the Congress and the people to execute any one power vested in the general government, and that the constitution and laws of every state are nullified and declared void, so far as they are or shall be inconsistent with this constitution, or the laws made in pursuance of it, or with treaties made under the authority of the United States. The government then, so far as it extends, is a complete one, and not a confederation. It is as much one complete government as that of New York or Massachusetts, has as absolute and perfect powers to make and execute all laws, to appoint officers, institute courts, declare offenses, and annex penalties, with respect to every object to which it extends, as any other in the world. So far therefore as its powers reach, all ideas of confederation are given up and lost. It is true this government is limited to certain objects, or to speak more properly, some small degree of power is still left to the states, but a little attention to the powers vested in the general government will convince every candid man that if it is capable of being executed, all that is reserved for the individual states must very soon be annihilated, except so far as they are barely necessary to the organization of the general government. The powers of the general legislature extend to every case that is of the least importance; there is nothing valuable to human nature, nothing dear to freemen, but what is within its power. It has authority to make laws which will affect the lives, the liberty, and property of every man in the United States; nor can the constitution or laws of any state in any way prevent or impede the full and complete execution of every power given. The legislative power is competent to lay taxes, duties, imposts, and excises. There is no limitation to this power, unless it be said that the clause which directs the use to which those taxes, and duties shall be applied, may be said to be a limitation; but this is no restriction of the power at all, for by this clause they are to be applied to pay the debts and provide for the common defense and general welfare of the United States, but the legislature have authority to contract debts at their discretion. They are the sole judges of what is necessary to provide for the common defense, and they only are to determine what is for the general welfare. This power therefore is neither more nor less than a power to lay and collect taxes, imposts, and excises, at their pleasure. Not only is the power to lay taxes unlimited, as to the amount they may require, but it is perfect and absolute to raise them in any mode they please. No state legislature, or any power in the state governments, have any more to do in carrying this into effect than the authority of one state has to do with that of another. In the business therefore of laying and collecting taxes, the idea of confederation is totally lost, and that of one entire republic is embraced. It is proper here to remark, that the authority to lay and collect taxes is the most important of any power that can be granted; it connects with it almost all other powers, or at least will in process of time draw all other after it. It is the great mean of protection, security, and defense in a good government, and the great engine of oppression and tyranny in a bad one. This cannot fail of being the case, if we consider the contracted limits which are set by this constitution, to the late governments on this article of raising money. No state can emit paper money lay any duties or imposts on imports or exports, but by consent of the Congress; and then the net produce shall be for the benefit of the United States. The only mean therefore left, for any state to support its government and discharge its debts is by direct taxation; and the United States have also power to lay and collect taxes in any way they please. Everyone who has thought on the subject must be convinced that but small sums of money can be collected in any country by direct taxes; when the federal government begins to exercise the right of taxation in all its parts, the legislatures of the several states will find it impossible to raise monies to support their governments. Without money they cannot be supported, and they must dwindle away and, as before observed, their powers absorbed in that of the general government.

It might be here shown that the power in the federal legislative, to raise and support armies at pleasure, as well in peace as in war, and their control over the militia tend not only to a consolidation of the government, but the destruction of liberty. I shall not, however, dwell upon these, as a few observations upon the judicial power of this government, in addition to the preceding, will fully evince the truth of the position.

The judicial power of the United States is to be vested in a supreme court, and in such inferior courts as Congress may from time to time ordain and establish. The powers of these courts are very extensive, their jurisdiction comprehends all civil causes, except such as arise between citizens of the same state, and it extends to all cases in law and equity arising under the constitution. One inferior court must be established, I presume, in each state, at least, with the necessary executive officers appendant thereto. It is easy to see that in the common course of things, these courts will eclipse the dignity, and take away from the respectability of the state courts. These courts will be in themselves, totally independent of the states, deriving their authority from the United States, and receiving from them fixed salaries; and in the course of human events it is to be expected that they will swallow up all the powers of the courts in the respective states.

How far the clause in the eighth section of the first article may operate to do away all idea of confederated states and to effect an entire consolidation of the whole into one general government, it is impossible to say. The powers given by this article are very general and comprehensive, and it may receive a construction to justify the passing almost any law. A power to make all laws which shall be *necessary and proper* for carrying into execution all powers vested by the constitution in the government of the United States or any department or officer thereof, is a power very comprehensive and definite and may, for ought I know, be exercised in a such manner as entirely to abolish the state legislatures. Suppose the legislature of a state should pass a law to raise money to support their government and pay the state debt. May the Congress repeal this law, because it may prevent the collection of a tax which they may think proper and necessary to lay to provide for the general welfare of the United States? For all laws made in pursuance of this constitution are the supreme law of the land, and the judges in every state shall be bound thereby, anything in the constitution or laws of the different states to the contrary notwithstanding. By such a law the government of a particular state might be overturned at one stroke, and thereby be deprived of every means of its support.

It is not meant by stating this case to insinuate that the constitution would warrant a law of this kind, or unnecessarily to alarm the fears of the people by suggesting that the federal legislature would be more likely to pass the limits assigned them by the constitution, than that of an individual state, further than they are less responsible to the people. But what is meant is that the legislature of the United States are vested with the great and uncontrollable powers of laying and collecting taxes, duties, imposts, and excises; of regulating trade, raising and supporting armies, organizing, arming, and disciplining the militia, instituting courts, and other general powers. And are by this clause invested with the power of making all laws *proper and necessary* for carrying all these into execution; and they may so exercise this power as entirely to annihilate all the state governments, and reduce this country to one single government. And if they may do it, it is pretty certain they will, for it will be found that the power retained by individual states, small as it is, will be a clog upon the wheels of the government of the United States; the latter therefore will be naturally inclined to remove it out of the way. Besides, it is a truth confirmed by the unerring experience of ages, that every man, and every body of men, invested with power, are ever disposed to increase it, and to acquire a superiority over everything that stands in their way. This disposition, which is implanted in human nature, will operate in the federal legislature to lessen and ultimately to subvert the state authority, and having such advantages, will most certainly succeed if the federal government succeeds at all. It must be very evident then, that what this constitution wants of being a complete consolidation of the several parts of the union into one complete government possessed of perfect legislative, judicial, and executive powers, to all intents and purposes, it will necessarily acquire in its exercise and operation.

Let us now proceed to inquire, as I at first proposed, whether it be best the thirteen United States should be reduced to one great republic or not. It is here taken for granted that all agree in this, that whatever government we adopt, it ought to be a free one; that it should be so framed as to secure the liberty of the citizens of America, and such an one as to admit of a full, fair, and equal representation of the people. The question then will be whether a government thus constituted and founded on such principles is practicable, and can be exercised over the whole United States, reduced into one state?

If respect is to be paid to the opinion of the greatest and wisest men who have ever thought or wrote on the science of government, we shall be constrained to conclude that a free republic cannot succeed over a country of such immense extent containing such a number of inhabitants, and these increasing in such rapid progression as that of the whole United States. Among the many illustrious authorities which might be produced to this point, I shall content myself with quoting only two. The one is the Baron de Montesquieu, *Spirit of Laws*, chap. xvi, vol. I. "It is natural to a republic to have only a small territory, otherwise it cannot long subsist. In a large republic there are men of large fortunes, and consequently of less moderation; there are trusts too great to be placed in any single subject; he has interest of his own; he soon begins to think that he may be happy, great and glorious, by oppressing his fellow citizens; and that he may raise himself to grandeur on the ruins of his country. In a large republic, the public good is sacrificed to a thousand views; it is subordinate to exceptions, and depends on accidents. In a small one, the interest of the public is easier perceived, better understood, and more within the reach of every citizen; abuses are of less extent, and of course are less protected." Of the same opinion is the Marquis Becarria.

History furnishes no example of a free republic anything like the extent of the United States. The Grecian republics were of small extent; so also was that of the Romans. Both of these, it is true, in process of time, extended their conquests over large territories of country; and the consequence was, that their governments were changed from that of free governments to those of the most tyrannical that ever existed in the world.

Not only the opinion of the greatest men, and the experience of mankind, are against the idea of an extensive republic, but a variety of reasons may be drawn from the reason and nature of things against it. In every government, the will of the sovereign is the law. In despotic governments, the supreme authority being lodged in one, his will is law, and can be as easily expressed to a large extensive territory as to a small one. In a pure democracy the people are the sovereign, and their will is declared by themselves; for this purpose they must all come together to deliberate and decide. This kind of government cannot be exercised, therefore, over a country of any considerable extent; it must be confined to a single city, or at least limited to such bounds as that the people can conveniently assemble, be able to debate, understand the subject submitted to them, and declare their opinion concerning it.

In a free republic, although all laws are derived from the consent of the people, yet the people do not declare their consent by themselves in person, but by representatives chosen by them, who are supposed to know the minds of their constituents and to be possessed of integrity to declare this mind.

In every free government, the people must give their assent to the laws by which they are governed. This is the true criterion between a free government and an arbitrary one. The former are ruled by the will of the whole, expressed in any manner they may agree upon; the latter by the will of one or a few. If the people are to give their assent to the laws by persons chosen and appointed by them, the manner of the choice and the number chosen must be such as to possess, be disposed, and consequently qualified to declare the sentiments of the people; for if they do not know, or are not disposed to speak the sentiments of the people, the people do not govern, but the sovereignty is in a few. Now, in a large extended country, it is impossible to have a representation possessing the sentiments and of integrity to declare the minds of the people, without having it so numerous and unwieldly, as to be subject in great measure to the inconvenience of a democratic government.

The territory of the United States is of vast extent; it now contains near three million souls, and is capable of containing much more than ten times that number. Is it practicable for a country, so large and so numerous as they will soon become, to elect a representation that will speak their sentiments without their becoming so numerous as to be incapable of transacting public business? It certainly is not.

In a republic, the manners, sentiments, and interests of the people should be similar. If this be not the case, there will be a constant clashing of opinions; and the representatives of one part will be continually striving against those of the other. This will retard the operations of government, and prevent such conclusions as will promote the public good. If we apply this remark to the condition of the United States, we shall be convinced that it forbids that we should be one government. The United States includes a variety of climates. The productions of the different parts of the union are very variant, and their interests, of consequence, diverse. Their manners and habits differ as much as their climates and productions; and their sentiments are by no means coincident. The laws and customs of the several states are, in many respects, very diverse, and in some opposite; each would be in favor of its own interests and customs, and, of consequence, a legislature formed of representatives from the respective parts, would not only be too numerous to act with any care or decision, but would be composed of such heterogenous and discordant principles as would constantly be contending with each other.

The laws cannot be executed in a republic of an extent equal to that of the United States with promptitude.

The magistrates in every government must be supported in the execution of the laws, either by an armed force, maintained at the public expense for that purpose, or by the people turning out to aid the magistrate upon his command in case of resistance.

In despotic governments, as well as in all the monarchies of Europe, standing armies are kept up to execute the commands of the prince or the magistrate, and are employed for this purpose when occasion requires. But they have always proved the destruction of liberty and abhorrent to the spirit of a free republic. In England, where they depend upon the parliament for their annual support, they have always been complained of as oppressive and unconstitutional, and are seldom employed in executing of the laws, never except on extraordinary occasions, and then under the direction of a civil magistrate.

A free republic will never keep a standing army to execute its laws. It must depend upon the support of its citizens. But when a government is to receive its support from the aid of the citizens, it must be so constructed as to have the confidence, respect, and affection of the people. Men who, upon the call of the magistrate, offer themselves to execute the laws, are influenced to do it either by affection to the government, or from fear. Where a standing army is at hand to punish offenders, every man is actuated by the latter principle and therefore, when the magistrate calls, will obey. But where this is not the case, the government must rest for its support upon the confidence and respect which the people have for their government and laws. The body of the people being attached, the government will always be sufficient to support and execute its laws, and to operate upon the fears of any faction which may be opposed to it, not only to prevent an opposition to the execution of the laws themselves, but also to compel the most of them to aid the magistrate. But the people will not be likely to have such confidence in their rulers, in a republic so extensive as the United States, as necessary for these purposes. The confidence which the people have in their rulers in a free republic arises from their knowing them, from their being responsible to them for their conduct, and from the power they have of displacing them when they misbehave. But in a republic of the extent of this continent, the people in general would be acquainted with very few of their rulers; the people at large would know little of their proceedings, and it would be extremely difficult to change them. The people in Georgia and New Hampshire would not know one another's mind, and therefore could not act in concert to enable them to effect a general change of representatives. The different parts of so extensive a country could not possibly be made acquainted with the conduct of their representatives, nor be informed of the reasons upon which measures were founded. The consequence will be [that] they will have no confidence in their legislature, suspect them of ambitious views, be jealous of every measure they adopt, and will not support the laws they pass. Hence the government will be nerveless and inefficient, and no way will be left to render it otherwise but by establishing an armed force to execute the laws at the point of the bayonet, a government of all others the most to be dreaded.

In a republic of such vast extent as the United States, the legislature cannot attend to the various concerns and wants of its different parts. It cannot be sufficiently numerous to be acquainted with the local condition and wants of the different districts and if it could, it is impossible it should have sufficient time to attend to and provide for all the variety of cases of this nature, that would be continually arising.

In so extensive a republic, the great officers of government would soon become above the control of the people, and abuse their power to the purpose of aggrandizing themselves and oppressing them. The trust committed to the executive offices, in a country of the extent of the United States, must be various and of magnitude. The command of all the troops and navy of the republic, the appointment of officers,

the power of pardoning offenses, the collecting of all the public revenues, and the power of expending them, with a number of other
powers, must be lodged and exercised in every state in the hands of a
few. When these are attended with great honor and emolument, as
they always will be in large states, so as greatly to interest men to
pursue them, and to be proper objects for ambitious and designing
men, such men will be ever restless in their pursuit after them. They
will use the power, when they have acquired it, to the purposes of
gratifying their own interest and ambition, and it is scarcely possible,
in a very large republic, to call them to account for their misconduct,
or to prevent their abuse of power.

These are some of the reasons by which it appears, that a free
republic cannot long subsist over a country of the great extent of these
states. If then this new constitution is calculated to consolidate the
thirteen states into one, as it evidently is, it ought not to be adopted.

Though I am of opinion that it is a sufficient objection to this government to reject it, that it creates the whole union into one government
under the form of a republic, yet if this objection was obviated, there
are exceptions to it which are so material and fundamental that they
ought to determine every man who is a friend to the liberty and happiness of mankind not to adopt it. I beg the candid and dispassionate
attention of my countrymen while I state these objections; they are
such as have obtruded themselves upon my mind upon a careful attention to the matter, and such as I sincerely believe are well founded.
There are many objections, of small moment, of which I shall take no
notice; perfection is not to be expected in anything that is the production of man, and if I did not in my conscience believe that this scheme
was defective in the fundamental principles in the foundation upon
which a free and equal government must rest, I would hold my peace.

*   *   *

It was intended in this Number to have prosecuted the inquiry into
the organization of this new system; particularly to have considered
the dangerous and premature union of the President and Senate,
and the mixture of legislative, executive, and judicial powers in the
Senate. But there is such an intimate connection between the several
branches in whom the different species of authority is lodged, and the
powers with which they are invested, that on reflection it seems
necessary first to proceed to examine the nature and extent of the
powers granted to the legislature.

This inquiry will assist us the better to determine whether the legislature is so constituted as to provide proper checks and restrictions for the security of our rights and to guard against the abuse of power. For the means should be suited to the end; a government should be framed with a view to the objects to which it extends: if these be few in number, and of such a nature as to give but small occasion or opportunity to work oppression in the exercise of authority, there will be less need of a numerous representation and special guards against abuse, than if the powers of the government are very extensive and include a great variety of cases. It will also be found necessary to examine the extent of these powers in order to form a just opinion how far this system can be considered as a confederation or a consolidation of the states. Many of the advocates for, and most of the opponents to this system, agree that the form of government most suitable for the United States is that of a confederation. The idea of a confederated government is that of a number of independent states entering into a compact, for the conducting certain general concerns, in which they have a common interest, leaving the management of their internal and local affairs to their separate governments. But whether the system proposed is of this nature cannot be determined without a strict inquiry into the powers proposed to be granted.

This constitution considers the people of the several states as one body corporate and is intended as an original compact. It will therefore dissolve all contracts which may be inconsistent with it. This not only results from its nature, but is expressly declared in the sixth *article* of it. The design of the constitution is expressed in the preamble, to be, "in order to form a more perfect union, to establish justice, insure domestic tranquility, provide for the common defense, promote the general welfare, and secure the blessings of liberty to ourselves and posterity." These are the ends this government is to accomplish, and for which it is invested with certain powers, among these is the power "to make all laws which are *necessary and proper* for carrying into execution the foregoing powers, and *all other* powers vested by this constitution in the government of the United States, or in any department or officer thereof." It is a rule in construing a law to consider the objects the legislature had in view in passing it, and to give it such an explanation as to promote their intention. The same rule will apply in explaining a constitution. The great objects then are declared in this preamble in general and indefinite terms to be to provide for the common defense, promote the general welfare, and an express power being vested in the legislature to make all laws which shall be necessary and proper for carrying into execution all the powers vested in the general government. The inference is natural that the legislature will have an authority to make all laws which they shall judge necessary for the common safety, and to promote the general welfare. This amounts to a power to make laws at discretion. No terms can be found more indefinite than these; it is obvious that the legislature alone must judge what laws are proper and necessary for the purpose. It may be said that this way of explaining the constitution is torturing and making it speak what it never intended. This is far from my intention, and I shall not even insist upon this implied power but join issue with those who say we are to collect the idea of the powers given from the express words of the clauses granting them; and it will not be difficult to show that the same authority is expressly given which is supposed to be implied in the foregoing [analysis].

In the first article, eighth section, it is declared, "that Congress shall have power to lay and collect taxes, duties, imposts and excises, to pay the debts, and provide for the common defense, and general welfare of the United States." In the preamble, the intent of the constitution, among other things, is declared to be to provide for the common defense, and promote the general welfare, and in this clause the power is in express words given to Congress "to provide for the common defense, and general welfare." And in the last paragraph of the same section there is an express authority to make all laws which shall be necessary and proper for carrying into execution this power. It is therefore evident that the legislature under this constitution may pass any law which they may think proper. It is true the ninth section restrains their power with respect to certain objects. But these restrictions are very limited, some of them improper, some unimportant, and others not easily understood, as I shall hereafter show. It has been urged that the meaning I give to this part of the constitution is not the true one, that the intent of it is to confer on the legislature the power to lay and collect taxes, etc. in order to provide for the common defense and general welfare. To this I would reply that the meaning and intent of the constitution is to be collected from the words of it, and I submit to the public whether the construction I have given it is not the most natural and easy. But admitting the contrary opinion to prevail I shall nevertheless be able to show that the same powers are substantially vested in the general government by several other articles in the constitution. It invests the legislature with authority to lay and collect taxes, duties, imposts and excises in order to provide for the common defense and promote the general welfare, and to pass all laws which shall be necessary and proper for carrying this power into effect. To comprehend the extent of this authority, it will be requisite to examine first, what is included in this power to lay and collect taxes, duties, imposts, and excises, second, what is implied in the authority to pass all laws which shall be necessary and proper for carrying this power into execution, and third, what limitation, if any, is set to the exercise of this power by the constitution.

First, to detail the particulars comprehended in the general terms, taxes, duties, imposts, and excises, would require a volume instead of a single piece in a newspaper. Indeed it would be a task far beyond my ability and to which no one can be competent unless possessed of a mind capable of comprehending every possible source of revenue; for they extend to every possible way of raising money, whether by direct or indirect taxation. Under this clause may be imposed a poll tax, a land tax, a tax on houses and buildings, on windows and fire places, on cattle and on all kinds of personal property. It extends to duties on all kinds of goods to any amount, to tonnage and poundage on vessels, to duties on written instruments, newspapers, almanacs, and books. It comprehends an excise on all kinds of liquors, spirits, wines, cider, beer, *etc.* And indeed it takes in duty or excise on every necessary or convenience of life, whether of foreign or home growth or manufactory. In short, we can have no conception of any way in which a government can raise money from the people, but what is included in one or other of three general terms. We may say then that this clause commits to the hands of the general legislature every conceivable source of revenue within the United States. Not only are these terms very comprehensive and extend to a vast number of objects, but the power to lay and collect has great latitude; it will lead to the passing a vast number of laws which may affect the personal rights of the citizens of the states, expose their property to fines and confiscation, and put their lives in jeopardy. It opens a door to the appointment of a swarm of revenue and excise officers to prey upon the honest and industrious part of the community, eat up their substance, and riot on the spoils of the country.

Second. We will next inquire into what is implied in the authority to pass all laws which shall be necessary and proper to carry this power into execution.

It is perhaps utterly impossible fully to define this power. The authority granted in the first clause can only be understood in its full extent by descending to all the particular cases in which a revenue can be raised; the number and variety of these cases are so endless, and as it were infinite, that no man living has as yet been able to reckon them up. The greatest geniuses in the world have been for ages employed in the research, and when mankind had supposed that the subject was exhausted they have been astonished with the refined improvements that have been made in modern times, and especially in the English nation on the subject. If then the objects of this power cannot be comprehended, how is it possible to understand the extent of that power which can pass all laws which shall be necessary and proper for carrying it into execution? It is truly incomprehensible. A case cannot be conceived of, which is not included in this power. It is well known that the subject of revenue is the most difficult and extensive in the science of government. It requires the greatest talents of a statesman, and the most numerous and exact provisions of the legislature. The command of the revenues of a state gives the command of everything in it. He that has the purse will have the sword, and they that have both, have everything; so that the legislature having every source from which money can be drawn under their direction, with a right to make all laws necessary and proper for drawing forth all the resource of the country, would have, in fact, all power.

Were I to enter into the detail, it would be easy to show how this power in its operation would totally destroy all the powers of the individual states. But this is not necessary for those who will think for themselves, and it will be useless to such as take things upon trust; nothing will awaken them to reflection, until the iron hand of oppression compel them to it.

I shall only remark that this power, given to the federal legislature, directly annihilates all the powers of the state legislatures. There cannot be a greater solecism in politics than to talk of power in a government, without the command of any revenue. It is as absurd as to talk of an animal without blood, or the subsistence of one without food. Now the general government having in their control every possible source of revenue, and authority to pass any law they may deem necessary to draw them forth, or to facilitate their collection; no source of revenue is therefore left in the hands of any state. Should any state attempt to raise money by law, the general government may repeal or arrest it in the execution, for all their laws will be the supreme law of the land: If then any one can be weak enough to believe that a government can exist without having the authority to raise money to pay a door-keeper to their assembly, he may believe that the state government can exist, should this new constitution take place.

It is agreed by most of the advocates of this new system, that the government which is proper for the United States should be a confederated one; that the respective states ought to retain a portion of their sovereignty, and that they should preserve not only the forms of their legislatures, but also the power to conduct certain internal concerns. How far the powers to be retained by the states shall extend, is the question. We need not spend much time on this subject, as it respects this constitution, for a government without the power to raise money is one only in name. It is clear that the legislatures of the respective states must be altogether dependent on the will of the general legislature for the means of supporting their government. The legislature of the United States will have a right to exhaust every source of revenue in every state and to annul all laws of the states which may stand in the way of effecting it; unless therefore we can suppose the state governments can exist without money to support the officers who execute them, we must conclude they will exist no longer than the general legislature choose they should. Indeed the idea of any government existing, in any respect, as an independent one, without any means of support in their own hands, is an absurdity. If therefore this constitution has in view, what many of its framers and advocates say it has, to secure and guarantee to the separate states the exercise of certain powers of government, it certainly ought to have left in their hands some sources of revenue. It should have marked the line in which the general government should have raised money, and set bounds over which they should not pass, leaving to the separate states other means to raise supplies for the support of their governments, and to discharge their respective debts. To this it is objected that the general government ought to have power competent to the purposes of the union; they are to provide for the common defense, to pay the debts of the United States, support foreign ministers, and the civil establishment of the union, and to do these they ought to have authority to raise money adequate to the purpose. On this I observe that the state governments have also contracted debts; they require money to support their civil officers, and how is this to be done, if they give to the general government a power to raise money in every way in which it can possibly be raised, with such a control over the state legislatures as to prohibit them, whenever the general legislature may think proper, from raising any money? It is again objected that it is very difficult, if not impossible, to draw the line of distinction between the powers of the general and state governments on this subject. The first, it is said, must have the power of raising the money necessary for the purposes of the union, if they are limited to certain objects the revenue may fall short of a sufficiency for the public exigencies, they must therefore have discretionary power. The line may be easily and accurately drawn between the powers of the two governments on this head. The distinction between external and internal taxes, is not a novel one in this country. It is a plain one and easily understood. The first includes impost duties on all imported goods; this species of taxes it is proper should be laid by the general government. Many reasons might be urged to show that no danger is to be apprehended from their exercise of it. They may be collected in few places, and from few hands with certainty and expedition. But few officers are necessary to be employed in collecting them, and there is no danger of oppression in laying them, because, if they are laid higher than trade will bear, the merchants will cease importing or smuggle their goods. We have therefore sufficient security, arising from the nature of the thing, against burdensome and intolerable impositions from this kind of tax. But the case is far otherwise with regard to direct taxes; these include poll taxes, land taxes, excises, duties on written instruments, on everything we eat, drink, or wear; they take hold of every species of property, and come home to every man's house and pocket. These are often so oppressive, as to grind the face of the poor, and render the lives of the common people a burden to them. The great and only security the people can have against oppression from this kind of taxes, must rest in their representatives. If they are sufficiently numerous to be well informed of the circumstances, and ability of those who send them, and have a proper regard for the people, they will be secure. The general legislature, as I have shown in a former paper, will not be thus qualified, and therefore, on this account, ought not to exercise the power of direct taxation. If the power of laying imposts will not be sufficient, some other specific mode of raising a revenue should have been assigned the general government. Many may be suggested in which their power may be accurately defined and limited, and it would be much better to give them authority to lay and collect a duty on exports, not to exceed a certain rate per cent, than to have surrendered every kind of resource that the country has, to the complete abolition of the state governments, and which will introduce such an infinite number of laws and ordinances, fines and penalties, courts, and judges, collectors, and excisemen, that when a man can number them, he may enumerate the stars of Heaven.

Maryland Farmer
Essay III (part I)
(Baltimore) Maryland Gazette
7 March, 1788

There are but two modes by which men are connected in society, the one which operates on individuals, this always has been, and ought still to be called, *national government;* the other which binds States and governments together (not corporations, for there is no considerable nation on earth, despotic, monarchical, or republican, that does not contain many subordinate corporations with various constitutions) this last has heretofore been denominated a *league or confederacy*. The term *federalists* is therefore improperly applied to themselves, by the friends and supporters of the proposed constitution. This abuse of language does not help the cause; every degree of imposition serves only to irritate, but can never convince. They are *national men*, and their opponents, or at least a great majority of them, are *federal*, in the only true and strict sense of the word.

Whether any form of *national* government is preferable for the Americans to a league or confederacy is a previous question we must first make up our minds upon. There will then remain still another. Whether, if any, the one proposed is the best, in our circumstances safe, and such a one as we should *unconditionally* receive? And if ever duty required deliberation before decision, it calls for it now, and in terms too strong to be resisted or evaded. Let the light come in *free* from every quarter. If reason cannot satisfy, experiment will determine. But even then, is it not the duty of those to whom the happiness of so great a proportion of the human species is entrusted, to conduct that experiment with the utmost coolness and fairness, with all those precautions which the wisdom of antiquity affords, and finally qualified with those securities to our liberty that, should it prove oppressive or impracticable, ourselves, or at least our posterity, may not be prevented by the power or influence of a civil or *military oligarchy*, from adopting the alternative?

The advantages or disadvantages of *national government* open too wide a field of discussion for my leisure or talents. Some few remarks I shall cursorily offer. That a *national government* will add to the dignity and increase the splendor of the United States abroad can admit of no doubt. It is essentially requisite for both. That it will render government and officers of government more dignified at home is equally certain. That these objects are more suited to the manners, if not genius and disposition of our people is, I fear, also true. That it is requisite in order to keep us at peace among ourselves is doubtful. That it is necessary to prevent foreigners from dividing us or interfering in our government, I deny positively; and after all, I have strong doubts whether all its advantages are not more *specious* than *solid*. We are vain; like other nations, we wish to make a noise in the world; and feel hurt that Europeans are not so attentive to America in *peace*, as they were to America in *war*. We are also, no doubt, desirous of cutting a figure in history. Should we not reflect that quiet is happiness? That content and pomp are incompatible? I have either read or heard this truth, which Americans should never forget, *that the silence of historians is the surest record of the happiness of a people.* The Swiss have been four hundred years the envy of mankind, and there is yet scarcely a history of their nation. What is history, but a disgusting and painful detail of the butcheries of conquerors, and the woeful calamities of the conquered? Many of us are proud, and are frequently disappointed that office confers neither respect or difference. No man of merit can ever be disgraced by office. A rogue in office may be feared in *some* governments; he will be respected in *none*. After all, what we call respect and difference only arise from contrast of situation, as most of our ideas come by comparison and relation. Where the people are free there can be no great contrast, or distinction among *honest* citizens *in* or *out* of office. In proportion as the people loose their freedom, every gradation of distinction between the *Governors* and *governed* obtains, until the former become *masters* and the latter become *slaves*. In all governments virtue will command reverence. The divine Cato knew every Roman citizen by name and never assumed any pre-eminence; yet Cato found, and his memory will find, respect and reverence in the bosoms of mankind, until this world returns into that nothing whence Omnipotence called it. That the people are not at present disposed for and are actually incapable of governments of simplicity and equal rights, I can no longer doubt. But whose fault is it? We make them bad, by bad governments, and then abuse and despise them for being so. Our people are capable of being made anything that human nature was or is capable of, if we would only have a little patience and give them good and wholesome institutions; but I see none such and very little prospect of such. Alas! I see nothing in my fellow citizens that will permit my still fostering the delusion that they are now capable of sustaining the weight of SELF-GOVERNMENT, a burden to which Greek and Roman shoulders proved unequal. The honor of supporting the dignity of the human character, seems reserved to the hardy Helvetians alone. If the body of the people will not govern themselves, and govern themselves *well too*, the consequence is unavoidable. A FEW will, and must govern *them*. Then it is that government becomes truly a government by *force* only, where men *relinquish part* of their natural rights to secure the *rest*, instead of an union of will and force to protect *all* their natural rights, which ought to be the foundation of every rightful social compact. Whether *national* government will be productive of internal peace, is too uncertain to admit of decided opinion. I only hazard a conjecture when I say, that our state disputes, *in a confederacy*, would be disputes of levity and passion, which would subside before injury. The people being free, government having no right to them, but they to government, they would separate and divide as interest or inclination prompted—as they do at this day, and always have done in Switzerland. In a *national* government, unless cautiously and fortunately administered, disputes will be the deep-rooted differences of interest, where part of the empire must be injured by the operation of general law; and then should the sword of government be once drawn (which Heaven avert) I fear it will not be sheathed, until we have waded through that series of desolation which France, Spain, and the other great kingdoms of the world have suffered, in order to bring so many separate states into uniformity of government and law; in which event the legislative power can only be entrusted to one man (as it is with them) who can have no *local attachments, partial interests,* or *private views* to gratify.

That a *national* government will prevent the influence or danger of foreign intrigue, or secure us from invasion, is in my judgment directly the reverse of the truth. The only *foreign,* or at *least evil foreign influence,* must be obtained through corruption. Where the government is lodged in the body of the people, as in Switzerland, they can never be corrupted; for no prince or people can have resources enough to corrupt the *majority of a nation;* and if they could, the play is not worth the candle. The facility of corruption is increased in proportion as power tends by representation or delegation, to a concentration in the *hands of a few.* The French have kept a minister in Switzerland for 300 years back to persuade them to place power in their general Assembly or Diet. The Swiss have always proved faithful allies and friends to France, but have laughed at her political advice as the assembly of Foxes treated with derision the curtailed Reynard who advised them to part with their cumbersome quantity of brush. As to any nation attacking a number of confederated independent republics, who are always as populous as brave, it is not to be expected, more especially as the wealth of the empire is there universally diffused and will not be collected into any one overgrown, luxurious, and effeminate capital to become a lure to the enterprizing ambitious. That extensive empire is a misfortune to be deprecated will not now be disputed. The balance of power has long engaged the attention of all the European world, in order to avoid the horrid evils of a general government. The same government pervading a vast extent of territory terrifies the minds of individuals into meanness and submission. All human authority, however organized, must have confined limits, or insolence and oppression will prove the offspring of its grandeur, and the difficulty or rather impossibility of escape prevents resistance. Gibbon relates that some Roman knights who had offended [the] government in Rome were taken up in Asia in a very few days after. It was the extensive territory of the Roman republic that produced a Sylla, a Marius, a Caligula, a Nero, and an Eliagabalus. In small independent States contiguous to each other, the people run away and leave despotism to reek its vengeance on itself; and thus it is that moderation becomes with them the law of self-preservation. These and such reasons founded on the eternal and immutable nature of things have long caused and will continue to cause much difference of sentiment throughout our wide extensive territories. From our divided and dispersed situation, and from the natural moderation of the American character, it has hitherto proved a warfare of argument and reason.

Agrippa
Letter IV
(Boston) Massachusetts Gazette
3 December, 1787

To the People:

Having considered some of the principal advantages of the happy form of government under which it is our peculiar good fortune to live, we find by experience that it is the best calculated of any form hitherto invented, to secure to us the rights of our persons and of our property, and that the general circumstances of the people show an advanced state of improvement never before known. We have found the shock given by the war in a great measure obliterated, and the public debt contracted at that time to be considerably reduced in the nominal sum. The Congress lands are fully adequate to the redemption of the principal of their debt, and are selling and populating very fast. The lands of this state at the west are, at the moderate price of eighteen pence an acre, worth near half a million pounds in our money. They ought, therefore, to be sold as quick as possible. An application was made lately for a large tract at that price, and continual applications are made for other lands in the eastern part of the state. Our resources are daily augmenting.

We find then that after the experience of near two centuries our separate governments are in full vigor. They discover, for all the purposes of internal regulation, every symptom of strength and none of decay. The new system is, therefore, for such purposes useless and burdensome.

Let us now consider how far it is practicable consistent with the happiness of the people and their freedom. It is the opinion of the ablest writers on the subject, that no extensive empire can be governed upon republican principles, and that such a government will degenerate to a despotism unless it be made up of a confederacy of smaller states, each having the full powers of internal regulation. This is precisely the principle which has hitherto preserved our freedom. No instance can be found of any free government of considerable extent which has been supported upon any other plan. Large and consolidated empires may indeed dazzle the eyes of a distant spectator with their splendor, but if examined more nearly are always found to be full of misery. The reason is obvious. In large states the same principles of legislation will not apply to all the parts. The inhabitants of warmer climates are more dissolute in their manners, and less industrious than in colder countries. A degree of severity is, therefore, necessary with one which would cramp the spirit of the other. We accordingly find that the very great empires have always been despotic. They have indeed tried to remedy the inconveniences to which the people were exposed by local regulations; but these contrivances have never answered the end. The laws not being made by the people who felt the inconveniences did not suit their circumstances. It is under such tyranny that the Spanish provinces languish, and such would be our misfortune and degradation if we should submit to have the concerns of the whole empire managed by one legislature. To promote the happiness of the people it is necessary that there should be local laws; and it is necessary that those laws should be made by the representatives of those who are immediately subject to the want of them. By endeavoring to suit both extremes, both are injured.

It is impossible for one code of laws to suit Georgia and Massachusetts. They must, therefore, legislate for themselves. Yet there is, I believe, not one point of legislation that is not surrendered in the proposed plan. Questions of every kind respecting property are determinable in a continental court, and so are all kinds of criminal causes. The continental legislature has, therefore, a right to make rules *in all cases* by which their judicial courts shall proceed and decide causes. No rights are reserved to the citizens. The laws of Congress are in all cases to be the supreme law of the land and paramount to the constitutions of the individual states. The Congress may institute what modes of trial they please, and no plea drawn from the constitution of any state can avail. This new system is, therefore, a consolidation of all the states into one large mass, however diverse the parts may be of which it is to be composed. The idea of an uncompounded republic, on an average, one thousand miles in length, and eight hundred in breadth, and containing six million white inhabitants all reduced to the same standard of morals or habits, and of laws, is in itself an absurdity and contrary to the whole experience of mankind. The attempt made by Great Britain to introduce such a system struck us with horror, and when it was proposed by some theorist that we should be represented in parliament, we uniformly declared that one legislature could not represent so many different interests for the purposes of legislation and taxation. This was the leading principle of the revolution, and makes an essential article in our creed. All that part therefore, of the new system, which relates to the internal government of the states, ought at once to be rejected.

Patrick Henry
Speeches given before the Virginia Ratifying Convention 4 and 5 June, 1788

Mr. Chairman, the public mind, as well as my own, is extremely uneasy at the proposed change of government. Give me leave to form one of that number of those who wish to be thoroughly acquainted with the reasons of this perilous and uneasy situation and why we are brought hither to decide on this great national question. I consider myself as the servant of the people of this Commonwealth, as a centinel over their rights, liberty, and happiness. I represent their feelings when I say that they are exceedingly uneasy, being brought from the state of full security which they enjoyed, to the present delusive appearance of things. A year ago the minds of our citizens were at perfect repose. Before the meeting of the late federal convention at Philadelphia, a general peace and an universal tranquility prevailed in this country; since that period they are exceedingly uneasy and disquieted. When I wished for an appointment to this convention, my mind was extremely agitated for the situation of public affairs. I conceive the republic to be in extreme danger. If our situation be thus uneasy, whence has arisen this fearful jeopardy? It arises from this fatal system. It arises from the proposal to change our government, a proposal that goes to the utter annihilation of the most solemn engagements of the States. A proposal of establishing nine States into a confederacy, to the eventual exclusion of four States. It goes to the annihilation of those solemn treaties we have formed with foreign nations. The present circumstances of France, the good offices rendered us by that kingdom, require our most faithful and most punctual adherence to our treaty with her. We are in alliance with the Spaniards, the Dutch, the Prussians. Those treaties bound us as thirteen states, confederated together. Yet, here is a proposal to sever this confederacy. Is it possible that we shall abandon all our treaties and national engagements? And for what? I expected to have heard the reasons of an event so unexpected to my mind, and many others. Was our civil polity, or public justice, endangered or sapped? Was the real existence of the country threatened—or was this preceded by a mournful progression of events?

This proposal of altering our federal government is of a most alarming nature. You ought to be extremely cautious, watchful, jealous of your liberty, for instead of securing your rights you may lose them forever. If a wrong step be now made, the republic may be lost forever. If this new government will not come up to the expectation of the people, and they should be disappointed, their liberty will be lost, and tyranny must and will arise. I repeat it again, and I beg gentlemen to consider, that a wrong step made now will plunge us in misery, and our republic will be lost. It will be necessary for this convention to have a faithful historical detail of the facts that preceded the session of the federal convention, and the reasons that actuated its members in proposing an entire alteration of government and demonstrate the dangers that awaited us. If they were of such awful magnitude as to warrant a proposal so extremely perilous as this, I must assert that this convention has an absolute right to a thorough discovery of every circumstance relative to this great event. And here I would make this inquiry of those worthy characters who composed a part of the late federal convention. I am sure they were fully impressed with the necessity of forming a great consolidated government, instead of a confederation. That this is a consolidated Government is demonstrably clear, and the danger of such a Government, is, to my mind, very striking. I have the highest veneration of those Gentlemen, but, Sir, give me leave to demand, what right had they to say, *We, the People.* My political curiosity, exclusive of my anxious solicitude for the public welfare, leads me to ask who authorized them to speak the language of *We, the People* instead of *We, the States?* States are the characteristics, and the soul of a confederation. If the states be not the agents of this compact, it must be one great consolidated national government of the people of all the states. I have the highest respect for those gentlemen who formed the convention, and were some of them not here, I would express some testimonial of my esteem for them. America had on a former occasion put the utmost confidence in them: a confidence which was well placed. And I am sure, sir, I would give up any thing to them; I would cheerfully confide in them as my representatives. But, sir, on this great occasion, I would demand the cause of their conduct. Even from that illustrious man [George Washington], who saved us by his valor, I would have a reason for his conduct. That liberty which he has given us by his valor tells me to ask this reason, and sure I am, were he here, he would give us that reason. But there are other gentlemen here who can give us this information. The people gave them no power to use their name. That they exceeded their power is perfectly clear. It is not mere curiosity that actuates me; I wish to hear the real actual existing danger, which should lead us to take those steps so dangerous in my conception. Disorders have arisen in other parts of America, but here, sir, no dangers, no insurrection or tumult, has happened; everything has been calm and tranquil. But notwithstanding this, we are wandering on the great ocean of human affairs. I see no landmark to guide us. We are running we know not whither. Difference in opinion has gone to a degree of inflammatory resentment in different parts of the country, occasioned by this perilous innovation. The federal convention ought to have amended the old system; for this purpose they were solely delegated. The object of their mission extended to no other consideration. You must therefore forgive the solicitation of one unworthy member, to know what danger could have arisen under the present confederation, and what are the causes of this proposal to change our government.

Mr. Chairman, I am much obliged to the very worthy gentleman for his encomium. I wish I was possessed of talents, or possessed of anything, that might enable me to elucidate this great subject. I am not free from suspicion. I am apt to entertain doubts. I rose yesterday to ask a question, which arose in my own mind. When I asked the question, I thought the meaning of my interrogation was obvious; the fate of this question and America may depend on this. Have they said, We the States? Have they made a proposal of a compact between states? If they had, this would be a confederation. It is otherwise most clearly a consolidated government. The question turns, sir, on that poor little thing, the expression, *We, the People* instead of the states of America. I need not take much pains to show that the principles of this system are extremely pernicious, impolitic, and dangerous. Is this a monarchy like England, a compact between prince and people, with checks on the former to secure the liberty of the latter? Is this a confederacy, like Holland, an association of a number of independent states, each of which retain its individual sovereignty? It is not a democracy, wherein the people retain all their rights securely. Had these principles been adhered to, we should not have been brought to this alarming transition from a confederacy to a consolidated government.

We have no detail of those great considerations which, in my opinion, ought to have abounded before we should recur to a government of this kind. Here is a revolution as radical as that which separated us from Great Britain. It is as radical, if in this transition our rights and privileges are endangered, and the sovereignty of the states be relinquished. And cannot we plainly see that this is actually the case? The rights of conscience, trial by jury, liberty of the press, all your immunities and franchises, all pretensions to human rights and privileges are rendered insecure, if not lost, by this change so loudly talked of by some, and inconsiderately by others. Is this same relinquishment of rights worthy of freemen? Is it worthy of that manly fortitude that ought to characterize republicans. It is said eight states have adopted this plan. I declare that if twelve states and an half had adopted it, I would with manly firmness, and in spite of an erring world, reject it. You are not to inquire how your trade may be increased, nor how you are to become a great and powerful people, but how your liberties can be secured, for liberty ought to be the direct end of your government.

Having premised these things I shall, with the aid of my judgment and information which I confess are not extensive, go into the discussion of this system more minutely. Is it necessary for your liberty that you should abandon those great rights by the adoption of this system? Is the relinquishment of the trial by jury and the liberty of the press necessary for your liberty? Will the abandonment of your most sacred rights tend to the security of your liberty? Liberty [is] the greatest of all earthly blessings; give us that precious jewel, and you may take everything else. But I am fearful I have lived long enough to become an old-fashioned fellow. Perhaps an invincible attachment to the dearest rights of man may in these refined enlightened days be deemed *old-fashioned*. If so, I am contented to be so. I say the time has been, when every pore of my heart beat for American liberty and which, I believe, had a counterpart in the breast of every true American. But suspicions have gone forth, suspicions of my integrity, publicly reported that my professions are not real. Twenty-three years ago was I supposed a traitor to my country; I was then said to be a bane of sedition, because I supported the rights of my country. I may be thought suspicious when I say our privileges and rights are in danger. But, sir, a number of the people of this country are weak enough to think these things are too true. I am happy to find that the honorable gentleman on the other side declares they are groundless. But, sir, suspicion is a virtue, as long as its object is the preservation of the public good, and as long as it stays within proper bounds.

We are come hither to preserve the poor Commonwealth of Virginia, if it can be possibly done. Something must be done to preserve your liberty and mine. The confederation, this same despised government, merits, in my opinion, the highest encomium. It carried us through a long and dangerous war. It rendered us victorious in that bloody conflict with a powerful nation. It has secured us a territory greater than any European monarch possesses. And shall a government which has been thus strong and vigorous, be accused of imbecility and abandoned for want of energy? Consider what you are about to do before you part with this government. Take longer time in reckoning things. Revolutions like this have happened in almost every country in Europe. Similar examples are to be found in ancient Greece and ancient Rome. Instances of the people losing their liberty by their own carelessness and the ambition of a few. We are cautioned by the honorable gentleman who presides [Edmund Pendleton] against faction and turbulence. I acknowledge that licentiousness is dangerous, and that it ought to be provided against. I acknowledge also the new form of government may effectually prevent it. Yet, there is another thing it will as effectually do; it will oppress and ruin the people. There are sufficient guards placed against sedition and licentiousness. For when power is given to this government to suppress these, or for any other purpose, the language it assumes is clear, express, and unequivocal; but when this Constitution speaks of privileges, there is an ambiguity, sir, a fatal ambiguity, an ambiguity which is very astonishing. In the clause under consideration, there is the strangest that I can conceive. I mean, when it says, that there shall not be more representatives than one for every 30,000. Now, sir, how easy is it to evade this privilege? "The number shall not exceed one for every 30,000." This may be satisfied by one representative from each state. Let our numbers be ever so great, this immense continent may, by this artful expression, be reduced to have but 13 representatives. I confess this construction is not natural, but the ambiguity of the expression lays a good ground for a quarrel. Why was it not clearly and unequivocally expressed that they *should* be entitled to have one for every 30,000? This would have obviated all disputes, and was this difficult to be done? What is the inference? When population increases, and a state shall send representatives in this proportion, Congress *may* remand them because the right of having one for every 30,000 is not clearly expressed. This possibility of reducing the number to one for each state approximates to probability by that other expression, "but each state shall at least have one representative." Now is it not clear that from the first expression the number might be reduced so much that some states should have no representative at all, were it not for the insertion of this last expression? And as this is the only restriction upon them, we may fairly conclude that they *may* restrain the number to one from each State.

Perhaps the same horrors may hang over my mind again. I shall be told I am continually afraid. But, sir, I have strong cause of apprehension. In some parts of the plan before you, the great rights of freemen are endangered, in other parts absolutely taken away. How does your trial by jury stand? In civil cases gone: not sufficiently secured in criminal, this best privilege is gone. But we are told that we need not fear because those in power being our representatives will not abuse the powers we put in their hands. I am not well versed in history but I will submit to your recollection, whether liberty has been destroyed most often by the licentiousness of the people, or by the tyranny of rulers? I imagine, sir, you will find the balance on the side of tyranny. Happy will you be if you miss the fate of those nations who, omitting to resist their oppressors or negligently suffering their liberty to be wrested from them, have groaned under intolerable despotism. Most of the human race are now in this deplorable condition. And those nations who have gone in search of grandeur, power and splendor have also fallen a sacrifice, and been the victims of their own folly. While they acquired those visionary blessings, they lost their freedom. My great objection to this government is that it does not leave us the means of defending our rights, or of waging war against tyrants. It is urged by some gentlemen that this new plan will bring us an acquisition of strength, an army, and the militia of the states. This is an idea extremely ridiculous; [the] gentlemen cannot be in earnest. This acquisition will trample on your fallen liberty. Let my beloved Americans guard against that fatal lethargy that has pervaded the universe. Have we the means of resisting disciplined armies when our only defense, the militia, is put into the hands of Congress? The honorable gentleman said that great danger would ensue if the convention rose without adopting this system. I ask, where is that danger? I see none. Other gentlemen have told us within these walls that the union is gone or, that the union will be gone. Is not this trifling with the judgment of their fellow citizens? Till they tell us the ground of their fears, I will consider them as imaginary. I rose to make inquiry where those dangers were; they could make no answer. I believe I never shall have that answer. Is there a disposition in the people of this country to revolt against the dominion of laws? Has there been a single tumult in Virginia? Have not the people of Virginia, when laboring under the severest pressure of accumulated distresses, manifested the most cordial acquiescence in the execution of the laws? What could be more awful than their unamious acquiescence under general distresses? Is there any revolution in Virginia? Whither is the spirit of America gone? Whither is the genius of America fled? It was but yesterday, when our enemies marched in triumph through our country. Yet the people of this country could not be appalled by their pompous armaments. They stopped their career, and victoriously captured them. Where is the peril now compared to that?

Let not gentlemen be told that it is not safe to reject this government. Wherefore is it not safe? We are told there are dangers, but those dangers are ideal; they cannot be demonstrated. To encourage us to adopt it, they tell us that there is a plain easy way of getting amendments. When I come to contemplate this part, I suppose that I am mad or that my countrymen are so. The way to amendment is, in my conception, shut. Let us consider this plain easy way: "The Congress, whenever two-thirds of both Houses shall deem it necessary, shall propose amendments to this Constitution, or, on the application of the Legislatures of two-thirds of the several states, shall call a convention for proposing amendments which, in either case, shall be valid to all intents and purposes, as part of this Constitution, when ratified by the Legislatures of three-fourths of the several states, or by Conventions in three-fourths thereof, as the one or the other mode of ratification may be proposed by the Congress. Provided that no amendment which may be made prior to the year 1808, shall in any manner affect the first and fourth clauses in the ninth section of the first article; and that no state, without its consent, shall be deprived of its equal suffrage in the Senate." Hence it appears that three-fourths of the states must ultimately agree to any amendments that may be necessary. Let us consider the consequences of this. However uncharitable it may appear, yet I must tell my opinion, that the most unworthy characters may get into power and prevent the introduction of amendments. Let us suppose (for the case is supposable, possible, and probable) that you happen to deal these powers to unworthy hands; will they relinquish powers already in their possession, or agree to amendments? Two-thirds of the Congress or of the state legislatures are necessary even to propose amendments. One-third of these being unworthy men may prevent the application for amendments; but what is destructive and mischievous is that three-fourths of the state legislatures, or of state conventions must concur in the amendments when proposed. In such numerous bodies, there must necessarily be some designing bad men. To suppose that so large a number as three-fourths of the states will concur is to suppose that they will possess genius, intelligence, and integrity approaching to miraculous. It would indeed be miraculous that they should concur in the same amendments or even in such as would bear some likeness to one another. For four of the smallest states that do not collectively contain one-tenth part of the population of the United States may obstruct the most salutary and necessary amendments. Nay, in these four states, six tenths of the people may reject these amendments; and suppose that amendments shall be opposed to amendments (which is highly probable) is it possible that three-fourths can ever agree to the same amendments? A bare majority in these four small states may hinder the adoption of amendments; so that we may fairly and justly conclude that one-twentieth part of the American people may prevent the removal of the most grievous inconveniences and oppression by refusing to accede to amendments. A trifling minority may reject the most salutary amendments. Is this an easy mode of securing the public liberty? It is, sir, a most fearful situation when the most contemptible minority can prevent the alteration of the most oppressive government; for it may in many respects prove to be such. Is this the spirit of republicanism? What, sir, is the genius of democracy? Let me read that clause of the Bill of Rights of Virginia, which relates to this: third clause. "That government is or ought to be instituted for the common benefit, protection, and security of the people, nation, or community. Of all the various modes and forms of government, that is best which is capable of producing the greatest degree of happiness and safety, and is most effectually secured against the danger of maladministration, and *that whenever any government shall be found inadequate, or contrary to these purposes, a majority of the community have an undubitable, unalienable, and indefeasible right to reform, alter, or abolish it, in such manner as shall be judged most conducive to the public weal.*" This, sir, is the language of democracy: that a majority of the community have a right to alter their government when found to be oppressive. But how different is the genius of your new Constitution from this.

The honorable gentleman's observations respecting the people's right of being the agents in the formation of this government are not accurate in my humble conception. The distinction between a national government and a confederacy is not sufficiently discerned. Had the delegates who were sent to Philadelphia a power to propose a consolidated government instead of a confederacy? Were they not deputed by states, and not by the people? The assent of the people in their collective capacity is not necessary to the formation of a federal government. The people have no right to enter into leagues, alliances, or confederations. They are not the proper agents for this purpose. States and sovereign powers are the only proper agents for this kind of government. Show me an instance where the people have exercised this business. Has it not always gone through the legislatures? I refer you to the treaties with France, Holland, and other nations. How were they made? Were they not made by the states? Are the people therefore in their aggregate capacity the proper persons to form a confederacy? This, therefore, ought to depend on the consent of the legislatures, the people having never sent delegates to make any proposition of changing the government. Yet I must say at the same time that it was made on grounds the most pure, and perhaps I might have been brought to consent to it so far as to the change of government; but there is one thing in it which I never would acquiesce in. I mean the changing it into a consolidated government, which is so abhorent to my mind.

The honorable gentleman then went on to the figure we make with foreign nations, the contemptible one we make in France and Holland, which, according to the system of my notes, he attributes to the present feeble government. An opinion has gone forth, we find that we are a contemptible people. The time has been when we were thought otherwise. Under this same despised government, we commanded the respect of all Europe. Wherefore are we now reckoned otherwise? The American spirit has fled from hence. It has gone to regions where it has never been expected. It has gone to the people of France in search of a splendid government, a strong energetic government. Shall we imitate the example of those nations who have gone from a simple to a splendid government? Are those nations more worthy of our imitation? What can make an adequate satisfaction to them for the loss they suffered in attaining such a government for the loss of their liberty? If we admit this consolidated government it will be because we like a great splendid one. Some way or other we must be a great and mighty empire; we must have an army, and a navy, and a number of things. When the American spirit was in its youth, the language of America was different; liberty, sir, was then the primary object. We are descended from a people whose government was founded on liberty. Our glorious forefathers of Great Britain made liberty the foundation of everything. That country is become a great, mighty, and splendid nation, not because their government is strong and energetic, but, sir, because liberty is its direct end and foundation. We drew the spirit of liberty from our British ancestors; by that spirit we have triumphed over every difficulty. But now, sir, the American spirit, assisted by the ropes and chains of consolidation, is about to convert this country to a powerful and mighty empire. If you make the citizens of this country agree to become the subjects of one great consolidated empire of America, your government will not have suffcient energy to keep them together. Such a government is incompatible with the genius of republicanism. There will be no checks, no real balances in this government. What can avail your specious imaginary balances, your rope-dancing, chain-rattling, ridiculous ideal checks and contrivances? But, sir, we are not feared by foreigners; we do not make nations tremble. Would this, sir, constitute happiness or secure liberty? I trust, sir, our political hemisphere will ever direct their operations to the security of *those* objects.

Yet this Constitution can counteract and suspend any of our laws that contravene its oppressive operation. They have the power of direct taxation which suspends our Bill of Rights; it is expressly provided that they can make all laws necessary for carrying their powers into execution, and it is declared paramount to the laws and constitutions of the states. Consider how the only remaining defense we have left is destroyed in this manner: besides the expenses of maintaining the Senate and other House in as much splendor as they please, there is to be a great and mighty president with very extensive powers: the powers of a king. He is to be supported in extravagant magnificence. So that the whole of our property may be taken by this American government by laying what taxes they please, giving themselves what salaries they please, and suspending our laws at their pleasure. I might be thought too inquisitive, but I believe I should take up but very little of your time in enumerating the little power that is left to the government of Virginia; for this power is reduced to little or nothing. Their garrisons, magazines, arsenals, and forts will be situated in the strongest places within the states. Their ten miles square, with all the fine ornaments of human life added to their powers and taken from the states, will reduce the power of the latter to nothing. The voice of tradition, I trust, will inform posterity of our struggles for freedom. If our descendants be worthy [of] the name of Americans, they will preserve and hand down to their latest posterity the transactions of the present times; and though I confess my exclamations are not worthy the hearing, they will see that I have done my utmost to preserve their liberty. For I never will give up the power of direct taxation, but for a scourge. I am willing to give it conditionally, that is, after noncompliance with requisitions. I will do more, sir, and what I hope will convince the most sceptical man that I am a lover of the American union; that in case Virginia shall not make punctual payment, the control of our custom houses and the whole regulation of trade shall be given to Congress, and that Virginia shall depend on Congress even for passports till Virginia shall have paid the last farthing and furnished the last soldier. Nay, sir, there is another alternative to which I would consent. Even that they should strike us out of the union and take away from us all federal privileges till we comply with federal requisitions; let it depend upon our own pleasure to pay our money in the most easy manner for our people. Were all the states more terrible than the mother country to join against us, I hope Virginia could defend herself; but, sir, the dissolution of the union is most abhorent to my mind. The first thing I have at heart is American *liberty*, the second thing is American union, and I hope the people of Virginia will endeavor to preserve that union. The increasing population of the southern states is far greater than that of New England. Consequently, in a short time they will be far more numerous than the people of that country. Consider this, and you will find this state more particularly interested to support American liberty, and not bind our posterity by an improvident relinquishment of our rights. I would give the best security for a punctual compliance with requisitions; but I beseech gentlemen, at all hazards, not to give up this unlimited power of taxation.

The honorable gentleman has told us these powers given to Congress are accompanied by a judiciary which will connect all. On examination you will find this very judiciary oppressively constructed, your jury trial destroyed, and the judges dependent on Congress. In this scheme of energetic government, the people will find two sets of tax gatherers: the state and the federal sheriffs. This it seems to me will produce such dreadful oppression as the people cannot possibly bear. The federal sheriff may commit what oppression, make what distresses he pleases, and ruin you with impunity. For how are you to tie his hands? Have you any sufficient decided means of preventing him from sucking your blood by speculations, commissions, and fees? Thus thousands of your people will be most shamefully robbed. Our state sheriffs, those unfeeling blood-suckers have, under the watchful eye of our Legislature, committed the most horrid and barbarous ravages on our people. It has required the most constant vigilance of the Legislature to keep them from totally ruining the people. A repeated succession of laws has been made to suppress their iniquitous speculations and cruel extortions; and as often have their nefarious ingenuity devised methods of evading the force of those laws. In the struggle they have generally triumphed over the Legislature. It is fact that lands have sold for five shillings, which were worth one hundred pounds. If sheriffs thus immediately under the eye of our state Legislature and judiciary have dared to commit these outrages, what would they not have done if their masters had been at Philadelphia or New York? If they perpetrate the most unwarrantable outrage on your persons or property, you cannot get redress on this side of Philadelphia or New York. And how can you get it there? If your domestic avocations could permit you to go thither, there you must appeal to judges sworn to support this Constitution, in opposition to that of any state, and who may also be inclined to favor their own officers. When these harpies are aided by excise men, who may search at any time your houses and most secret recesses, will the people bear it? If you think so you differ from me.

This Constitution is said to have beautiful features, but when I come to examine these features, sir, they appear to me horridly frightful. Among other deformities, it has an awful squinting; it squints towards monarchy. And does not this raise indignation in the breast of every American? Your president may easily become king. Your Senate is so imperfectly constructed that your dearest rights may be sacrificed by what may be a small minority; and a very small minority may continue forever unchangeably this government, although horridly defective. Where are your checks in this government? Your strongholds will be in the hands of your enemies. It is on a supposition that our American governors shall be honest, that all the good qualities of this government are founded. But its defective and imperfect construction puts it in their power to perpetrate the worst of mischiefs, should they be bad men. And, sir, would not all the world, from the Eastern to the Western hemisphere, blame our distracted folly in resting our rights upon the contingency of our rulers being good or bad? Show me that age and country where the rights and liberties of the people were placed on the sole chance of their rulers being good men, without a consequent loss of liberty? I say that the loss of that dearest privilege has ever followed with absolute certainty every such mad attempt.

Where is the responsibility, that leading principle in the British government? In that government a punishment, certain and inevitable, is provided. But in this there is no real actual punishment for the grossest maladministration. They may go without punishment, though they commit the most outrageous violation on our immunities. That paper may tell me they will be punished. I ask, by what law? They must make the law; for there is no existing law to do it. What? Will they make a law to punish themselves? This, sir, is my great objection to the Constitution; that there is no true responsibility, and that the preservation of our liberty depends on the single chance of men being virtuous enough to make laws to punish themselves. In the country from which we are descended, they have real, and not imaginary, responsibility; for there, maladministration has cost their heads to some of the most saucy geniuses that ever were. The Senate by making treaties may destroy your liberty and laws for want of responsibility. Two-thirds of those that shall happen to be present can, with the president, make treaties that shall be the supreme law of the land. They may make the most ruinous treaties, and yet there is no punishment for them. Whoever shows me a punishment provided for them will oblige me. So, sir, notwithstanding there are eight pillars, they want another. Where will they make another?

I trust, sir, the exclusion of the evils wherewith this system is replete in its present form will be made a condition precedent to its adoption by this or any other state. The transition from a general unqualified admission to offices to a consolidation of government seems easy; for though the American states are dissimilar in their structure, this will assimilate them. This, sir, is itself a strong consolidating feature, and is not one of the least dangerous in that system. Nine states are sufficient to establish this government over those nine. Imagine that nine have come into it. Virginia has certain scruples. Suppose she will consequently refuse to join with those states. May not they still continue in friendship and union with her? If she sends her annual requisitions in dollars, do you think their stomachs will be so squeamish that they will refuse her dollars? Will they not accept her regiments? They would intimidate you into an inconsiderate adoption, and frighten you with ideal evils, and that the union shall be dissolved. 'Tis a bugbear, sir. The fact is, sir, that the eight adopting states can hardly stand on their own legs. Public fame tells us that the adopting states have already heart-burnings and animosity, and repent their precipitate hurry. This, sir, may occasion exceeding great mischief. When I reflect on these and many other circumstances, I must think those states will be fond to be in confederacy with us. If we pay our quota of money annually, and furnish our ratable number of men when necessary, I can see no danger from a rejection. The history of Switzerland clearly proves we might be in amicable alliance with those states without adopting this Constitution. Switzerland is a confederacy, consisting of dissimilar governments. This is an example which proves that governments of dissimilar structure may be confederated; that confederate republic has stood upwards of 400 years, and although several of the individual republics are democratic and the rest aristocratic, no evil has resulted from this dissimilarity, for they have braved all the power of France and Germany during that long period. The Swiss spirit, sir, has kept them together. They have encountered and overcome immense difficulties with patience and fortitude. In this vicinity of powerful and ambitious monarchs, they have retained their independence, republican simplicity, and valor.

Look at the peasants of that country and of France, and mark the difference. You will find the condition of the former far more desirable and comfortable. No matter whether a people be great, splendid, and powerful if they enjoy freedom. The Turkish Grand Seignior alongside of our president would put us to disgrace. But we should be abundantly consoled for this disgrace when our citizen should be put in contrast with the Turkish slave. The most valuable end of government is the liberty of the inhabitants. No possible advantages can compensate for the loss of this privilege. Show me the reason why the American union is to be dissolved. Who are those eight adopting states? Are they averse to give us a little time to consider before we conclude? Would such a disposition render a junction with them eligible, or is it the genius of that kind of government to precipitate people hastily into measures of the utmost importance, and grant no indulgence? If it be, sir, is it for us to accede to such a government? We have a right to have time to consider; we shall therefore insist upon it. Unless the government be amended, we can never accept it.

Chapter III:

The Antifederalist Views of Republicanism

Only upon considering the question of federalism clarified did Antifederalists freely entertain the next question, namely, that the system ought to be republican. In America this had two senses: the national system had to be republican to agree with the states, while the states, already republican, had to confederate to preserve their form. We are concerned with the claim that the national arrangement ought to be republican within the context of federal principles.

The chief constraint on instituting republicanism in a confederal arrangement is the problem of sovereignty. In effect, sovereignty must be placed in those hands ultimately responsible for the character of the government. This would be the people with respect to the local governments and the local governments with respect to the national government. "The exercise of sovereignty does not consist in choosing masters, such as the senators would be, who, when chosen, would be beyond control, but in the power of dismissing, impeaching, or the like, those to whom authority is delegated." The Constitution on the other hand left it to the representatives to impeach themselves and to regulate their own qualifications for office. That implied that the people's sovereignty—hence, the authority of the local governments— could be alienated or divided. It made the representative not a representative or delegate but a sovereign in the ancient sense. Antifederalist thought envisioned an indivisible sovereignty, requiring a power above the representative capable of arresting his activity at any moment.

Depending on the question of sovereignty were the questions of suffrage, powers, and revenues. The republican right freely to elect representatives had to be firmly established, and the organs of government had to be severely limited in their ability to alter the essential republican forms. Similar reasonings formed the basis for the critique of the powers granted to the national government. Antifederalists presumed that such extensive powers must eventuate in the destruction of state governments—hence, a transformation of the system into a consolidated, despotic government.

Aside from the question of federalism, two reasons were cited to

137

prove that the system could not be republican. First was the arrangement of offices itself. Second was the extensive territory. With respect to the territory—

> It is natural, says Montesquieu, to a republic to have only a small territory, otherwise it cannot long subsist: in a large one, there are men of large fortunes, and consequently of less moderation. . . . In large republics the public good is sacrificed to a thousand views; in a small one, the interest of the public is easily perceived, better understood, and more within the reach of every citizen; abuses have a less extent, and of course are less protected.

Because they argued that the proposed system would necessarily become consolidated, Antifederalists insisted on treating it as a single republic. As such its bounds exceeded all examples of permissible extent.

Antifederalist political science prescribed modes for concentrating the power of the people and eliminating for officeholders temptations to evil. The heart of their method was to arrange representation in such a manner as to safeguard interests and to avoid the clashes of factions. They generally conceived that this demanded a certain homogeneity of interests, as opposed to the encouragement of diverse interests. The latter approach they rejected as dangerous. Their political science, then, explicitly rejected John Adams's mixed-regime theories and also Publius's confounding of classes in *Federalist* 10. They placed their faith in the virtue of "middling" Americans, coupled with holding their representatives "in the greatest responsibility to their constituents."

Antifederalist notions of responsibility assumed the triune expression of faith in rotation in office, frequent elections (and provisions for recall), and a right in the constituents to give instructions to their representatives. Additionally, they sought to ensure that the elections of representatives would not confine choices to the talented few, but rather should draw from the bulk, the great middling classes of society. As Melancton Smith phrased it, they wished to assure that representatives as a whole would constitute a "mirror of the society." Theoretically, Antifederalists conceived of representation as a device to facilitate the direct expression of the will of the people. Federalists regarded representation as a device to facilitate deliberation. Antifederalists, on the other hand, conceived of the deliberation pre-requisite to sound governing as primarily social; that is, taking place within the body of the people. That is the reason they emphasized so strongly the need to safeguard social stability and homogeneity.

Respecting the arrangement of offices, the system again departs from the perceived prescription of Montesquieu. It had not the checks "of the British monarchy." It had a partially limited, but partially absolute executive. And it had defective legislative branches, neither being wholly democratic or wholly aristocratic. "Are not all defects and corruption founded on" these perils? As noted above, the tendency of the Constitution (in Antifederalist eyes) was to treat indivisible sovereignty as if it were divisible. Thus Antifederalists viewed the arrangement of offices in this light, the creation of mutually independent sovereigns. Recurring to Montesquieu again, they inferred that such independent rulers would "erect an interest separate from the ruled, which will tend to enslave them." To the extent that this government was not free presidents, senators, and representatives would tend to lose their republican mores and adopt the habits of a different regime. Their new mores would be translated into the government itself.

The Antifederalist conclusion: unless executive power was yet more limited, representation was broadened, presidents and senators were made more responsible to the people or the people's immediate representatives—unless the arrangement was significantly modified—the proposed regime would necessarily destroy political liberty by destroying the sovereignty of the people, the litmus test of republicanism.

James Monroe
Observations on the Constitution
June, 1788

Gentlemen,

When you did me the honor to elect me into the convention to decide for you upon the constitution submitted to the states from Philadelphia, I had not at that time examined it with that attention its importance required, and of course could give you no decided opinion respecting it. Other cares had unavoidably taken my attention from it. After you had reposed that trust in me it became my duty to pay it a more serious attention. Having given it the best investigation that my limited capacity is capable of, and perhaps formed in some measure my opinion respecting it, subject however to alteration when I shall be convinced that I am in an error, I should think myself unpardonable if I witheld it from you. To you it belongs to approve or correct this opinion, for although it would give me pain to be compelled to take a course which my own mind did not approve, yet I have too high a respect for your rights, too just a sense of my duty, and too strong an impression of gratitude for the confidence you have reposed in me to act contrary to your wishes. Under this impression I have thought proper to make to you the following unreserved communication of my sentiments upon this all important subject.

It will readily occur to you that this plan of government is not submitted for your decision in an ordinary way, not to one branch of the government in its legislative character and confined under the constitution to the sphere it has assigned it, but to the people to whom it belongs and from whom all power originates, in convention assembled. In this situation your present state constitution was or should have been formed, and in this situation you are of course able to alter or change it at pleasure. You are therefore to observe that whatever act you now enter into, will be paramount to all others either of law or constitution, and that in adopting this it becomes in reality the constitution of the state and binding on you as such. Whether it will absolutely annul and do away that of the state is perhaps doubtful; my own apprehension is it will not, except in those cases wherein they disagree. In these it will of course prevail, and control all the departments of the state government, being the ulterior act of the people. You will therefore perceive it is a subject of great extent and importance upon which you have to decide and that you owe it to your country, yourselves, and posterity that it be well examined in all its consequences before it is determined.

When we contemplate the causes that might probably have contributed to make it necessary to submit to your decision the propriety of such a change in your political situation, we are naturally led into one of the following conclusions; either that the morals of the people have become corrupted; that the passions of mankind by nature render them unfit for the enjoyment of equal liberty; or that the form of the government itself under which we live is radically defective, and capable of such improvement as will extend to us its blessings in a higher degree, and make them of longer duration. Believing firmly that the body of the people are virtuous, at least sufficiently so to bear a free government, that it was the design of their Creator in forming such an order of beings that they should enjoy it, and that it is only by a strange and unaccountable perversion of his benevolent intentions to mankind that they are ever deprived of it, I will proceed to examine the latter hypothesis which supposes such defects in the present form as to make a change advisable. If we find that they really do exist, I will then proceed to suggest such remedies as will enable us comparatively to determine on the merits of that supposed to be substituted in its stead. I feel myself deeply impressed with the importance of this undertaking and am too well acquainted with my own inability even to hope that I shall conduct myself with propriety through it; but from a sincere desire to establish a perfect good understanding between us, and prevent the possibility of any future anxiety on this subject, I find myself constrained however painful it may be, and however ungracefully I may do it, not only to avow my sentiments respecting it but the principles on which they are founded. . . .

It is to be observed that by the second article [Articles of Confederation] the individual states retain their respective sovereignties, jurisdictions and rights in all cases not expressly ceded to the confederacy. And by the fifth they reserve the right of appointing, continuing or removing their respective delegations at pleasure. To these articles we are to look for the tone and character of this government, for upon these does its good or bad qualities depend. It is upon this point that the present commotion hath taken place in America, and upon the merits of which we have to decide.

The deputies from each state being amenable for their conduct, and depending on it for their hopes and prospects, necessarily negotiate for its interests. This property or distinction pervades the whole body, and thus their general council or the Congress becomes a diplomatic corps, or a corps formed of ministers or representatives from sovereign states acting for whatever may be the powers of the union over the several members that compose it, will be to shield itself from the common burdens of the government. To effect this all the arts of intrigue and negociation will be constantly exerted. What is the obvious course of a government organized on such principles? Are not the seeds of dissolution deeply engrafted in it? The most powerful principles of human action, the hope of reward and the fear of punishment, are in the hands of each state, and while mankind is subject to their influence or the passions and affections of the human heart continue as they have been, its course will always be the same. This government, it is manifest, can never be an efficient one. Strong necessity and imminent danger may make it so occasionally, but whenever this cause ceases to operate, its repellant principles will prevail. If this position is just, I am perhaps right in supposing it a consequence necessarily resulting from it that the stronger the powers of the government are, the more repellent will its qualities be, and the sooner its dissolution; at least certain it is that the conflict between the general and state governments will be proportionally more violent, and its or their ruin the sooner accomplished, for it must soon terminate either in that of the one or the other, I mean as an efficient government. The higher toned those of the states were, the more rapid would the progress be. I think I may venture to affirm that a confederacy formed of principalities would not last long, for the pride of princes would not brook those familiarities and insults which a free discussion of rights and interests, especially if they interfere sometimes unavoidably occasions; and when an absolute prince takes offense he wields the state with him. But this is not the case with democracies, for although their chief magistrates may be offended, it is difficult for them to communicate at the same time the same passions and dispositions to the whole community which they themselves possess. This is a caution however which I hope it is not necessary to suggest here, for I am satisfied the state governments will never take this turn of themselves, nor while that of the confederacy is preserved and properly supported.

But to carry this government a little further into practice let us submit the concerns and interests of different states or individuals within them to this corps formed of representatives from each negotiating for that to which they respectively belong, and what kind of justice may we expect from its decisions? If magazines were to be established or troops raised and stationed in some quarter of the union for public defense, might we not expect that these arrangements would take stronger bias from the combination of the day than any sentiment of propriety? If states or individuals within them had claims founded on the same principles with those upon which a decision had already been had in favor of others, are we to calculate with certainty upon a similar decree? In short apply it to every case that may possibly arise, either of states or individuals, in the full scope of its powers, and we shall find its decisions depend more upon negotiation, the bargain of the day, than any established maxim of justice or policy.

On the other hand, how are its treaties, laws, or ordinances to be carried into effect? Are they of authority and in force immediately within the states as soon as they are passed? Or does it require the intervention of a state law to give them validity? And if the law is necessary may not the state refuse to pass it, and if she does how shall she be compelled? It is well known from the practice of all the states in the confederacy that no act of Congress, of what nature soever it may be, is of force within them until it is recognized by their own legislatures; prior to that event it is a nullity, and to that only does it owe its authority. This view of the subject demonstrates clearly that the present government in its ordinary administration, though a league of independent states for common good and possessed of extensive powers, must always be void of energy, slow in its operation, sometimes oppressive, and often altogether suspended. It can never be calculated on by foreign powers, and of course they will form no treaties or compacts whatever with it that stipulate anything, at least on equal terms. In fine, very little dependence can be placed in it by the states themselves, for destitute of the power of coercion, to say nothing as to the justice or propriety of the measures themselves, *these* will not be forward to comply with its demands, while *those* may refuse with impunity. On the other hand, the illustrious event which has placed them in the rank of independent states demonstrates with equal certainty that it is competent to external defense and perfect security from abroad, for how otherwise could it have been achieved? These are the defects or the principal defects of the present government, and they are inseparable from a league of independent states, for to that circumstance and that alone they are to be attributed. We have then to weigh these evils, and compare them with the probable benefits and dangers that may accompany a change, and then see in which scale the balance preponderates.

It may be now asked are we reduced to this alternative either to subvert the state sovereignties or submit to these evils? Is the state sovereignty a vain and illusory hope, is it incompatible with its own and the general interests of the confederacy? Or is there any other alternative? The practice of nations and the field of inquiry is open before us, and we have everything that is sacred and dear to mankind depending on the event. Two species of remedy only present themselves to my mind, and these contemplate either a complete annihilation of the state governments, or a partial one with considerable reduction of their powers. A complete annihilation and the organization of a general government over the whole would unquestionably remove all the objections which have been stated above, and apply to it as a federal government; and I will be free to own that if it were in reality a practicable thing, there is no object which my mind has ever contemplated the attainment of which would give it such high gratification. To collect the citizens of America who have fought and bled together, by whose joint and common efforts they have been raised to the comparatively happy and exalted theatre on which they now stand; to lay aside all those jarring interests and discordant principles which state legislatures if they do not create, certainly foment and increase, arrange them under one government and make them one people, is an idea not only elevated and sublime, but equally benevolent and humane. Whether it contains within it a territory as extensive as the Russian or German empires, or is confined in its operation to the narrow scale of their smallest principalities or provinces, yet it is the business of state legislation to pursue its destined course, "the interests of those who live under it." For a legislature to contemplate other objects and make a sacrifice of their own for the good of other people or even decline availing itself of the legitimate exercise of its powers for that purpose, upon every opportunity which chance or fortune may present in its way, is a degree of liberality to which the human heart has not as yet attained. A society of philosophers of the ancient stoic sect might perhaps be capable of such extended philanthropy; but this sect is now altogether at an end, and at its height, never formed but an inconsiderable part of any community, and was by all the rest of the world considered as affecting objects without the pale of human nature. How much more delightful, therefore, is it to the mind to contemplate one legislature organized over the whole continent, containing all the free inhabitants of the American states within it, nourishing, protecting, and promoting their interests in every line and extending its genial influence to every part; commerce flourishing, arts increasing, lands rising in value, with all those other happy concomitants that attend a well formed and wisely directed government, than thirteen different legislatures in pursuit of local objects, acting upon partial and confined considerations, without system or policy, jealous of their particular rights, dissatisfied with, and preying upon each other. If it were practicable, I should embrace this change with the utmost pleasure, and consider it the goal at which all our efforts should bend, the polar star that should direct all our movements. I should consider the abolition of the state legislatures as a most fortunate event for America, and congratulate my country on the commencement of a new era in her affairs from whence to date the dawn of better hopes and happier days.

But is it practicable; can it be accomplished? Can a legislature be organized upon such principles as to comprehend the territory lying between the Mississippi, the St. Lawrence, the Lakes, and the Atlantic ocean, with such a variety of soil and climate, contain within it all the vital parts of a democracy and those provisions which the wisdom of ages has pointed out as the best security for liberty, and be at the same time a strong, efficient, and energetic government? Would it be possible to form in every respect a complete consolidation of interest and how otherwise would its operation affect the weaker party?

It is true the improvement of government under this form, by representation, the discovery of which is attributed to modern times, might make some difference in this respect; but are there no bounds within which it should still be restrained? Shall it attempt things that seem from the concurrent testimony of all history to be the appropriate object of despotism? Maladies that are incurable after they have afflicted the body with all the pain and anguish incident to a frail and feverish being, exhausted its efforts, and worn out its constitution, complete the work by terminating its existence. This government too, after having experienced the vicisitudes of fortune that might accompany its natural imperfections, of laws badly formed and indifferently executed, of anarchy, disorder, and confusion; after having worn out and broken the spirits of the people would also have its end. But what form it would then assume is left for time to develop. The diseases of every government suggest its remedy. Other circumstances, it is true, give it a bias, but these have a principal influence in directing its course. Those of the federal system, and which owed their birth and enormity to the want of strength in the federal head, had disposed the people to agree to an annihilation of their state governments, which yielded to the present one. Had this change been accomplished by the designs of wicked and abandoned men, by the usurpations of a tyrant, or the seductions of art and intrigue, it is to be presumed, and the experience of other countries has proved it, that the people would now return to that they had forsaken with a degree of zeal and fervor proportioned to the sufferings they had borne.* But if a long and patient experience had shown its defects, a calm and dispassionate appeal had been made to their understandings, and a recollection of the great calamities it had inflicted on them demonstrated it was neither calculated for the care of their liberties, their safety, or common interests, they would make a new experiment and take a different course. From the causes above stated the incapacity of the legislative branch to form happy, wise, or uniform laws for the government of a territory so extensive, and of a people in pursuit of objects so opposite in their nature, had perhaps already often clogged its operations and suspended its course. This had gradually alienated the affections of the people and created in them a contempt for this branch of the government. The powers of the executive had of course been proportionably increased, for it is natural for the latter to supply the defects of the former. Accustomed to behold it in miniature, and to derive relief from its friendly interference, the people are at length prepared to have recourse to a royal government as the last resort, the only safe asylum for the miserable and oppressed. And this perhaps would be the issue of the present government, and for these reasons I should dread its establishment over these states. For to however low and pitiable a condition we may have fallen, however deservedly we may have

---

*As in the restoration of Charles II in England.

acquired the contempt and scorn of nations, yet I had rather submit in peace and quiet to those reproaches which the proud and disdainful may throw upon us, than by commencing on a stage upon which the fortunes of all nations have been wrecked, however splendid and meteor like our transient exhibition might be, risk the enjoyment of those blessings we now possess.

But may not some middle course be struck, some plan be adopted to give the general government those rights of internal legislation necessary for its safety, and well being, in all cases and yet leave to the states other powers they might exercise to advantage? If by this it is intended to comprehend the right of direct taxation and excise with the absolute control of the resources of the union, it will be easy to perceive its consequences. Those who are in any degree acquainted with the principles of government, or with those of the human heart well know that upon this point, the equal distribution of the resources of the union between the two governments, will their balance depend. If you place the whole into the hands of one, it will require no casuist, no great degree of depth in this science to determine which will preponderate. Acting on the bowels the body will soon decay and die away. The pageant ornaments and trappings of power will not last long, for the reason and good sense of mankind turn with disgust upon the mockery of empty forms. Such an arrangement would therefore, in my apprehension, embark us on a more perilous and stormy sea than even a complete annihilation of the state governments.

If then such a government as I have above described in either view presents an impracticable alternative, or such an one as we should not without a nearer and better view of it embrace, the other mode only remains, or that which proposes the organization of a general government over the states forming a part of and acknowledged by the constitution of each, leaving at the same time a qualified government in each state for local objects. Let us examine this then since it is the only safe or even plausible course for us to take.

To organize a general government that shall contain within it a particular one for each state or, in other words, to form a constitution for each state which shall acknowledge that of the union, is no easy thing, for there never was an example of the kind before. The Amphictionic council, Achaean, Belgic, or Helvetic confederacies were but leagues of independent states, somewhat similar to the present one. To mark the precise point at which the powers of the general government shall cease, and that from whence those of the states shall commence, to poise them in such manner as to prevent either destroying the other, will require the utmost force of human wisdom and ingenuity. No possible ground of variance or even interference should be left, for there would the conflict commence that might perhaps prove fatal to both. As the very being or existence of the republican form in America, and of course the happiness and interests of the people depend on this point, the utmost clearness and perspicuity should be used to trace the boundary between them. The obvious line of separation is that of general and local interests. All those subjects that may fall within the former distinction should be given to the confederacy, and those of the latter retained to the states. If the federal government has a right to exercise direct legislation within the states, their respective sovereignties are at an end, and a complete consolidation or incorporation of the whole into one, established in their stead. For in government it is, as in physics, a maxim that two powers cannot occupy the same space at the same time. Let this therefore be the characteristic line of the division; internal legislation or the management of those concerns which are entirely local shall belong to the states, and that of those which have a foreign aspect and in which they have a national concern, to the confederacy.

In forming a constitution on these principles, the same rule should be observed that has been in forming those of individual states, defining the powers given, and qualifying the mode in which they shall be exercised. All powers not ceded, it is true, belong to the people, but those given in a constitution are expressed in general terms, as that the Congress shall levy and collect duties. This involves in it the right of making laws for the purpose, for the means are included in the power, otherwise it is a nullity. The species of evidence and the mode of trial are subordinate objects under it, and does it not follow that the Congress might regulate these at pleasure? How are we secured in the trial by jury? This most excellent mode of trial which has been found in those few countries where it has been adopted the bulwark of their rights, and which is the terror of despotic governments for it disarms them of half their power, is but a matter of police, of human invention; if then we gave general powers, unless we qualified their exercise by securing this, might they not regulate it otherwise? I would not be understood to insinuate it would be the case, but that it were possible is improper. The spirit of the times might secure the people of America perhaps for a great length of time against it; but fundamental principles form a check, even when the spirit of the times has changed, indeed they retard and control it. As it is with the trial by jury so it is with the liberty of conscience, that of the press, and many others. As to the powers themselves, the distinction being drawn, the enumeration would be of course. To those of the former Congress some few might be added, or from those of the constitution, some few taken away, for nominally there is not so great a difference between them as some people suppose. To the former for instance, let the absolute control of commerce with the revenues arising from it be added. Let the right of apportionment be as in the constitution, for the ground on which the states have met on that point is certainly a happy compromise, being that indeed which had been long recommended by Congress. Let them regulate the discipline and training of the militia, the calling them forth and commanding them in service; for the militia of a country is its only safe and proper defense. All countries are more or less exposed to danger, either from insurrection or invasion and the greater the authority of Congress over this respectable body of men, in whose hands everything would be safe, the less necessity there would be, to have recourse to that bane of all societies, the destroyer of the rights of men, a standing army. But it may be urged the revenues from the impost would not be sufficient for national purposes, and that without the right of direct taxation, the government would be forced to have recourse, to the expedient of requisitions, the inefficacy of which had already been sufficiently experienced. The position in the first instance as to the insufficiency of the revenues is doubtful; but the apprehension of the states neglecting requisitions under this as they have done under the late government still more so. When the United States became in effect a national government by being incorporated with those of the states, possessed considerable revenues, had at their command a fleet and army, with the absolute control of trade; I cannot but believe that their constitutional demands, or requisitions would be complied with. Let the individual states also be restrained from exercising improper powers, making war, emitting paper bills of credit and the like. All restraints that were necessary for the wise administration of a good and virtuous government would have my ready assent. It is not my intention to draft a form, a general idea is all I aim at, and in this perhaps I am tedious. . . .

It has been long established by the most celebrated writers, but particularly illustrated and explained by the President Montesquieu and Mr. Locke, that the division of the powers of a government over one state or one people only into three branches, the legislative, executive, and judiciary, is absolutely necessary for the preservation of liberty. This is now admitted by all who are not the friends of despotism, and I am persuaded it has already been demonstrated in the course of these observations that such a division is, if possible, more necessary in a government to be organized over more than one. Taking this position then as established, I will proceed to an examination of the principles upon which this organization should be formed.

If the states as such or in their legislative character appoint any of the officers of this government, the effect will be the same, provided the rotative principle is preserved, which will I hope never be given up, that has already been experienced; for in the appointment is involved that of responsibility. It should therefore proceed from the people immediately, or by means of electors chosen for the purpose. This will make them amenable to the people only for their conduct, or to such constitutional tribunals where they are practicable, as they shall establish to take cognizance of offenses. This we apprehend would contribute much to the establishment of a national government; each would move in the sphere the constitution had appointed for it and be accountable to the people only for their conduct, the high and pure source whence they respectively derived their authorities.

The legislative branches are in all democratic governments, and of course would be so in this, the immediate representatives of the people. They should therefore be kept as dependent on them as possible, having in all respects the same interests with themselves. For offenses in these branches the general government can provide no punishment, for there can be no tribunal under it to take cognizance of them. Charges of corruption or prosecutions for it or other offenses, committed by those in these branches, should not be allowed from those in the others, for this might either unite them in malpractices against their country or create endless strife between them, and thereby destroy the balance of the government. A free people are the only proper judges of the merits of those who serve them, and they only should bring them to justice. This shows the necessity of frequent elections. The members of each should in my opinion return to the body of the people, those of the house of representatives at the expiration of every two years, and those of the senate of every four years, capable however always of re-election. Both these branches should if possible be filled on the principles of representation from all the states. For the house of representatives, the rule adopted in the constitution is perhaps the proper one. Let twice that number or a still greater ratio of numbers to that of representation be the rule for the senate. The members of both branches should be incapable of appointment to other offices while in these, otherwise a wide door will be left open for corruption. This is not an idle or visionary precaution, but in a great measure the pivot upon which the upright and faithful administration of the government will depend. The experience of Britain has demonstrated how often the most valuable interests of the people have been bartered away by leading members of the house of commons for a seat in the house of peers, or some lucrative office in the government; how much greater then should our apprehension be of danger in the present instance, when we recollect that the government is organized upon such principles as to acknowledge no responsibility to the states, and comprehends within it such an extent of territory, as to put it out of the power of those who inhabit its extremities to have any knowledge of the conduct of their servants! The possibility of this kind of traffic should therefore be absolutely prohibited . . .

Having now taken a view as concisely as I have been able of the defects of the present system, suggested the remedy with the principles upon which it is founded, examined the constitution by that standard, and shown wherein I have approved or disapproved of it, perhaps it may be expected (as a deduction from the foregoing principles) that I should make some calculation of the probable course and ultimate fate of the government should it be adopted in its present form, since it might have some influence upon your opinion in the present instance. This must however be altogether conjectural, for in the operation of government, as in that of all other powers after consequences have been clearly demonstrated, as resulting from certain causes, oftentimes some incident not contemplated nor taken into the combination, or extra circumstances arises, that gives it a different direction. To form any estimate in this respect some peculiarities present themselves to view very deserving of attention. The mixture between the general and state governments, being partly a consolidated and partly a confederated one, suggests a balance between sovereignties that is new and interesting. So far as it proceeds from the people and its powers embrace the care of their interests, it partakes of the qualities of the former, and so far as the state governments remain, of the latter. In weighing the momentum of their relative strength or force it is no less difficult to determine which will preponderate. Founded alike by the people, by the people also may either be changed at pleasure. If the precise boundary had been drawn between them, the proper checks established, and the general government well poised, it might for a long time, and I should hope forever, be stationary; defective in these respects it will probably soon experience a change. Pursuing a natural course under those shocks it must expect, without any foreign impression to give it the fairest hopes, let us inquire what the interests of the people will dictate, for let that be its direction. Independent state sovereignties or partial confederacies have been reprobated in its commencement. Its foundation has been laid on the ruin of all schemes that had that tendency, and it is presumable it would in no event embrace either, at least until it had experienced a great vicissitude of fortunes. If then it escaped the first paroxysms the severe struggles and violent efforts against it exposed it to, its establishment might be considered as complete. And suppressing the spirit of opposition, its constitutional basis will be found broad and extensive. It is not the aid of the Delphic oracle, the blind zeal of enthusiasm, that will be called in to its support. It has the protection of the true religion, of divine authority itself to shield it from danger. The exercise of powers in common that will be allowed of in its commencement must yield on the part of the states to its acquiring strength. And wielding those the constitution has given it, without availing itself of such as were constructive, the state governments under this progress would soon become a burden to the people. The confederated principle or the spirit of state sovereignty would however not be inactive, but operate so as to bring on the crisis; and the constitution itself presents a fruitful source of controversy, for the spirit of accommodation or the mutual fear of danger must be great where the line between them is not exactly drawn, if they do not interfere. If this government had been organized over one state with a moderate extent of territory, its natural progress through the Senate would be to aristocracy. But as it is I am inclined to believe that, although in its operation it may bear that tone, yet when it becomes convulsed and experiences a change it will hold a different direction. Even the construction of that branch in its operation will contribute to hurry it into monarchy, and our earnest hopes and prayers should be, every circumstance considered, that it be a limited one. For these reasons and not that I fear any danger to the liberties of our country from the effective force of the government, exerted immediately against the good people of America, could I wish those checks and guards adopted, omitted at present from neglect and an overconfidence of our security, but which it is possible if the present opportunity is lost, we may contend for hereafter in vain. Political institutions, we are taught by melancholy experience, have their commencement, maturity and decline; and why should we not in early life, take these precautions that are calculated to prolong our days, and guard against the diseases of age? Or shall we rather follow the example of the strong, active, and confident young man, who in the pride of health, regardless of the admonitions of his friends, pursues the gratification of unbridled appetites, and falls a victim to his own indiscretion, even in the morn of life and before his race had been fairly begun.

I have to apologize for the trouble I have given you in the perusal of these observations. I owe it to myself however to observe that the bounds within which I have been under the necessity of confining this letter has prevented my going into that detail, often necessary, especially on so intricate a subject for the sake of illustration; and the want of leisure has I fear, prevented even a tolerable degree of correctness. But if I have been able to explain myself to your satisfaction I shall be contented. Upon the whole it results that although I am for a change, and a radical one, of the confederation, yet I have some strong and invincible objections to that proposed to be substituted in its stead. Those of less weight might be yielded for the sake of accommodation; but until an experiment shall prove the contrary, I shall always believe that the exercise of direct taxation and excise by one body, over the very extensive territory contained within the bounds of the United States, will terminate either in anarchy and a dissolution of the government, or a subversion of liberty . . .

The subject now submitted to you is no less interesting than it is important. Providence has long seen nine-tenths of the habitable globe immersed and groaning under the dreadful oppressions of slavery. To the people of America, to you it belongs to correct the opposite extreme. To form a government that shall shield you from danger from abroad, and promote your general and local interests, protect in safety the life, liberty, and property, of the peaceful, the virtuous, and the weak against the encroachments of the disorderly and licentious. Whether they are now endangered, whether the plan now before you, presented under the most faithful and illustrious auspices (under the auspices of men of whose abilities and integrity you have long had the most satisfactory proofs, and who to the most important services, by abandoning the enjoyments of a peaceful and happy retirement, have added this further testimony of their never failing attachment to the interests of their country), will accomplish this end or is capable of still further improvement, belongs to you to determine. To differ in any respect from these men is no pleasant thing to me; but being called upon an awful stage upon which I must now bear a part, I have thought it my duty to explain to you the principles on which my opinions were founded, under this further assurance, that if after a candid review, they shall appear indefensible, I will most cheerfully submit to be governed by your wishes, and obey other instructions.

John DeWitt
Essay V
(Boston) American Herald
December, 1787

To the Free Citizens of the Commonwealth of Massachusetts:

The chief blessings of society, like individuals, are fond of association, and have a mutual dependence upon each other. They form links of one chain, and are all actuated by the same cause. Where freedom prevails, industry and science there also prevail. Industry produces wealth, and science preserves freedom in purity. The majority of the people in all such countries become so active in their different pursuits, that they are deprived both of their time and opportunity to inform themselves of the principles of the government by which those great blessings are secured to them, and almost implicitly rely both for the explaining and for the enforcing of those principles upon the patriotism of those, their fellow citizens, who labor but in the field of inquiry, and who spend their whole time in researches after knowledge. Thanks be to heaven that in America, that majority always retaining the power, the others have never dared to enforce their principles without previous explanation; and it has become natural to mankind, wherever they have a system of any kind, a favorite, if it is as genuine and honest in principle as in appearance, they leave no active powers of the mind unessayed in elucidating, explaining, and enlarging upon its benefits to those whom they wish should adopt it. All its good qualities are delineated, and every exertion is made to refute all objections offered against it, which exertions will be crowned with success, if the objections in themselves are futile and will not bear the force of light and argument.

The malevolent passions of the heart are not called in, private faults of individuals are not raked from oblivion and magnified, invidious representations are not made, neither are the slanderous, envenomed darts of malice and envy hurled against those characters, who yesterday were deemed praiseworthy and held sacred for a series of obligations conferred by them upon their country, but today are execrated with passion because they do not in all points see as other men see. On the contrary, cool reasoning and dispassionate argument are of themselves sufficient to build up such a system, to unravel all its mysteries, and to present to the people in expressive, legible colors the blessings that will result from its adoption. Where this mode of conduct is not pursued by its advocates, where instead of cool reasoning upon the subject in question artful evasions are presented, the system itself is winked out of sight. Instead of dispassionate endeavors to remove difficulties arising in honest minds, which are offered with decency to the public in order to be refuted, those who make them are loaded with the opprobrious terms of *insurgents*, *destroyers of all government*, *bankrupts*, *defaulters*, and *anti federalists*, which is worse than *jacobitism*. Where, instead of promoting free discussions upon the most important subject ever before a community, attempts are made to fetter and suppress such discussions, by threatening the printer and dropping the papers that contain them. Where, instead of coming forward like men, in the full exercise of reason, like fellow citizens warmed with a patriotic ardor for their country, emulous to secure and preserve its sacred principles, and with proper weapons disarming their fellow citizens of those objections, they blast and asperse their characters (the dernier resort of all supporters of a bad cause). I say the people have a fair, undoubted right to presume those objections unanswerable, the system itself essentially defective, and that its advocates are, by their conduct, endeavoring not to reason, but to surprise the people into a hasty approbation of it.

That this is the case with the supporters of the proceedings of the federal convention, far be it from me to declare. Judge, my fellow-citizens, for yourselves; examine the public prints from the promulgation of this Constitution. Objections there you will find in score. Are they offered with decency? Do they attack men or measures? Are they answered in the same manner? And do you discover a desire in those who wish you to embrace this government to inform you of its principles, and the consequences which will probably ensue from such principles? Why have they taken from you the sinews of your present government, and instead of revising and amending your Confederation, have handed you a new one, contrasted in the plenitude of its powers? As you answer these questions, so you must make up your opinion upon that which is before you.

They have the power of "organizing, arming and disciplining the militia, and of governing them when in service of the United States, giving to the separate states the appointment of the officers, and the authority of training the militia according to the discipline prescribed by Congress." Let us inquire why they have assumed this power, for if it is for the purpose of forming you into one uniform, solid body throughout the United States, making you respectable both at home and abroad, of arming you more completely and exercising you oftener, of strengthening the power which is now lodged in your hands, and relying upon you and you solely for aid and support to the civil power in the execution of all the laws of the New Congress, it certainly can be no where better placed under the restrictions therein mentioned than in that body. But is this probable? Does the complexion of the proceedings countenance such a supposition? When they unprecedentedly claim the power of raising and supporting standing armies, do they tell you for what purposes they are to be raised? How they are to be employed? How many they are to consist of, and where to be stationed? Is this power fettered with any one of these necessary restrictions which will show they depend upon the militia, and not upon this infernal engine of oppression, to execute their civil laws? The nature of the demand in itself contradicts such a supposition, and forces you to believe that it is for none of these causes, but rather for the purpose of consolidating and finally destroying your strength, as your respective governments are to be destroyed.

They well know the impolicy of putting or keeping arms in the hands of a nervous people at a distance from the seat of government, upon whom they mean to exercise the powers granted in that government. They have no idea of calling upon the party aggrieved to support and enforce their own grievances. They are aware of the necessity of catching Samson asleep to trim him of his locks. It is asserted by the most respectable writers upon government that a well regulated militia, composed of the yeomanry of the country has ever been considered as the bulwark of a free people; and, says the celebrated Mr. Hume, "without it, it is folly to think any free government will have stability or security. When the sword is introduced, as in our constitution (speaking of the British), the person entrusted will always neglect to discipline the militia in order to have a pretext for keeping up a standing army; and it is evident this is a mortal distemper in the British parliament, of which it must finally inevitably perish." If they have not the same design, why do they wish a standing army unrestrained? It is universally agreed that a militia and a standing body of troops never yet flourished in the same soil. Tyrants have uniformly depended upon the latter at the expense of the former. Experience has taught them that a standing body of regular forces, wherever they can be completely introduced, are always efficacious in enforcing their edicts, however arbitrary; and slaves by profession themselves are "nothing loath" to break down the barriers of freedom with a *gout*. No, my fellow citizens, this plainly shows they do not mean to depend upon the citizens of the states alone to enforce their powers, wherefore it is their policy to neglect them, and lean upon something more substantial and summary. It is true they have left the appointment of officers in the breast of the several states, but this to me appears an insult rather than a priviledge. For what avails this right, if they in their pleasure should choose to neglect to arm, organize and discipline the men over whom such officers are to be appointed? It is a bait, that you might be led to suppose they did intend to apply to them in all cases and to pay particular attention to making them the bulwark of this continent. And would they not be equal to such an undertaking? Are they not abundantly able to give security and stability to your government as long as it is free? Are they not the only proper persons to do it? Are they not the most respectable body of yeomanry in that character upon earth? Have they not been deeply engaged in some of the most brilliant actions in America, and more than once decided the fate of armies? In short, do they not preclude the necessity of any standing army whatsoever, unless in case of invasion, and in that case it would be time enough to raise them; for no free government under heaven, with a well disciplined militia, was ever yet subdued by mercenary troups.

The advocates at the present day for a standing army in the New Congress pretend it is necessary for the respectability of government. I defy them to produce an instance in any country, in the Old or New World, where they have not finally done away the liberties of the people. Every writer upon government, Locke, Sidney, Hamden, and a list of others have uniformly asserted that standing armies are a solecism in any government; that no nation ever supported them, that did not resort to, rely on, and finally become a prey to them. No Western historians have yet been hardy enough to advance principles that look a different way. What historians have asserted, all the Grecian republics have verified. They are brought up to obedience and unconditional submission. With arms in their hands, they are taught to feel the weight of rigid discipline. They are excluded from the enjoyments which liberty gives to its votaries; they, in consequence, hate and envy the rest of the community in which they are placed and indulge a malignant pleasure in destroying those privileges to which they never can be admitted. "Without them," says the Marquis of Beccaria, "in every society there is an effort constantly tending to confer on one part the height of power, and to reduce the other to the extreme of weakness and misery, and this is of itself sufficient to employ the people's attention." There is no instance of any government being reduced to a confirmed tyranny without military oppression; and the first policy of tyrants has been to annihilate all other

means of national activity and defense, and to rely solely upon standing troops. Repeated were the trials before the sovereigns of Europe
dared to introduce them upon any pretext whatever; and the whole
record of the transactions of mankind cannot furnish an instance
(unless the proceedings of the convention may now be called a part of
that record) where the motives which caused their establishment were
not completely disguised. Pisistratus in Greece, and Dyonysius in
Syracuse, Charles in France, and Henry in England all cloaked their
villainous intentions under an idea of raising a small body for a guard
to their persons; and Spain could not succeed in the same nefarious
plan, until through the influence of the ambitious priest, they were
called upon to resist the progress of the infidels. "Caesar, who first
attacked the commonwealth with *mines*, very soon opened his *batteries*." Notwithstanding all these objections to this engine of oppression
which are made by the most experienced men, and confirmed by every
country where the rays of freedom ever extended. Yet in America,
which has hitherto been her favorite abode; in this civilized territory
where property is valuable, and men are found with feelings that will
not patiently submit to arbitrary control, in this western region where,
my fellow countrymen, it is confessedly proper that you should associate and dwell in society from choice and reflection, and not be kept
together by force and fear, you are modestly requested to engraft into
the component parts of your Constitution, a standing army, without
any qualifying restraints whatever, certainly to exist somewhere within
the bowels of your country in time of peace. It is very true, that the
celebrated Mr. Wilson, a member of the convention and who we may
suppose breathes, in some measure the spirit of that body, tells you it
is for the purpose of forming cantonments upon your frontiers, and for
the dignity and safety of your country, as it respects foreign nations.
No man that loves his country could object to their being raised for the
first of these causes, but for the last it cannot be necessary. GOD has so
separated us by an extensive ocean from the rest of mankind. He has
so liberally endowed us with privileges, and so abundantly taught us
to esteem them precious, it would be impossible, while we retain our
integrity and advert to first principles, for any nation whatever to
subdue us. We have succeeded in an opposition to the most powerful
people upon the globe; and the wound that America received in the
struggle, where is it? As speedily healed as the track in the ocean is
buried by the succeeding wave. It has scarcely stopped her progress,
and our private dissentions only at this moment tarnish the luster of
the most illustrious infant nation under heaven.

You cannot help suspecting this gentleman when he goes on to tell you, "that standing armies in time of peace, have always been a topic of *popular declamation*, but Europe has found them necessary to maintain the appearance of strength in a season of the most profound tranquility." This shows you his opinion, and that he, as one of the convention, was for unequivocally establishing them in time of peace; and to object to them is mere popular declamation. But I will not, my countrymen, I cannot believe you to be of the same sentiment. Where is the standing army in the world that, like the musket they make use of, has been, in time of peace, brightened and burnished for the sake only of maintaining an appearance of strength, without being put to a different use, without having had a pernicious influence upon the morals, the habits, and the sentiments of society, and finally, taking a chief part in executing its laws. But some say that there is a control over them, and that consists in the appropriation of monies for their support. Turn your attention to England, and see the popular part of this constitution by the influence of money, by the influence of military and revenue officers, brought gravely to give their annual assent to the existence of a standing army, and for monies to support it. It has long since been an insult on the good sense of that nation.

It may not be amiss to remind you of that swarm of revenue, excise, impost and stamp officers, continental assessors and collectors that your new Constitution will introduce among you. They will, of themselves, be a STANDING ARMY to you, and you will see them at your elections, active and industrious to secure the seats of those men who put them into office. They will be very adequate to give you a surfeit of their company, to make you tired in meddling with government, and disposed to become indifferent about the exercise of it without the blessed assistance of any military corps.

Upon the whole, my countrymen, it appears to me that this power as it now stands is decidedly improper and dangerous. That Congress ought to have the power of raising armies when invaded by our enemies is certain; that they ought not to have it for any other cause is equally so. If they did not or do not mean to employ them in any other way, they ought in express terms to say so in a Bill of Rights. They never ought to exist at all, but in subordination to civil authority. If the people are not in general disposed to execute the powers of government, it is time to suspect there is something wrong in that government, and rather than employ a standing army, they had better have another. For, in my humble opinion, it is yet much too early to set it down for a fact that mankind cannot be governed but by force.

Cato
Letters V, VI, and VII
New York Journal
22 November, 1787, 3 January, 1788

To the Citizens of the State of New York:

In my last number I endeavored to prove that the language of the article relative to the establishment of the executive of this new government was vague and inexplicit, that the great powers of the President, connected with his duration in office would lead to oppression and ruin. That he would be governed by favorites and flatterers, or that a dangerous council would be collected from the great officers of state. That the ten miles square, if the remarks of one of the wisest men drawn from the experience of mankind may be credited, would be the asylum of the base, idle, avaricious and ambitious, and that the court would possess a language and manners different from yours, that a vice-president is as unnecessary as he is dangerous in his influence, that the president cannot represent you because he is not of your own immediate choice, that if you adopt this government, you will incline to an arbitrary and odious aristocracy or monarchy, that the president possessed of the power given him by this frame of government differs but very immaterially from the establishment of monarchy in Great Britain, and I warned you to beware of the fallacious resemblance that is held out to you by the advocates of this new system between it and your own state governments.

And here I cannot help remarking that inexplicitness seems to pervade this whole political fabric; certainty in political compacts which Mr. Coke calls *the mother and nurse of repose and quietness,* the want of which induced men to engage in political society, has ever been held by a wise and free people as essential to their security; as, on the one hand it fixes barriers which the ambitious and tyrannically disposed magistrate dare not overleap, and on the other, becomes a wall of safety to the community, otherwise stipulations between the governors and governed are nugatory. You might as well deposit the important powers of legislation and execution in one or a few and permit them to govern according to their disposition and will; but the world is too full of examples which prove that *to live by one man's will became the cause of all men's misery.* Before the existence of express political compacts it was reasonably implied that the magistrate should govern with wisdom and justice, but mere implication was too feeble to restrain the unbridled ambition of a bad man, or afford security against negligence, cruelty, or any other defect of mind. It is alleged that the opinions and manners of the people of America are capable to resist and prevent an extension of prerogative or oppression. But you must recollect that opinion and manners are mutable, and may not always be a permanent obstruction against the encroachments of government; that the progress of a commercial society begets luxury, the parent of inequality, the foe to virtue, and the enemy to restraint, and that ambition and voluptuousness aided by flattery will teach magistrates where limits are not explicitly fixed to have separate and distinct interests from the people; besides it will not be denied that government assimilates the manners and opinions of the community to it. Therefore, a general presumption that rulers will govern well is not a sufficient security. You are then under a sacred obligation to provide for the safety of your posterity, and would you now basely desert their interests, when by a small share of prudence you may transmit to them a beautiful political patrimony, which will prevent the necessity of their travelling through seas of blood to obtain that, which your wisdom might have secured. It is a duty you owe likewise to your own reputation, for you have a great name to lose. You are characterised as cautious, prudent and jealous in politics; whence is it therefore, that you are about to precipitate yourselves into a sea of uncertainty, and adopt a system so vague, and which has discarded so many of your valuable rights. Is it because you do not believe that an American can be a tyrant? If this be the case you rest on a weak basis; Americans are like other men in similar situations, when the manners and opinions of the community are changed by the causes I mentioned before, and your political compact inexplicit, your posterity will find that great power connected with ambition, luxury, and flattery will as readily produce a Caesar, Caligula, Nero, and Domitian in America as the same causes did in the Roman empire.

But the next thing to be considered in conformity to my plan is the first article of this new government, which comprises the erection of the house of representatives and senate, and prescribes their various powers and objects of legislation. The most general objections to the first article are that biennial elections for representatives are a departure from the safe democratic principle of annual ones, that the number of representatives are too few, that the apportionment and principles of increase are unjust, that no attention has been paid to either the numbers or property in each state in forming the senate, that the mode in which they are appointed and their duration will lead to the establishment of an aristocracy, that the senate and president are improperly connected, both as to appointments and the making of treaties, which are to become the supreme law of the land, that the judicial in some measure, to wit, as to the trial of impeachments, is placed in the senate, a branch of the legislative and some times a branch of the executive. That Congress have the improper power of making or altering the regulations prescribed by the different legislatures respecting the time, place, and manner of holding elections for representatives, and the time and manner of choosing senators. That standing armies may be established, and appropriation of money made for their support for two years, that the militia of the most remote state may be marched into those states situated at the opposite extreme of this continent. That the slave trade is, to all intents and purposes permanently established, and a slavish capitation, or poll tax, may at any time be levied. These are some of the many evils that will attend the adoption of this government.

But with respect to the first objection, it may be remarked that a well digested democracy has this advantage over all others; to wit, that it affords to many the opportunity to be advanced to the supreme command, and the honors they thereby enjoy fill them with a desire of rendering themselves worthy of them. Hence, this desire becomes part of their education, is matured in manhood, and produces an ardent affection for their country; and it is the opinion of the great Sidney and Montesquieu that this is in a great measure produced by annual election of magistrates.

If annual elections were to exist in this government, and learning and information to become more prevalent, you never will want men to execute whatever you could design. Sidney observes *that a well governed state is as fruitful to all good purposes as the seven headed serpent is said to have been in evil; when one head is cut off, many rise up in the place of it.* He remarks further, that *it was also thought that free cities, by frequent elections of magistrates, became nurseries of great and able men, every man endeavoring to excel others that he might be advanced to the honor he had no other title to than what might arise from his merit, or reputation,* but the framers of this *perfect government,* as it is called, have departed from this democratic principle, and established biennial elections for the house of representatives who are to be chosen by the people, and sextennial for the senate, who are to be chosen by the legislatures of the different states. [They] have given to the executive the unprecedented power of making temporary senators, in case of vacancies, by resignation or otherwise, and so far forth establishing a precedent for virtual representation (though in fact, their original appointment is virtual), thereby influencing the choice of the legislatures, or if they should not be so complaisant as to conform to his appointment, offense will be given to the executive and the temporary members will appear ridiculous by rejection; this temporary member, during his time of appointment, will of course act by a power derived from the executive, and for and under his immediate influence.

It is a very important objection to this government that the representation consists of so few; too few to resist the influence of corruption, and the temptation to treachery, against which all governments ought to take precautions. How guarded you have been on this head, in your own state constitution, and yet the number of senators and representatives proposed for this vast continent does not equal those of your own state. How great the disparity if you compare them with the aggregate numbers in the United States. The history of representation in England from which we have taken our model of legislation is briefly this; before the institution of legislating by deputies, the whole free part of the community usually met for that purpose. When this became impossible by the increase of numbers, the community was divided into districts, from each of which was sent such a number of deputies as was a complete representation of the various numbers and orders of citizens within them; but can it be asserted with truth that six men can be a complete and full representation of the numbers and various orders of the people in this state? Another thing may be suggested against the small number of representatives, that but few of you will have the chance of sharing even in this branch of the legislature; and that the choice will be confined to a very few. The more complete it is, the better will your interests be preserved, and the greater the opportunity you will have to participate in government, one of the principal securities of a free people. But this subject has been so ably and fully treated by a writer under the signature of Brutus that I shall content myself with referring you to him thereon, reserving further observations on the other objections I have mentioned for my future numbers . . . The next objection that arises against this proffered constitution is that the apportionment of representatives and direct taxes are unjust. The words as expressed in this article are, "representatives and direct taxes shall be apportioned among the several states which may be included in this union, according to their respective numbers, which shall be determined by adding to the whole number of free persons, including those bound to service for a term of years, and excluding Indians not taxed, three fifths of all other persons." In order to elucidate this, it will be necessary to repeat the remark in my last number, that the mode of legislation in the infancy of free communities was by the collective body, and this consisted of free persons, or those whose age admitted them to the rights of mankind and citizenship, whose sex made them capable of protecting the state, and whose birth may be denominated free born, and no traces can be found that ever women, children, and slaves, or those who were not sui juris, in the early days of legislation meeting with the free members of the community to deliberate on public measures. Hence, is derived this maxim in free governments, that representation ought to bear a proportion to the number of free inhabitants in a community; this principle your own state constitution and others have observed in the establishment of a future census, in order to apportion the representatives, and to increase or diminish the representation to the ratio of the increase or diminution of electors. But, what aid can the community derive from the assistance of women, infants, and slaves in their deliberation or in their defense? and what motive therefore could the convention have in departing from the just and rational principle of representation, which is the governing principle of this state and of all America?

The doctrine of taxation is a very important one, and nothing requires more wisdom and prudence than the regulation of that portion, which is taken from, and of that which is left to, the subject; and if you anticipate, what will be the enormous expense of this new government added also to your own, little will that portion be which will be left to you. I know there are politicians who believe that you should be loaded with taxes, in order to make you industrious and, perhaps, there are some of this opinion in the convention, but it is an erroneous principle. For what can inspire you with industry if the greatest measures of your labor are to be swallowed up in taxes? The advocates for this new system hold out an idea that you will have but little to pay for, that the revenues will be so managed as to be almost wholly drawn from the source of trade or duties on imports, but this is delusive. For this government to discharge all its incidental expenses, besides paying the interests on the home and foreign debts, will require more money than its commerce can afford; and if you reflect one moment, you will find that if heavy duties are laid on merchandise, as must be the case if government intend to make this the prime medium to lighten the people of taxes, that the price of the commodities, useful as well as luxurious, must be increased. The consumers will be fewer. The merchants must import less; trade will languish, and this source of revenue in a great measure be dried up. But if you examine this a little further, you will find that this revenue managed in this way will come out of you and be a very heavy and ruinous one, at last. The merchant no more than advances the money for you to the public, and will not, nor cannot pay any part of it himself; and if he pays more duties, he will sell his commodities at a price proportionably raised. Thus the laborer, mechanic, and farmer must feel it in the purchase of their utensils and clothing; wages, etc. must rise with the price of things, or they must be ruined. And that must be the case with the farmer, whose produce will not increase in the ratio with labor, utensils, and clothing, [because] he must sell at the usual price or lower, perhaps caused by the decrease of trade. The consequence will be that he must mortgage his farm, and then comes inevitable bankruptcy.

In what manner then will you be eased, if the expenses of government are to be raised solely out of the commerce of this country; do you not readily apprehend the fallacy of this argument? But government will find that to press so heavily on commerce will not do, and therefore must have recourse to other objects; these will be a capitation or poll tax, window lights, etc. etc. and a long train of impositions which their ingenuity will suggest. But will you submit to be numbered like the slaves of an arbitrary despot? What will be your reflections when the taxmaster thunders at your door for the duty on that light which is the bounty of heaven? It will be the policy of the great landholders who will chiefly compose this senate, and perhaps a majority of this house of representatives, to keep their lands free from taxes; and this is confirmed by the failure of every attempt to lay a land tax in this state. Hence, recourse must and will be had to the sources I mentioned before. The burdens on you will be insupportable, your complaints will be inefficacious; this will beget public disturbances, and I will venture to predict, without the spirit of prophecy, that you and the government, if it is adopted, will one day be at issue on this point. The force of government will be exerted, this will call for an increase of revenue, and will add fuel to the fire. The result will be that either you will revolve to some other form, or that government will give peace to the country by destroying the opposition. If government therefore can, notwithstanding every opposition, raise a revenue on such things as are odious and burdensome to you, they can do anything.

But why should the number of individuals be the principle to apportion the taxes in each state, and to include in that number, women, children and slaves? The most natural and equitable principle of apportioning taxes would be in a ratio to their property, and a reasonable impost in a ratio to their trade; but you are told to look for the reason of these things in accommodation. But this much admired principle, when stripped of its mystery, will in this case appear to be no less than a basis for an odious poll tax, the offspring of despotic governments, a thing so detestable that the state of Maryland, in their bill of rights, declares, "that the levying taxes by the poll is grievous and oppressive and ought to be abolished." A poll tax is at all times oppressive to the poor, and their greatest misfortune will consist in having more prolific wives than the rich.

In every civilized community, even in those of the most democratic kind, there are principles which lead to an aristocracy; these are superior talents, fortunes, and public employments. But in free governments, the influence of the two former is resisted by the equality of the laws, and the latter by the frequency of elections, and the chance that everyone has in sharing in public business. But when this natural and artificial eminence is assisted by principles interwoven in this government; when the senate, so important a branch of the legislature, is so far removed from the people, as to have little or no connection with them; when their duration in office is such as to have the resemblance of perpetuity; when they are connected with the executive, by the appointment of all officers and also, to become a judiciary for the trial of officers of their own appointments; added to all this, when none but men of oppulence will hold a seat, what is there left to resist and repel this host of influence and power? Will the feeble efforts of the house of representatives, in whom your security ought to subsist, consisting of about seventy-three, be able to hold the balance against them when, from the fewness of the number in this house, the senate will have in their power to poison even a majority of that body by douceurs of office for themselves or friends? From causes like this both Montesquieu and Hume have predicted the decline of the British government into that of an absolute one. But the liberties of this country, if this system is adopted, will be strangled in their birth; for whenever the executive and senate can destroy the independence of the majority in the house of representatives, then where is your security? They are so intimately connected that their interests will be one and the same; and will the slow increase of numbers be able to afford a repelling principle? But you are told to adopt this government first, and you will always be able to alter it afterwards. This would be first submitting to be slaves and then taking care of your liberty; when your chains are on, then act like freemen.

Complete acts of legislation, which are to become the supreme law of the land, ought to be the united act of all the branches of government. But one of the most important duties may be managed by the senate and executive alone, and to have all the force of the law paramount without the aid or interference of the house of representatives; that is the power of making treaties. This power is a very important one, and may be exercised in various ways, so as to affect your person and property, and even the domain of the nation. By treaties you may defalcate part of the empire; engagements may be made to raise an army, and you may be transported to Europe to fight the wars of ambitious princes. Money may be contracted for, and you must pay it; and a thousand other obligations may be entered into; all which will become the supreme law of the land; and you are bound by it. If treaties are erroneously or wickedly made, who is there to punish? The executive can always cover himself with the plea that he was advised by the senate, and the senate being a collective body are not easily made accountable for maladministration. On this account we are in a worse situation than Great Britain, where they have secured, by a ridiculous fiction, the King from accountability by declaring that he can do no wrong, by which means the nation can have redress against his minister. But with us infallibility pervades every part of the system, and neither the executive nor his council, who are a collective body, and his advisers, can be brought to punishment for maladministration . . .

. . . That the senate and president are further improperly connected will appear, if it is considered that their dependence on each other will prevent either from being a check upon the other; they must act in concert, and whether the power and influence of the one or the other is to prevail will depend on the character and abilities of the men who hold those offices at the time. The senate is vested with such a proportion of the executive that it would be found necessary that they should be constantly sitting. This circumstance did not escape the convention, and they have provided for the event in the second article, which declares that the executive may, on extraordinary occasions, *convene both houses or either of them.* No occasion can exist for calling the assembly without the senate; the words *or either of them* must have been intended to apply only to the senate. Their wages are already provided for; and it will be therefore readily observed that the partition between a perpetuation of their sessions and a perpetuation of their offices, in the progress of the government, will be found to be but thin and feeble. Besides, the senate who have the sole power to try all impeachments, in case of the impeachment of the president, are to determine as judges, the propriety of the advice they gave him as senators. Can the senate in this, therefore, be an impartial judicature? And will they not rather serve as a screen to great public defaulters?

Among the many evils that are incorporated in this new system of government, is that of congress having the power of making or altering the regulations prescribed by the different legislatures, respecting the time, place, and manner of holding elections for representatives, and the time and manner of choosing senators. If it is inquired, in what manner this regulation may be exercised to your injury, the answer is easy.

By the first article the house of representatives shall consist of members chosen every second year by the people of the several states, who are qualified to vote for members of their several state assemblies. It can therefore readily be believed that the different state legislatures, provided such can exist after the adoption of this government, will continue those easy and convenient modes for the election of representatives for the national legislature that are in use, for the election of members of assembly for their own states. But the congress has, by the constitution, a power to make other regulations, or alter those in practice, prescribed by your own state legislatures. Hence, instead of having the places of elections in the precincts, and brought home almost to your own doors. Congress may establish a place, or places, at either the extremes, center, or outer parts of the states, at a time and season too, when it may be very inconvenient to attend; and by these means destroy the rights of election. But in opposition to this reasoning, it is asserted that it is a necessary power because the states might omit making rules for the purpose, and thereby defeat the existence of that branch of the government. This is what logicians call *argumentum absurdum*, for the different states, if they will have any security at all in this government, will find it in the house of representatives, and they, therefore, would not be very ready to eradicate a principle in which it dwells, or involve their country in an instantaneous revolution. Besides, if this was the apprehension of the framers, and the ground of that provision, why did not they extend this controlling power to the other duties of the several state legislatures? To exemplify this the states are to appoint senators and electors for choosing of a president, but the time is to be under the direction of congress. Now suppose they were to omit the appointment of senators and electors, though congress was to appoint the time, which might well be apprehended as the omission of regulations for the election of members of the house of representatives, provided they had that power; or suppose they were not to meet at all. Of course, the government cannot proceed in its exercise. And from this motive or apprehension, congress ought to have taken these duties entirely in their own hands and, by a decisive declaration, annihilated them, which they in fact have done by leaving them without the means of support or at least resting on their bounty. To this, the advocates for this system oppose the common, empty declamation that there is no danger that congress will abuse this power; but such language, as relative to so important a subject, is mere vapor, and sound without sense. Is it not in their power, however, to make such regulations as may be inconvenient to you? It must be admitted because the words are unlimited in their sense. It is a good rule, in the construction of a contract, to suppose that what may be done will be. Therefore, in considering this subject, you are to suppose that in the exercise of this government, a regulation of congress will be made for holding an election for the whole state at Poughkeepsie at New York, or perhaps at Fort Stanwix. Who will then be the actual electors for the house of representatives? Very few more than those who may live in the vicinity of these places. Could any others afford the expense and time of attending? And would not the government by this means have it in their power to put whom they pleased in the house of representatives? You ought certainly to have as much or more distrust with respect to the exercise of these powers by congress, than congress ought to have with respect to the exercise of those duties which ought to be entrusted to the several states, because over them congress can have a legislative controlling power.

Hitherto we have tied up our rulers in the exercise of their duties by positive restrictions; if the cord has been drawn too tight, loosen it to the necessary extent, but do not entirely unbind them. I am no enemy to placing a reasonable confidence in them; but such an unbounded one as the advocates and framers of this new system advise you to would be dangerous to your liberties. It has been the ruin of other governments, and will be yours, if you adopt with all its latitudinal powers; unlimited confidence in governors as well as individuals is frequently the parent of deception. What facilitated the corrupt designs of Philip of Macedon and caused the ruin of Athens, but the unbounded confidence in their statesmen and rulers? Such improper confidence Demosthenes was so well convinced had ruined his country that in his second Philippic oration he remarks, "that there is one common bulwark with which men of prudence are naturally provided, the guard and security of all people, particularly of free states, against the assaults of tyrants. What is this? Distrust. Of this be mindful, to this adhere, preserve this carefully, and no calamity can affect you." Montesquieu observes that, "the course of government is attended with an insensible descent to evil, and there is no reascending to good without very great efforts." The plain inference from this doctrine is that rulers in all governments will erect an interest separate from the ruled, which will have a tendency to enslave them. There is therefore no other way of interrupting this insensible descent and warding off the evil as long as possible, than by establishing principles of distrust in your constituents, and cultivating the sentiment among yourselves. But let me inquire of you, my countrymen, whether the freedom and independence of elections is a point of magnitude? If it is, what kind of a spirit of amity, deference and concession is that which has put in the power of congress at one stroke to prevent your interference in government and do away your liberties forever? Does either the situation or circumstances of things warrant it?

John Lansing
Speech given before the New York Ratifying Convention 24 June, 1788

. . . I trust the committee will indulge me with a few additional observations. It has been an argument urged with considerable zeal, that, if the state legislatures possessed the power of recall, its exercise would be governed by faction or caprice, and be subject to the impulses of the moment. Sir, it has been sufficiently proven to the committee that, although there have been factions in the state governments, though they have been subject in some instances to inconstant humors and a disaffected spirit, they have never yet exercised the power of recall which was vested in them. As far, therefore, as experience is satisfactory, we may safely conclude that none of these factious humors will operate to produce the evils which the gentlemen apprehend. If, however, the legislature should be so deluded as to recall an honest and faithful senator, certainly every opportunity would be allowed him of defending himself, of explaining his motives which influenced him, and of convincing them of the injustice of the imputation. If the state has been imposed upon by ambitious and designing men, the intrigue, on full examination, will be detected and exposed. If misinformation or false views have produced the measure, the error may easily be corrected.

It has been observed that the power of recall might be exercised to the destruction of the union. Gentlemen have expressed their apprehensions that, if one part of the continent was invaded, the states most distant from the danger might refuse their aid and consequently the whole fall a sacrifice. Is this reasoning upon probability? Is not every state fully convinced that her interest and safety are involved in those of the union? It is impossible, sir, for such an event to happen till, in the decline of the human species the social principles, on which our union is founded, are utterly lost and forgotten. It is by no means necessary that the state which exercises the power contended for should continue unrepresented. I have no objection that a clause should be added to the amendment, obliging the state, in case of a recall, to choose immediately other senators to fill the vacancy. Such a provision would probably in some measure remove the apprehensions which are entertained.

In the gentlemen's reasoning on the subject, there appears an inconsistency which I cannot but notice. It is observed that one design of the Senate, as it is now organized, is to form a counterpoise to the local prejudices which are incompatible with a liberal view of national objects, and which commonly accompany the representatives of a state. On the other hand, it is said the amendment will have a tendency to lessen the attachment of the senators to their constituents, and make them regardless of the public sentiments, by removing the motive to virtue: that is, a continuation of honors and employments. This reasoning seems to be calculated upon the idea of dependence on the state governments, and a close connection between the interest of the several states and that of their representatives. But this dependence, say the gentlemen, is the very source of all those local prejudices which are so unfavorable to good government, and which the design of the senate was to correct and remove. I am, however, sir, by no means in sentiment with the honorable gentleman, that the rotation proposed would diminish the senator's ambition to merit the good will of the people. Though, at the expiration of his office, he would be incapacitated for a term of six years, yet to the end of this term he would look forward with as earnest ambition as if he were constantly the object of the public suffrages. Nay, while in office, he would have an additional motive to act well; for conscious of the people's inconstant disposition, he would be obliged; in order to secure a future election, to fix in their minds the most lasting impression of his services. It is entirely probable that local interests, opinions, and prejudices will ever prevail in the general government in a greater or less degree. It was upon this presumption that the small states were induced to join themselves to the union.

Melancton Smith
Speech given before the New York Ratifying Convention
20 June, 1788

Mr. *Smith* again rose. He most heartily concurred in sentiment with the honorable gentleman who opened the debate yesterday, that the discussion of the important question now before them ought to be entered on with a spirit of patriotism, with minds open to conviction, with a determination to form opinions only on the merits of the question, from those evidences which should appear in the course of the investigation.

How far the general observations made by the honorable gentleman accorded with these principles, he left to the House to determine.

It was not, he said, his intention to follow that gentleman through all his remarks. He should only observe that what had been advanced did not appear to him to apply to the subject under consideration.

He was as strongly impressed with the necessity of a union, as anyone could be. He would seek it with as much ardor. In the discussion of this subject, he was disposed to make every reasonable concession, and indeed to sacrifice everything for a union, except the liberties of his country, than which he could contemplate no greater misfortune. But he hoped we were not reduced to the necessity of sacrificing or even endangering our liberties to preserve the union. If that was the case, the alternative was dreadful. But he would not now say that the adoption of the Constitution would endanger our liberties; because that was the point to be debated, and the premises should be laid down previously to the drawing of any conclusion. He wished that all observations might be confined to this point, and that declamation and appeals to the passions might be omitted.

Why, said he, are we told of our weaknesses? Of the defenseless condition of the southern parts of our state? Of the exposed situation of our capital? Of Long Island surrounded by water, and exposed to the incursions of our neighbors in Connecticut? Of Vermont having separated from us and assumed the powers of a distinct government, and of the northwest part of our state being in the hands of a foreign enemy? Why are we to be alarmed with apprehensions that the Eastern states are inimical, and disinclined to form alliances with us? He was sorry to find that such suspicions were entertained. He believed that no such disposition existed in the Eastern states. Surely it could not be supposed that those states would make war upon us for exercising the rights of freemen, deliberating and judging for ourselves on a subject the most interesting that ever came before any assembly. If a war with our neighbor was to be the result of not acceding, there was no use in debating here; we had better receive their dictates, if we were unable to resist them. The defects of the old Confederation needed as little proof as the necessity of an union. But there was no proof in all this that the proposed Constitution was a good one. Defective as the old Confederation is, he said, no one could deny but it was possible we might have a worse government. But the question was not whether the present Confederation be a bad one, but whether the proposed Constitution be a good one.

It had been observed that no examples of federal republics had succeeded. It was true that the ancient confederated republics were all destroyed; so were those which were not confederated, and all ancient governments of every form had shared the same fate. Holland had undoubtedly experienced many evils from the defects in her government, but with all these defects, she yet existed; she had under her confederacy made a principal figure among the nations of Europe, and he believed few countries had experienced a greater share of internal peace and prosperity. The Germanic Confederacy was not the most pertinent example to produce on this occasion. Among a number of absolute princes who consider their subjects as their property, whose will is law, and to whose ambition there are no bounds, it was no difficult task to discover other causes from which the convulsions in that country rose, than the defects of their confederation. Whether a confederacy of states under any form be a practicable government was a question to be discussed in the course of investigating this Constitution.

He was pleased that thus early in the debate, the honorable gentleman had himself shown, that the intent of the Constitution was not a confederacy, but a reduction of all the states into a consolidated government. He hoped the gentleman would be complaisant enough to exchange names with those who disliked the Constitution, as it appeared from his own concession that they were Federalists, and those who advocated it Antifederalists. He begged leave, however, to remind the gentleman that Montesquieu, with all the examples of modern and ancient republics in view, gives it as his opinion that a confederated republic has all the internal advantages of a republic, with the external force of a monarchical government. He was happy to find an officer of such high rank recommending to the other officers of government, and to those who are members of the Legislature, to be unbiased by any motives of interest or state importance. Fortunately for himself, he was out of the verge of temptations of this kind, not having the honor to hold any office under the state. But then he was exposed, in common with other gentlemen of the convention, to another temptation, against which he thought it necessary that we should be equally guarded. If, said he, this constitution is adopted, there will be a number of honorable and lucrative offices to be filled, and we ought to be cautious lest an expectancy of some of them should influence us to adopt without due consideration.

We may wander, said he, in the fields of fancy without end and gather flowers as we go. It may be entertaining, but it is of little service to the discovery of truth. We may on one side compare the scheme advocated by our opponents to *golden images, with feet part of iron and part of clay;* and on the other, *to a beast dreadful and terrible, and strong exceedingly, having great iron teeth, which devours, breaks in pieces, and stamps the residue with his feet.* And after all, said he, we shall find that both these allusions are taken from the same *vision;* and their true meaning must be discovered by sober reasoning.

He would agree with the honorable gentleman, that perfection in any system of government was not to be looked for. If that was the object, the debates on the one before them might soon be closed. But he would observe that this observation applied with equal force against changing any systems, especially against material and radical changes. Fickleness and inconstancy, he said, was characteristic of a free people; and in framing a Constitution for them it was perhaps the most difficult thing to correct this spirit, and guard against the evil effects of it. He was persuaded it could not be altogether prevented without destroying their freedom; it would be like attempting to correct a small indisposition in the habit of the body by fixing the patient in a confirmed consumption. This fickle and inconstant spirit was the more dangerous in bringing about changes in the government. The instance that had been adduced by the gentleman from sacred history was an example in point to prove this. The nation of Israel having received a form of civil government from heaven, enjoyed it for a considerable period; but at length laboring under pressures which were brought upon them by their own misconduct and imprudence, instead of imputing their misfortunes to their true causes, and making a proper improvement of their calamities by a correction of their errors, they imputed them to a defect in their constitution. They rejected their Divine Ruler, and asked Samuel to make them a king to judge them like other nations. Samuel was grieved at their folly; but still, by the command of God, he harkened to their voice, though not until he had solemnly declared unto them the manner in which the king should reign over them. "This, (says Samuel) shall be the manner of the king that shall reign over you. He will take your sons and appoint them for himself, for his chariots, and for his horsemen, and some shall run before his chariots; and he will appoint him captains over thousands, and captains over fifties, and will set them to ear his ground, and to reap his harvest, and to make his instruments of war, and instruments of his chariots. And he will take your daughters to be confectionaries, and to be cooks, and to be bakers. And he will take your fields, and your vineyards, and your oliveyards, even the best of them, and give them to his servants. And he will take the tenth of your seed, and of your vineyards, and give to his officers and to his servants. And he will take your men servants and your maid servants, and your goodliest young men, and your asses, and put them to his work. He will take the tenth of your sheep, and ye shall be his servants. And ye shall cry out in that day, because of your king which ye have chosen you, and the Lord will not hear you in that day." How far this was applicable to the subject he would not now say; it could be better judged of when they had gone through it. On the whole he wished to take up this matter with candor and deliberation.

He would now proceed to state his objections to the clause just read, (section two of article one, clause three.) His objections were comprised under three heads: first, the rule of apportionment is unjust; second, there is no precise number fixed on below which the house shall not be reduced; third, it is inadequate. In the first place the rule of apportionment of the representatives is to be according to the whole number of the white inhabitants, with three fifths of all others; that is, in plain English, each state is to send representatives in proportion to the number of freemen, and three fifths of the slaves it contains. He could not see any rule by which slaves are to be included in the ratio of representation. The principle of a representation, being that every free agent should be concerned in governing himself, it was absurd to give that power to a man who could not exercise it; slaves have no will of their own. The very operation of it was to give certain privileges to those people who were so wicked as to keep slaves. He knew it would be admitted that this rule of apportionment was founded on unjust principles, but that it was the result of accommodation; which he supposed we should be under the necessity of admitting, if we meant to be in union with the southern states, though utterly repugnant to his feelings. In the second place, the number was not fixed by the Constitution, but left at the discretion of the Legislature. Perhaps he was mistaken; it was his wish to be informed. He understood from the

Constitution that sixty-five members were to compose the House of Representatives for three years; that after that time a census was to be taken, and the numbers to be ascertained by the Legislature on the following principles. First, they shall be apportioned to the respective states according to numbers; second, each state shall have one at least; third, they shall never exceed one to every thirty thousand. If this was the case, the first Congress that met might reduce the number below what it now is, a power inconsistent with every principle of a free government: to leave it to the discretion of the rulers to determine the number of the representatives of the people. There was no kind of security except in the integrity of the men who were entrusted; and if you have no other security, it is idle to contend about constitutions. In the third place, supposing Congress should declare that there should be one representative for every thirty thousand of the people, in his opinion it would be incompetent to the great purposes of representation. It was, he said, the fundamental principle of a free government, that the people should make the laws by which they were to be governed. He who is controlled by another is a slave; and that government which is directed by the will of any one or a few, or any number less than is the will of the community, is a government for slaves.

The next point was, how was the will of the community to be expressed? It was not possible for them to come together; the multitude would be too great. In order, therefore, to provide against this inconvenience, the scheme of representation had been adopted by which the people deputed others to represent them. Individuals entering into society became one body, and that body ought to be animated by one mind; and he conceived that every form of government should have that complexion. It was true that notwithstanding all the experience we had from others, it had not appeared that the experiment of representation had been fairly tried. There was something like it in the ancient republics in which, being of small extent, the people could easily meet together, though instead of deliberating, they only considered of those things which were submitted to them by their magistrates. In Great Britain representation had been carried much further than in any government we knew of, except our own; but in that country it now had only a name. America was the only country in which the first fair opportunity had been offered. When we were colonies, our representation was better than any that was then known. Since the revolution we had advanced still nearer to perfection. He considered it as an object of all others the most important, to have it fixed on its true principle; yet he was convinced that it was impracticable to have such a representation in a consolidated government.

However, said he, we may approach a great way towards perfection by increasing the representation and limiting the powers of Congress. He considered that the great interests and liberties of the people could only be secured by the state governments. He admitted that if the new government was only confined to great national objects, it would be less exceptionable; but it extended to everything dear to human nature. That this was the case could be proved without any long chain of reasoning; for that power which had both the purse and the sword had the government of the whole country, and might extend its powers to any and to every object. He had already observed, that by the true doctrine of representation, this principle was established; that the representative must be chosen by the free will of the majority of his constituents. It therefore followed that the representative should be chosen from small districts. This being admitted, he would ask, could 65 men for 3,000,000 or 1 for 30,000 be chosen in this manner? Would they be possessed of the requisite information to make happy the great number of souls that were spread over this extensive country? There was another objection to the clause. If great affairs of government were trusted to a few men, they would be more liable to corruption. Corruption, he knew, was unfashionable among us, but he supposed that Americans were like other men, and though they had hitherto displayed great virtues, still they were men; and therefore such steps should be taken as to prevent the possibility of corruption. We were now in that stage of society, in which we could deliberate with freedom; how long it might continue God only knew! Twenty years hence, perhaps, these maxims might become unfashionable; we already hear, said he, in all parts of the country gentlemen ridiculing that spirit of patriotism and love of liberty which carried us through all our difficulties in times of danger. When patriotism was already nearly hooted out of society, ought we not to take some precautions against the progress of corruption?

He had one more observation to make, to show that the representation was insufficient. Government, he said, must rest for its execution on the good opinion of the people, for if it was made in heaven, and had not the confidence of the people, it could not be executed; that this was proved by the example given by the gentleman of the Jewish theocracy. It must have a good setting out, or the instant it takes place there is an end of liberty. He believed that the inefficacy of the old Confederation had arisen from that want of confidence; and this caused in a great degree by the continual declamation of gentlemen of importance against it from one end of the continent to the other, who had frequently compared it to a rope of sand. It had pervaded every class of citizens and their misfortunes; the consequences of idleness and extravagance were attributed to the defects of that system. At the close of the war, our country had been left in distress, and it was impossible that any government on earth could immediately retrieve it; it must be time and industry alone that could effect it. He said he would pursue these observations no further at present, and concluded with making the following motion:

"*Resolved,* That it is proper that the number of representatives be fixed at the rate of one for every twenty thousand inhabitants, to be ascertained on the principles mentioned in the second section of the first article of the Constitution, until they amount to three hundred; after which they shall be apportioned among the states in proportion to the number of inhabitants of the states respectively. And that before the first enumeration shall be made, the several states shall be entitled to choose double the number of representatives for that purpose, mentioned in the Constitution."

Federal Farmer
Letters II, III, and XII
(Poughkeepsie) Country Journal
9 and 10 October, 1787, 12 January, 1788

The essential parts of a free and good government are a full and equal representation of the people in the legislature, and the jury trial of the vicinage in the administration of justice. A full and equal representation is that which possesses the same interests, feelings, opinions, and views the people themselves would were they all assembled. Fair representation, therefore, should be so regulated that every order of men in the community, according to the common course of elections, can have a share in it. In order to allow professional men, merchants, traders, farmers, mechanics, etc. to bring a just proportion of their best informed men respectively into the legislature, the representation must be considerably numerous. We have about 200 state senators in the United States; and a less number than that of federal representatives clearly cannot be a full representation of this people in the affairs of internal taxation and police, were there but one legislature for the whole union. The representation cannot be equal, or the situation of the people proper for one government only, if the extreme parts of the society cannot be represented as fully as the central. It is apparently impracticable that this should be the case in this extensive country; it would be impossible to collect a representation of the parts of the country five, six, and seven hundred miles from the seat of government.

Under one general government alone, there could be but one judiciary, one supreme and a proper number of inferior courts. I think it would be totally impracticable in this case to preserve a due administration of justice, and the real benefits of the jury trial of the vicinage. There are now supreme courts in each state in the union, and a great number of county and other courts subordinate to each supreme court; most of these supreme and inferior courts are itinerant, and hold their sessions in different parts every year of their respective states, counties and districts. With all these moving courts, our citizens from the vast extent of the country must travel very considerable distances from home to find the place where justice is administered. I am not for bringing justice so near to individuals as to afford them any temptation to engage in law suits, though I think it one of the greatest benefits in a good government, that each citizen should find a court of justice within a reasonable distance perhaps within a day's travel of his home; so that, without great inconveniences and enormous expenses, he may have the advantages of his witnesses and jury. It would be impracticable to derive these advantages from one judiciary. The one supreme court at most could only set in the center of the union, and move once a year into the center of the eastern and southern extremes of it. In this case, each citizen on an average would travel 150 or 200 miles to find this court. That, however, inferior courts might be properly placed in the different counties and districts of the union, the appellate jurisdiction would be intolerable and expensive.

If it were possible to consolidate the states, and preserve the features of a free government, it is evident that the middle states, the parts of the union about the seat of government, would enjoy great advantages, while the remote states would experience the many inconveniences of remote provinces. Wealth, offices, and the benefits of government would collect in the center, and the extreme states and their principal towns become much less important.

There are other considerations which tend to prove that the idea of one consolidated whole on free principles is ill-founded. The laws of a free government rest on the confidence of the people, and operate gently, and never can extend their influence very far, if they are executed on free principles about the center, where the benefits of the government induce the people to support it voluntarily; yet they must be executed on the principles of fear and force in the extremes. This has been the case with every extensive republic of which we have any accurate account.

There are certain unalienable and fundamental rights which, in forming the social compact, ought to be explicitly ascertained and fixed. A free and enlightened people, in forming this compact, will not resign all their rights to those who govern, and they will fix limits to their legislators and rulers, which will soon be plainly seen by those who are governed, as well as by those who govern; and the latter will know they cannot be passed unperceived by the former, and without giving a general alarm. These rights should be made the basis of every constitution; and if a people be so situated, or have such different opinions that they cannot agree in ascertaining and fixing them, it is a very strong argument against their attempting to form one entire society to live under one system of laws only. I confess, I never thought the people of these states differed essentially in these respects, they having derived all these rights from one common source, the British system, and having in the formation of their state constitutions discovered that their ideas relative to these rights are very similar. However, it is now said that the states differ so essentially in these respects, and even in the important article of the trial by jury, that when assembled in convention, they can agree to no words by which to establish that trial, or by which to ascertain and establish many other of these rights as fundamental articles in the social compact. If so, we proceed to consolidate the states on no solid basis whatever.

But I do not pay much regard to the reasons given for not bottoming the new constitution on a better bill of rights. I still believe a complete federal bill of rights to be very practicable. Nevertheless I acknowledge the proceedings of the convention furnish my mind with many new and strong reasons against a complete consolidation of the states. They tend to convince me that it cannot be carried with propriety very far, that the convention have gone much farther in one respect than they found it practicable to go in another; that is, they propose to lodge in the general government very extensive powers, *powers* nearly, if not altogether, complete and unlimited, over the purse and the sword. But in its organization, they furnish the strongest proof that the proper limbs, or parts of a government to support and execute those powers on proper principles (or in which they can be safely lodged) cannot be formed. These powers must be lodged somewhere in every society, but then they should be lodged where the strength and guardians of the people are collected. They can be wielded or safely used in a free country only by an able executive and judiciary, a respectable senate, and a secure, full, and equal representation of the people. I think the principles I have premised or brought into view are well founded, I think they will not be denied by any fair reasoner. It is in connection with these, and other solid principles, we are to examine the constitution. It is not a few democratic phrases, or a few well formed features that will prove its merits; or a few small omissions that will produce its rejection among men of sense. They will inquire what are the essential powers in a community, and what are nominal ones, where and how the essential powers shall be lodged to secure government, and to secure true liberty.

In examining the proposed constitution carefully, we must clearly perceive an unnatural separation of these powers from the substantial representation of the people. The state governments will exist with all their governors, senators, representatives, officers and expenses; in these will be nineteen-twentieths of the representatives of the people. They will have a near connection, and their members an immediate intercourse with the people; and the probability is that the state governments will possess the confidence of the people, and be considered generally as their immediate guardians.

The general government will consist of a new species of executive, a small senate, and a very small house of representatives. As many citizens will be more than three hundred miles from the seat of this government as will be nearer to it, its judges and officers cannot be very numerous without making our governments very expensive. Thus will stand the state and the general governments, should the constitution be adopted without any alterations in their organization; but as to powers, the general government will possess all essential ones, at least on paper, and those of the states a mere shadow of power. And therefore, unless the people shall make some great exertions to restore to the state governments their powers in matters of internal police; as the powers to lay and collect, exclusively, internal taxes, to govern the militia, and to hold the decisions of their own judicial courts upon their own laws final, the balance cannot possibly continue long. But the state governments must be annihilated, or continue to exist for no purpose.

It is, however, to be observed that many of the essential powers given the national government are not exclusively given; and the general government may have prudence enough to forbear the exercise of those which may still be exercised by the respective states. But this cannot justify the impropriety of giving powers, the exercise of which prudent men will not attempt, and imprudent men will, or probably can, exercise only in a manner destructive of free government. The general government, organized as it is, may be adequate to many valuable objects, and be able to carry its laws into execution on proper principles in several cases; but I think its warmest friends will not contend that it can carry all the powers proposed to be lodged in it into effect without calling to its aid a military force, which must very soon destroy all elective governments in the country, produce anarchy, or establish despotism. Though we cannot have now a complete idea of what will be the operations of the proposed system, we may, allowing things to have their common course, have a very tolerable one. The powers lodged in the general government, if exercised by it, must intimately affect the internal police of the states, as well as external concerns; and there is no reason to expect the numerous state governments and their connections will be very friendly to the execution of federal laws in those internal affairs, which hitherto have been under their own immediate management. There is more reason to believe that the general government, far removed from the people and none of its members elected oftener than once in two years, will be forgot or neglected, and its laws in many cases disregarded, unless a multitude of officers and military force be continually kept in view, and employed to enforce the execution of the laws, and to make the government feared and respected. No position can be truer than this, that in this country either neglected laws or a military execution of them must lead to a revolution and to the destruction of freedom. Neglected laws must first lead to anarchy and confusion, and a military execution of laws is only a shorter way to the same point: despotic government . . .

. . . The great object of a free people must be so to form their government and laws, and so to administer them as to create a confidence in and respect for the laws; and thereby to induce the sensible and virtuous part of the community to declare in favor of the laws and to support them without an expensive military force. I wish, though I confess I have not much hope, that this may be the case with the laws of congress under the new constitution. I am fully convinced that we must organize the national government on different principles, and make the parts of it more efficient, and secure in it more effectually the different interests in the community, or else leave in the state governments some powers proposed to be lodged in it, at least till such an organization shall be found to be practicable. Not sanguine in my expectations of a good federal administration and satisfied, as I am, of the impracticability of consolidating the states, and at the same time of preserving the rights of the people at large, I believe we ought still to leave some of those powers in the state governments, in which the people, in fact, will still be represented; to define some other powers proposed to be vested in the general government more carefully, and to establish a few principles to secure a proper exercise of the powers given it. It is not my object to multiply objections, or to contend about inconsiderable powers or amendments. I wish the system adopted with a few alterations, but those, in my mind, are essential ones; if adopted without, every good citizen will acquiesce though I shall consider the duration of our governments, and the liberties of this people, very much dependent on the administration of the general government. A wise and honest administration may make the people happy under any government; but necessity only can justify even our leaving open avenues to the abuse of power by wicked, unthinking, or ambitious men. I will examine first, the organization of the proposed government in order to judge, second, with propriety, what powers are improperly, at least prematurely lodged in it. I shall examine, third, the undefined powers, and fourth, those powers, the exercise of which is not secured on safe and proper ground.

First, as to the organization, the house of representatives, the democratic branch as it is called, is to consist of 65 members; that is, about one representative for fifty thousand inhabitants to be chosen biennially. The federal legislature may increase this number to one for each thirty thousand inhabitants, abating fractional numbers in each state. Thirty-three representatives will make a quorum for doing business, and a majority of those present determine the sense of the house. I have no idea that the interests, feelings, and opinions of three or four millions of people, especially touching internal taxation, can be collected in such a house. In the nature of things, nine times in ten, men of the elevated classes in the community only can be chosen. Connecticut, for instance, will have five representatives; not one man in a hundred of those who form the democratic branch in the state legislature will, on a fair computation, be one of the five. The people of this country in one sense may all be democratic; but if we make the proper distinction between the few men of wealth and abilities and consider them, as we ought, as the natural aristocracy of the country, and the great body of the people, the middle and lower classes, as the democracy, this federal representative branch will have but very little democracy in it. Even this small representation is not secured on proper principles. The branches of the legislature are essential parts of the fundamental compact, and ought to be so fixed by the people, that the legislature cannot alter itself by modifying the elections of its own members. This, by a part of article one, section four, the general legislature may do; it may evidently so regulate elections as to secure the choice of any particular description of men. It may make the whole state one district, make the capital or any places in the state the place or places of election. It may declare that the five men (or whatever the number may be the state may choose) who shall have the most votes shall be

considered as chosen. In this case it is easy to perceive how the people who live scattered in the inland towns will bestow their votes on different men, and how a few men in a city, in any order or profession, may unite and place any five men they please highest among those that may be voted for; and all this may be done constitutionally and by those silent operations, which are not immediately perceived by the people in general. I know it is urged that the general legislature will be disposed to regulate elections on fair and just principles. This may be true; good men will generally govern well with almost any constitution. But why in laying the foundation of the social system, need we unnecessarily leave a door open to improper regulations? This is a very general and unguarded clause, and many evils may flow from that part which authorizes the congress to regulate elections. Were it omitted, the regulations of elections would be solely in the respective states, where the people are substantially represented, and where the elections ought to be regulated, [in order] to secure a representation from all parts of the community. In making the constitution, we ought to provide for dividing each state into a proper number of districts, and for confining the electors in each district to the choice of some men, who shall have a permanent interest and residence in it; and also for this essential object: that the representative elected shall have a majority of the votes of those electors who shall attend and give their votes.

In considering the practicability of having a full and equal representation of the people from all parts of the union, not only distances and different opinions, customs, and views, common in extensive tracts of country are to be taken into view, but many differences peculiar to eastern, middle, and southern states. These differences are not so perceivable among the members of congress, and men of general information in the states, as among the men who would properly form the democratic branch. The eastern states are very democratic, and composed chiefly of moderate freeholders; they have but few rich men and no slaves. The southern states are composed chiefly of rich planters and slaves; they have but few moderate freeholders, and the prevailing influence in them is generally a dissipated aristocracy. The middle states partake partly of the eastern, and partly of the southern character.

Perhaps nothing could be more disjointed, unwieldly, and incompetent to doing business with harmony and dispatch than a federal house of representatives properly numerous for the great objects of taxation, et cetera collected from the several states. Whether such men would ever act in concert, whether they would not worry along a few years, and then be the means of separating the parts of the union is very

problematical. View this system in whatever form we can, propriety brings us still to this point; a federal government possessed of general and complete powers, as to those national objects which cannot well come under the cognizance of the internal laws of the respective states, and this federal government, accordingly, consisting of branches not very numerous.

The house of representatives is on the plan of consolidation, but the senate is entirely on the federal plan. Delaware will have as much constitutional influence in the senate as the largest state in the union; and in this senate are lodged legislative, executive and judicial powers. Ten states in this union urge that they are small states, nine of which were present in the convention. They were interested in collecting large powers into the hands of the senate, in which each state still will have its equal share of power. I suppose it was impracticable for the three large states, as they were called, to get the senate formed on any other principles. But this only proves that we cannot form one general government on equal and just principles, and proves that we ought not to lodge in it such extensive powers before we are convinced of the practicability of organizing it on just and equal principles. The senate will consist of two members from each state chosen by the state legislatures every sixth year. The clause referred to respecting the elections of representatives, empowers the general legislature to regulate the elections of senators also, "except as to the places of choosing senators." There is, therefore, but little more security in the elections than in those of representatives. Fourteen senators make a quorum for business, and a majority of the senators present give the vote of the senate, except in giving judgment upon an impeachment, or in making treaties, or in expelling a member, when two-thirds of the senators present must agree. The members of the legislature are not excluded from being elected to any military offices or any civil offices, except those created, or the emoluments of which shall be increased by themselves. Two-thirds of the members present of either house may expel a member at pleasure. The senate is an independent branch of the legislature, a court for trying impeachments, and also a part of the executive, having a negative in the making of all treaties and in appointing almost all officers.

The vice-president is not a very important, if not an unnecessary part of the system. He may be a part of the senate at one period, and act as the supreme executive magistrate at another. The election of this officer, as well as of the president of the United States seems to be properly secured; but when we examine the powers of the president, and the forms of the executive, we shall perceive that the general

government, in this part, will have a strong tendency to aristocracy, or the government of the few. The executive is, in fact, the president and senate in all transactions of any importance. The president is connected with, or tied to the senate; he may always act with the senate, but never can effectually counteract its views. The president can appoint no officer, civil or military, who shall not be agreeable to the senate; and the presumption is, that the will of so important a body will not be very easily controlled, and that it will exercise its powers with great address.

In the judicial department, powers ever kept distinct in well balanced governments are no less improperly blended in the hands of the same men; in the judges of the supreme court is lodged the law, the equity, and the fact. It is not necessary to pursue the minute organical parts of the general government proposed. There were various interests in the convention to be reconciled, especially of large and small states, of carrying and non-carrying states, and of states more and states less democratic. Vast labor and attention were by the convention bestowed on the organization of the parts of the constitution offered; still it is acknowledged there are many things radically wrong in the essential parts of this constitution; but it is said that these are the result of our situation. On a full examination of the subject, I believe it; but what do the laborious inquiries and determinations of the convention prove? If they prove anything, they prove that we cannot consolidate the states on proper principles. The organization of the government presented proves that we cannot form a general government in which all power can be safely lodged; and a little attention to the parts of the one proposed will make it appear very evident that all the powers proposed to be lodged in it will not be then well deposited, either for the purposes of government, or the preservation of liberty. I will suppose no abuse of powers in those cases in which the abuse of it is not well guarded against; I will suppose the words authorizing the general government to regulate the elections of its own members struck out of the plan, or free district elections in each state amply secured. That the small representation provided for shall be as fair and equal as it is capable of being made. I will suppose the judicial department regulated on pure principles, by future laws, as far as it can be by the constitution, and consistent with the situation of the country; still there will be an unreasonable accumulation of powers in the general government, if all be granted, enumerated in the plan proposed. The plan does not present a well balanced government. The senatorial branch of the legislative and the executive are substantially united, and the president, or the first executive magistrate may aid the senatorial interest when weakest, but never can effectually support the democratic; however it may be oppressed. The excellency, in my mind, of a well balanced government is that it consists of distinct branches, each sufficiently strong and independent to keep its own station, and to aid either of the other branches which may occasionally want aid.

The convention found that any but a small house of representatives would be expensive, and that it would be impracticable to assemble a large number of representatives. Not only the determination of the convention in this case, but the situation of the states, proves the impracticability of collecting, in any one point, a proper representation.

The formation of the senate, and the smallness of the house, being, therefore, the result of our situation, and the actual state of things, the evils which may attend the exercise of many powers in this national government may be considered as without a remedy.

All officers are impeachable before the senate only before the men by whom they are appointed or who are consenting to the appointment of these officers. No judgment of conviction in an impeachment can be given unless two-thirds of the senators agree. Under these circumstances the right of impeachment in the house can be of but little importance, the house cannot expect often to convict the offender, and, therefore, probably will but seldom or never exercise the right. In addition to the insecurity and inconveniences attending this organization beforementioned, it may be observed that it is extremely difficult to secure the people against the fatal effects of corruption and influence. The power of making any law will be in the president, eight senators, and seventeen representatives, relative to the important objects enumerated in the constitution. Where there is a small representation a sufficient number to carry any measure may with ease be influenced by bribes, offices and civilities; they may easily form private juntos and outdoor meetings, agree on measures, and carry them by silent votes.

Impressed as I am with a sense of the difficulties there are in the way of forming the parts of a federal government on proper principles, and seeing a government so unsubstantially organized, after so arduous an attempt has been made, I am led to believe that powers ought to be given to it with great care and caution.

In the second place it is necessary, therefore, to examine the extent, and the probable operations of some of those extensive powers proposed to be vested in this government. These powers, legislative, executive, and judicial, respect internal as well as external objects. Those respecting external objects, as all foreign concerns, commerce, imposts, all causes arising on the seas, peace and war, and Indian affairs, can be lodged no where else with any propriety, but in this government. Many powers that respect internal objects ought clearly to be lodged in it, as those to regulate trade between the states, weights and measures, the coin or current monies, post-offices, naturalization, etc. These powers may be exercised without essentially affecting the internal police of the respective states. But powers to lay and collect internal taxes, to form the militia, to make bankrupt laws, and to decide on appeal questions arising on the internal laws of the respective states are of a very serious nature, and carry with them almost all other powers. These taken in connection with the others, and powers to raise armies and build navies proposed to be lodged in this government, appear to me to comprehend all the essential powers in the community, and those which will be left to the states will be of no great importance.

A power to lay and collect taxes at discretion is in itself of very great importance. By means of taxes, the government may command the whole or any part of the subject's property. Taxes may be of various kinds; but there is a strong distinction between external and internal taxes. External taxes are impost duties which are laid on imported goods; they may usually be collected in a few seaport towns and of a few individuals, though ultimately paid by the consumer. A few officers can collect them, and they can be carried no higher than trade will bear or smuggling permit; in the very nature of commerce, bounds are set to them. But internal taxes, as poll and land taxes, excises, duties on all written instruments, etc. may fix themselves on every person and species of property in the community; they may be carried to any lengths, and in proportion as they are extended, numerous officers must be employed to assess them, and to enforce the collection of them. In the United Netherlands the general government has complete powers as to external taxation; but as to internal taxes, it makes requisitions on the provinces. Internal taxation in this country is more important, as the country is so very extensive. As many assessors and collectors of federal taxes will be above three hundred miles from the seat of the federal government as will be less. Besides, to lay and collect internal taxes in this extensive country must require a great number of congressional ordinances, immediately operating upon the body of the people; these must continually interfere with the state laws, and thereby produce disorder and general dissatisfaction till the one system of laws or the other, operating upon the same subjects, shall be abolished. These ordinances alone, to say nothing of those respecting the militia, coin, commerce, federal judiciary, etc. etc. will probably soon defeat the operations of the state laws and governments.

Should the general government think it politic, as some administrations (if not all) probably will, to look for a support in a system of influence, the government will take every occasion to multiply laws, and officers to execute them, considering these as so many necessary props for its own support. Should this system of policy be adopted, taxes more productive than the impost duties will probably be wanted to support the government, and to discharge foreign demands without leaving any thing for the domestic creditors. The internal sources of taxation then must be called into operation, and internal tax laws and federal assessors and collectors spread over this immense country. All these circumstances considered, is it wise, prudent, or safe, to vest the powers of laying and collecting internal taxes in the general government, while imperfectly organized and inadequate; and to trust to amending it hereafter, and making it adequate to this purpose? It is not only unsafe but absurd to lodge power in a government before it is fitted to receive it? It is confessed that this power and representation ought to go together. Why give the power first? Why give the power to the few, who, when possessed of it, may have address enough to prevent the increase of representation? Why not keep the power and when necessary, amend the constitution, and add to its other parts this power, and a proper increase of representation at the same time? Then men who may want the power will be under strong inducements to let in the people by their representatives into the government, to hold their due proportion of this power. If a proper representation be impracticable, then we shall see this power resting in the states where it at present ought to be, and not inconsiderately given up.

When I recollect how lately congress, conventions, legislatures, and people contended in the cause of liberty, and carefully weighed the importance of taxation. I can scarcely believe we are serious in proposing to vest the powers of laying and collecting internal taxes in a government so imperfectly organized for such purposes. Should the United States be taxed by a house of representatives of two hundred members, which would be about fifteen members for Connecticut, twenty-five for Massachusetts, etc. still the middle and lower classes of people could have no great share in fact in taxation. I am aware it is said that the representation proposed by the new constitution is sufficiently numerous; it may be for many purposes. But to suppose that this branch is sufficiently numerous to guard the rights of the people in the administration of the government, in which the purse and sword is placed, seems to argue that we have forgot what the true meaning of representation is. I am sensible also that it is said that congress will not attempt to lay and collect internal taxes; that it is necessary for them to have the power, though it cannot probably be exercised. I admit that it is not probable that any prudent congress will attempt to lay and collect internal taxes, especially direct taxes; but this only proves that the power would be improperly lodged in congress, and that it might be abused by imprudent and designing men.

I have heard several gentlemen, to get rid of objections to this part ' of the constitution, attempt to construe the powers relative to direct taxes as those who object to it would have them; as to these, it is said, that congress will only have power to make requisitions, leaving it to the states to lay and collect them. I see but very little color for this construction, and the attempt only proves that this part of the plan cannot be defended. By this plan there can be no doubt, but that the powers of congress will be 'complete as to all kinds of taxes whatever. Further, as to internal taxes, the state governments will have concurrent powers with the general government, and both may tax the same objects in the same year; and the objection that the general government may suspend a state tax as a necessary measure for promoting the collection of a federal tax is not without foundation. As the states owe large debts and have large demands upon them individually, there clearly would be a propriety in leaving in their possession exclusively some of the internal sources of taxation, at least until the federal representation shall be properly increased. The power in the general government to lay and collect internal taxes will render its powers respecting armies, navies and the militia the more exceptionable. By the constitution it is proposed that congress shall have power "to raise and support armies, but no appropriation of money to that use shall be for a longer term than two years, to provide and maintain a navy, to provide for calling forth the militia to execute the laws of the union, suppress insurrections, and repel invasions, to provide for organizing, arming, and disciplining the militia, reserving to the states the right to appoint the officers, and to train the militia according to the discipline prescribed by congress. Congress will have unlimited power to raise armies, and to engage officers and men for any number of years; but a legislative act applying money for their support can have operation for no longer term than two years. If a subsequent congress do not within the two years renew the appropriation, or further appropriate monies for the use of the army, the army will be left to take care of itself. When an army shall once be raised for a number of years, it is not probable that it will find much difficulty in getting congress to pass laws for applying monies to its support. I see so many men in America fond of a standing army, and especially among those who probably will have a large share in administering the federal system; it is very evident to me that we shall have a large standing army as soon as the monies to support them can be possibly found. An army is a very agreeable place of employment for the young gentlemen of many families. A power to raise armies must be lodged somewhere; still this will not justify the lodging this power in a bare majority of so few men without any checks, or in the government in which the great body of the people, in the nature of things, will be only nominally represented. In the state governments the great body of the people, the yeomanry, etc. of the country, are represented. It is true they will choose the members of congress, and may now and then choose a man of their own way of thinking; but it is impossible for forty, or thirty thousand people in this country one time in ten to find a man who can possess similar feelings, views, and interests with themselves. Powers to lay and collect taxes and to raise armies are of the greatest moment; for carrying them into effect laws need not be frequently made, and the yeomanry, etc of the country ought substantially to have a check upon the passing of these laws. This check ought to be placed in the legislatures, or at least in the few men the common people of the country will probably have in congress, in the true sense of the word, "from among themselves." It is true, the yeomanry of the country possess the lands, the weight of property, possess arms, and are too strong a body of men to be openly offended; and, therefore, it is urged they will take care of themselves, that men who shall govern will not dare pay any disrespect to their opinions. It is easily perceived that if they have not their proper negative upon passing laws in congress, or on the passage of laws relative to taxes and armies, they may in twenty or thirty years be by means imperceptible to them totally deprived of that boasted weight and strength. This may be done in a great measure by congress, if disposed to do it, by modelling the militia. Should one fifth, or one eighth part of the men capable of bearing arms be made a select militia, as has been proposed, and those the young and ardent part of the community, possessed of but little or no property, and all the others put upon a plan that will render them of no importance, the former will answer all the purposes of an army, while the latter will be defenseless. The state must train the militia in such form and according to such systems and rules as congress shall prescribe; and the only actual influence the respective states will have respecting the militia will be in appointing the officers. I see no provision made for calling out the *posse comitatus* for executing the laws of the union, but provision is made for congress to call forth the militia for the execution of them. And the militia in general, or any select part of it, may be called out under military officers instead of the sheriff, to enforce an execution of federal laws in the first instance and thereby introduce an entire military execution of the laws. I know that powers to raise taxes, to regulate the military strength of the community on some uniform plan, to provide for its defense and internal order, and for duly executing the laws, must be lodged somewhere; but still we ought not so to lodge them as evidently to give one order of men in the community undue advantages over others, or commit the many to the mercy, prudence, and moderation of the few. And so far as it may be necessary to lodge any of the peculiar powers in the general government, a more safe exercise of them ought to be secured, by requiring the consent of two-thirds or three-fourths of congress thereto, until the federal representation can be increased, so that the democratic members in congress may stand some tolerable chance of a reasonable negative in behalf of the numerous, important, and democratic part of the community.

I am not sufficiently acquainted with the laws and internal police of all the states to discern fully how general bankrupt laws, made by the union, would affect them, or promote the public good. I believe the property of debtors, in the several states, is held responsible for their debts in modes and forms very different. If uniform bankrupt laws can be made without producing real and substantial inconveniences, I wish them to be made by Congress.

There are some powers proposed to be lodged in the general government in the judicial department, I think very unnecessarily. I mean powers respecting questions arising upon the internal laws of the respective states. It is proper the federal judiciary should have powers co-extensive with the federal legislature; that is, the power of deciding finally on the laws of the union. By article three, section two, the powers of the federal judiciary are extended (among other things) to all cases between a state and citizens of another state, between citizens of different states, between a state or the citizens thereof, and foreign states, citizens or subjects. Actions in all these cases, except against a state government are now brought and finally determined in the law courts of the states respectively; and as there are no words to exclude these courts of their jurisdiction in these cases, they will have concurrent jurisdiction with the inferior federal courts in them. Therefore, if the new constitution be adopted without any amendment in this respect, all those numerous actions now brought in the state courts between our citizens and foreigners, between citizens of different states, by state governments against foreigners, and by state governments against citizens of other states, may also be brought in the federal courts; and an appeal will lay in them from the state courts or federal inferior courts, to the supreme judicial court of the union. In almost all these cases, either party may have the trial by jury in the state courts, excepting paper money and tender laws, which are wisely guarded against in the proposed constitution. Justice may be obtained in these courts on reasonable terms; they must be more competent to proper decisions on the laws of their respective states than the federal courts can possibly be. I do not, in any point of view, see the need of opening a new jurisdiction to these causes, of opening a new scene of expensive law suits, of suffering foreigners and citizens of different states to drag each other many hundred miles into the federal courts. It is true those courts may be so organized by a wise and prudent legislature as to make the obtaining of justice in them tolerably easy; they may in general be organized on the common law principles of the country. But this benefit is by no means secured by the constitution. The trial by jury is secured only in those few criminal cases, to which the federal laws will extend, as crimes committed on the seas, against the laws of nations, treason, and counterfeiting the federal securities and coin. But even in these cases, the jury trial of the vicinage is not secured; particularly in the large states, a citizen may be tried for a crime committed in the state, and yet tried in some states 500 miles from the place where it was committed. But the jury trial is not secured at all in civil causes. Though the convention have not established this trial, it is to be hoped that congress, in putting the new system into execution, will do it by a legislative act, in all cases in which it can be done with propriety. Whether the jury trial is not excluded from the supreme judicial court is an important question. By article three section two all cases affecting ambassadors, other public ministers, and consuls, and in those cases in which a state shall be party, the supreme court shall have jurisdiction. In all the other cases beforementioned, the supreme court shall have appellate jurisdiction, both as to *law and fact*, with such exception, and under such regulations, as the congress shall make. By court is understood a court consisting of judges; and the idea of a jury is excluded. This court or the judges are to have jurisdiction on appeals in all the cases enumerated, as to law and fact; the judges are to decide the law and try the fact, and the trial of the fact being assigned to the judges by the constitution, a jury for trying the fact is excluded. However, under the exceptions and powers to make regulations, congress may perhaps introduce the jury to try the fact in most necessary cases.

There can be but one supreme court in which the final jurisdiction will center in all federal causes, except in cases where appeals by law shall not be allowed. The judicial powers of the federal courts extends in law and equity to certain cases, and, therefore, the powers to determine on the law in equity and as to the fact all will concenter in the supreme court. These powers, which by this constitution are blended in the same hands, the same judges, are in Great Britain deposited in different hands; to wit, the decision of the law in the law judges, the decision in equity in the chancellor, and the trial of the fact in the jury. It is a very dangerous thing to vest in the same judge power to decide on the law, and also general powers in equity; for if the law restrain him, he is only to step into his shoes of equity, and give what judgment his reason or opinion may dictate. We have no precedents in this country as yet, to regulate the divisions in equity as in Great Britain; equity, therefore, in the supreme court for many years will be mere discretion. I confess in the constitution of this supreme court, as left by the constitution, I do not see a spark of freedom or a shadow of our own or the British common law.

This court is to have appellate jurisdiction in all the other cases before mentioned. Many sensible men suppose that cases before mentioned respect as well the criminal cases as the civil ones, mentioned antecedently in the constitution, if so an appeal is allowed in criminal cases, contrary to the usual sense of law. How far it may be proper to admit a foreigner or the citizen of another state to bring actions against state governments which have failed in performing so many promises made during the war is doubtful. How far it may be proper so to humble a state, as to oblige it to answer to an individual in a court of law, is worthy of consideration; the states are now subject to no such actions, and this new jurisdiction will subject the states and many defendants to actions and processes which were not in the contemplation of the parties when the contract was made. All engagements existing between citizens of different states, citizens and foreigners, states and foreigners, and states and citizens of other states were made [with] the parties contemplating the remedies then existing on the laws of the states, and the new remedy proposed to be given in the federal courts can be founded on no principle whatever . . .

. . . On carefully examining the parts of the proposed system, respecting the elections of senators, and especially of the representatives, they appear to me to be both ambiguous and very defective. I shall endeavor to pursue a course of reasoning, which shall fairly lead to establishing the impartiality and security of elections, and then to point out an amendment in this respect.

It is well observed by Montesquieu that in republican governments, the forms of elections are fundamental, and that it is an essential part of the social compact to ascertain by whom, to whom, when, and in what manner suffrages are to be given.

Wherever we find the regulation of elections have not been carefully fixed by the constitution or the principles of them, we constantly see the legislature new modifying its own form and changing the spirit of the government to answer partial purposes.

By the proposed plan it is fixed that the qualifications of the electors of the federal representatives shall be the same as those of the electors of state representatives; though these vary some in the several states the electors are fixed and designated.

The qualifications of the representatives are also fixed and designated, and no person under 25 years of age, not an inhabitant of the state, and not having been seven years a citizen of the United States, can be elected; the clear inference is that all persons 25 years of age and upwards, inhabitants of the state, and having been, at any period or periods, seven years citizens of the United States, may be elected representatives. They have a right to be elected by the constitution, and the electors have a right to choose them. This is fixing the federal representation, as to the elected, on a very broad basis. It can be no objection to the elected that they are Christians, Pagans, Mahometans, or Jews; that they are of any color, rich or poor, convict or not. Hence, many men may be elected who cannot be electors. Gentlemen who have commented so largely upon the wisdom of the constitution, for excluding from being elected young men under a certain age, would have done well to have recollected that it positively makes pagans, convicts, etc. eligible. The people make the constitution; they exclude a few persons, by certain descriptions, from being elected, and all not thus excluded are clearly admitted. Now a man 25 years old, an inhabitant of the state, and having been a citizen of the states seven years, though afterwards convicted may be elected, because not within any of the excluding clauses; the same of a beggar, an absentee, etc.

The right of the electors and eligibility of the elected being fixed by the people, they cannot be narrowed by the state legislatures, or congress. It is established that a man being (among other qualifications) an inhabitant of the state shall be eligible. Now it would be narrowing the right of the people to confine them in their choice to a man, an inhabitant of a particular county or district in the state. Hence it follows that neither the state legislatures or congress can establish district elections; that is, divide the state into districts and confine the electors of each district to the choice of a man resident in it. If the electors could be thus limited in one respect, they might in another be confined to choose a man of a particular religion, of certain property, etc. and thereby half of the persons made eligible by the constitution be excluded. All laws, therefore, for regulating elections must be made on the broad basis of the constitution.

Next, we may observe that representatives are to be chosen by the people of the state. What is a choice by the people of the state? If each given district in it choose one, will that be a choice within the meaning of the constitution? Must the choice be by plurality of votes or a majority? In connection with these questions, we must take article one, section four, where it is said the state legislatures shall prescribe the times, places, and manner of holding elections; but congress may make or alter such regulations. By this clause, I suppose, the electors of different towns and districts in the state may be assembled in different places to give their votes; but when so assembled, by another clause they cannot by congress or the state legislatures be restrained from giving their votes for any man an inhabitant of the state, and qualified as to age, and having been a citizen the time required. But I see nothing in the constitution by which to decide whether the choice shall be by a plurality or a majority of votes; this, in my mind, is by far the most important question in the business of elections. When we say a representative shall be chosen by the people, it seems to imply that he shall be chosen by a majority of them; but states which use the same phraseology in this respect practice both ways. I believe a majority of the states choose by pluralities, and I think it probable that the federal house of representatives will decide that a choice of its members by pluralities is constitutional. A man who has the most votes is chosen in Great Britain. It is this, among other things, that gives every man fair play in the game of influence and corruption. I believe that not much stress was laid upon the objection that congress may assemble the electors at some out of the way place. However, the advocates seem to think they obtain a victory of no small glory and importance when they can show, with some degree of color, that the evil is rather a possibility than a probability.

When I observed that the elections were not secured on proper principles, I had an idea of far more probable and extensive evils, secret mischiefs, and not so glaring transgressions, the exclusions of proper district elections and of the choice by a majority.

It is easy to perceive that there is an essential difference between elections by pluralities and by majorities, between choosing a man in a small or limited district, and choosing a number of men promiscuously by the people of a large state; and while we are almost secure of judicious unbiased elections by majorities in such districts, we have no security against deceptions, influence, and corruption in states or large districts in electing by pluralities. When a choice is made by a plurality of votes, it is often made by a very small part of the electors who attend and give their votes, when by a majority, never by so few as one half of them. The partialities and improprieties attending the former mode may be illustrated by a case that lately happened in one of the middle states. Several representatives were to be chosen by a large number of inhabitants compactly settled, among whom there were four or five thousand voters. Previous to the time of election a number of lists of candidates were published, to divide and distract the voters in general. About half a dozen men of some influence, who had a favorite list to carry, met several times, fixed their list, and agreed to hand it about among all who could probably be induced to adopt it, and to circulate the other lists among their opponents, to divide them. The poll was opened, and several hundred electors, suspecting nothing, attended and put in their votes; the list of the half dozen was carried, and men were found to be chosen, some of whom were very disagreeable to a large majority of the electors. Though several hundred electors voted, men on that list were chosen who had only 45, 43, 44, etc. votes each; they had a plurality, that is, more than any other persons. The votes generally were scattered, and those who made even a feeble combination succeeded in placing highest upon the list several very unthought of and very unpopular men. This evil never could have happened in a town where all the voters meet in one place, and consider no man as elected unless he have a majority, or more than half of all the votes; clear it is, that the men on whom thus but a small part of the votes are bestowed cannot possess the confidence of the people or have any considerable degree of influence over them.

But as partial, as liable to secret influence, and corruption as the choice by pluralities may be, I think we cannot avoid it without essentially increasing the federal representation and adopting the principles of district elections. There is but one case in which the choice by the majority is practicable, and that is where districts are formed of such moderate extent that the electors in each can conveniently meet in one place, and at one time, and proceed to the choice of a representative, when, if no man have a majority, or more than half of all the votes the first time, the voters may examine the characters of those brought forward, accommodate, and proceed to repeat their votes till some one shall have that majority. This, I believe, cannot be a case under the constitution proposed in its present form. To explain my ideas, take Massachusetts, for instance; she is entitled to eight representatives. She has 370,000 inhabitants, about 46,000 to one representative. If the elections be so held that the electors throughout the state meet in their several towns or places, and each elector puts in his vote for eight representatives, the votes of the electors will ninety-nine times in a hundred be so scattered that on collecting the votes from the several towns or places, no men will be found, each of whom have a majority of the votes, and therefore the election will not be made. On the other hand, there may be such a combination of votes, that in thus attempting to choose eight representatives, the electors may choose even fifteen. Suppose 10,000 voters to attend and give their votes, each voter will give eight votes, one for each of eight representatives; in the whole 80,000 votes will be given eight men, each having 5001 votes, in the whole 40,008, will have each a majority and be chosen; 39,092 votes will be bestowed on other men, and if they all be bestowed on seven men, they may have each a considerable majority and also be chosen. This indeed is a very rare combination, but the bestowing all the votes pretty equally upon nine, ten, or eleven men, and choosing them all, is an event too probable not to be guarded against.

If Massachusetts be divided into eight districts, each having about 46,000 inhabitants, and each district directed to choose one representative, it will be found totally impracticable for the electors of it to meet in one place; and when they meet in several towns and places in the district, they will vote for different men, and nineteen times in twenty, so scatter their votes that no one man will have a majority of the whole and be chosen. We must, therefore, take the man who has the most votes, whether he has three quarters, one quarter, or one tenth part of the whole; the inconveniences of scattering votes will be increased, as men not of the district, as well as those that are in it, may be voted for.

I might add many other observations to evince the superiority and solid advantages of proper district elections, and a choice by a majority, and to prove that many evils attend the contrary practice; these evils we must encounter as the constitution now stands.

I see no way to fix elections on a proper footing and to render tolerably equal and secure the federal representation, but by increasing the representation so as to have one representative for each district, in which the electors may conveniently meet in one place, and at one time, and choose by a majority. Perhaps this might be effected pretty generally, by fixing one representative for each twelve thousand inhabitants; dividing, or fixing the principles for dividing the states into proper districts; and directing the electors of each district to the choice by a majority of some men having a permanent interest and residence in it. I speak of a representation tolerably equal, etc. because I am still of opinion that it is impracticable in this extensive country to have a federal representation sufficiently democratic, or substantially drawn from the body of the people; the principles just mentioned may be the best practical ones we can expect to establish. By thus increasing the representation, we not only make it more democratic and secure, strengthen the confidence of the people in it, and thereby render it more nervous and energetic, but it will also enable the people essentially to change for the better the principles and forms of elections. To provide for the people's wandering throughout the state for a representative may sometimes enable them to elect a more brilliant or an abler man than by confining them to districts, but generally this latitude will be used to pernicious purposes, especially connected with the choice by plurality when a man in the remote part of the state, perhaps obnoxious at home, but ambitious and intriguing, may be chosen to represent the people in another part of the state far distant, and by a small part of them, or by a faction, or by a combination of some particular description of men among them. This has been long the case in Great Britain; it is the case in several of the states. Nor do I think that such pernicious practices will be merely possible in our federal concerns but highly probable. By establishing district elections, we exclude none of the best men from being elected; and we fix what, in my mind, is of far more importance than brilliant talents, I mean a sameness, as to residence and interests between the representative and his constituents; and by the election by a majority, he is sure to be the man, the choice of more than half of them.

Though it is impossible to put elections on a proper footing as the constitution stands, yet I think regulations respecting them may be introduced of considerable service. It is not only, therefore, important to inquire how they may be made, but also what body has the controlling power over them. An intelligent, free, and unbiased choice of representatives by the people is of the last importance; we must then carefully guard against all combinations, secret arts, and influence to the contrary. Various expedients have been adopted in different countries and states to effect genuine elections; as the constitution now stands, I confess I do not discover any better than those adopted in Connecticut in the choice of counselors beforementioned.

The federal representatives are to be chosen every second year (an odd mode of expression). In all the states, except South Carolina, the people, the same electors, meet twice in that time to elect state representatives. For instance, let the electors in Massachusetts, when they meet to choose state representatives, put in their votes for eight federal representatives, the number that state may choose (merely for distinction sake, we may call these the votes of nomination), and return a list of the men voted for in the several towns and places to the legislature or some proper body. Let this list be immediately examined and published, and some proper number, say 15 or 20, who shall have the most votes upon the list, be sent out to the people; and when the electors shall meet the next year to choose state representatives, let them put in their votes for the eight federal representatives, confining their votes to the proper number so sent out, and let the eight highest of those thus voted for in the two votes (which we may call, by way of distinction, votes of election), be the federal representatives. Thus a choice may be made by the people, once in two years without much trouble and expense, and, I believe, with some degree of security. As soon as the votes of nomination shall be collected and made known, the people will know who are voted for, and who are candidates for their votes the succeeding year; the electors will have near a year to inquire into their characters and politics, and also into any undue means, if any were taken, to bring any of them forward. And such as they find to be the best men, and agreeable to the people, they may vote for in giving the votes of election. By these means the men chosen will ultimately always have a majority, or near a majority of the votes of the electors who shall attend and give their votes. The mode itself will lead to the discovery of truth and of political characters, and to prevent private combinations by rendering them in a great measure of no effect. As the choice is to be made by the people, all combinations and checks must be confined to their votes. No supplying the want of a majority by the legislatures, as in Massachusetts in the choice of senators, etc. can be admitted. The people generally judge right when informed, and, in giving their votes the second time, they may always correct their former errors.

I think we are all sufficiently acquainted with the progress of elections to see that the regulations as to times, places, and the manner merely of holding elections may under the constitution, easily be made useful or injurious. It is important then to inquire, who has the power to make regulations, and who ought to have it. By the constitution, the state legislatures shall prescribe the times, places, and manner of holding elections, but congress may make or alter such regulations. Power in congress merely to alter those regulations, made by the states, could answer no valuable purposes; the states might make, and congress alter them *ad infinitum*, and when the state should cease to make, or should annihilate its regulations, congress would have nothing to alter. But the states shall make regulations, and congress may make such regulations as the clause stands. The true construction is that when congress shall see fit to regulate the times, places, and manner of holding elections, congress may do it, and state regulations, on this head, must cease; for if state regulations could exist, after congress should make a system of regulations, there would or might be two incompatible systems of regulations relative to the same subject.

It has been often urged that congress ought to have power to make these regulations, otherwise the state legislatures, by neglecting to make provision for elections, or by making improper regulations, may destroy the general government. It is very improbable that any state legislature will adopt measures to destroy the representation of its own constituents in congress, especially when the state must, represented in congress or not, pay its proportion of the expense of keeping up the government, and even of the representatives of the other states, and be subject to their laws. Should the state legislatures be disposed to be negligent, or to combine to break up congress, they have a very simple way to do it, as the constitution now stands they have only to neglect to choose senators, or to appoint the electors of the president, and vice-president. There is no remedy provided against these last evils, nor is it to be presumed that if a sufficient number of state legislatures to break up congress should, by neglect or otherwise, attempt to do it, that the people who yearly elect those legislatures would elect under the regulations of congress. These and many other reasons must evince that it was not merely to prevent an annihilation of the federal government that congress has power to regulate elections.

It has been urged also that the state legislatures choose the federal senators, one branch, and may injure the people, who choose the other, by improper regulations; that therefore congress, in which the people will immediately have one, the representative branch, ought to have power to interfere in behalf of the people, and rectify such improper regulations. The advocates have said much about the opponents dwelling upon possibilities; but to suppose the people will find it necessary to appeal to congress to restrain the oppressions of the state legislatures, is supposing a possibility indeed. Can any man in his senses suppose that the state legislatures, which are so numerous as almost to be the people themselves, all branches of them depending yearly, for the most part, on the elections of the people, will abuse them in regulating federal elections and make it proper to transfer the power to congress, a body one branch of which is chosen once in six years by these very legislatures, and the other biennially, and not half so numerous as even the senatorial branches in those legislatures?

Senators are to be chosen by the state legislatures; where there are two branches the appointment must be, I presume, by a concurrent resolution, in passing which, as in passing all other legislative acts each branch will have a negative. This will give the senatorial branch just as much weight in the appointment as the democratic; the two branches form a legislature only when acting separately, and therefore, whenever the members of the two branches meet, mix, and vote individually in one room for making an election, it is expressly so directed by the constitutions. If the constitution, by fixing the choice to be made by the legislatures, has given each branch an equal vote, as I think it has, it cannot be altered by any regulations.

On the whole, I think, all general principles respecting electors ought to be carefully established by the constitution, as the qualifications of the electors and of elected, the number of the representatives, and the inhabitants of each given district called on to choose a man from among themselves by a majority of votes, leaving it to the legislature only so to regulate from time to time the extent of the districts so as to keep the representatives proportionate to the number of inhabitants in the several parts of the country. And so far as regulations as to elections cannot be fixed by the constitution, they ought to be left to the state legislatures, they coming far nearest to the people themselves; at most, congress ought to have power to regulate elections only where a state shall neglect to make them.

Brutus
Essays IV, XI, XII, and XV
New York Journal
29 November, 1787, 31 January, 1788,
7 and 14 February, 1788

To the People of the State of New York:

There can be no free government where the people are not possessed of the power of making the laws by which they are governed, either in their own persons, or by others substituted in their stead.

Experience has taught mankind that legislation by representatives is the most eligible and the only practicable mode in which the people of any country can exercise this right, either prudently or beneficially. But then it is a matter of the highest importance in forming this representation, that it be so constituted as to be capable of understanding the true interests of the society for which it acts, and so disposed as to pursue the good and happiness of the people as its ultimate end. The object of every free government is the public good, and all lesser interests yield to it. That of every tyrannical government is the happiness and aggrandizement of one or a few, and to this the public felicity and every other interest must submit. The reason of this difference in these governments is obvious. The first is so constituted as to collect the views and wishes of the whole people in that of their rulers, while the latter is so framed as to separate the interests of the governors from that of the governed. The principle of self love, therefore, that will influence the one to promote the good of the whole will prompt the other to follow its own private advantage. The great art, therefore, in forming a good constitution appears to be this: so to frame it as that those to whom the power is committed shall be subject to the same feelings, and aim at the same objects as the people do, who transfer to them their authority. There is no possible way to effect this but by an equal, full, and fair representation; this, therefore, is the great desideratum in politics. However fair an appearance any government may make, though it may possess a thousand plausible articles and be decorated with ever so many ornaments, yet if it is deficient in this essential principle of a full and just representation of the people, it will be only like a painted sepulcher. For, without this it cannot be a free government; let the administration of it be good or ill, it still will be a government, not according to the will of the people, but according to the will of a few.

To test this new constitution then, by this principle, is of the last importance. It is to bring to it the touchstone of national liberty, and I hope I shall be excused, if, in this paper, I pursue the subject commenced in my last number, to wit, the necessity of an equal and full representation in the legislature. In that, I showed that it was not equal, because the smallest states are to send the same number of members to the senate as the largest, and, because the slaves, who afford neither aid nor defense to the government, are to increase the proportion of members. To prove that it was not a just or adequate representation, it was urged that so small a number could not resemble the people or possess their sentiments and dispositions; that the choice of members would commonly fall upon the rich and great, while the middling class of the community would be excluded; and that in so small a representation there was no security against bribery and corruption.

The small number which is to compose this legislature will not only expose it to the danger of that kind of corruption and undue influence which will arise from the gift of places of honor and emolument, or the more direct one of bribery, but it will also subject it to another kind of influence no less fatal to the liberties of the people, though it be not so flagrantly repugnant to the principles of rectitude. It is not to be expected that a legislature will be found in any country that will not have some of its members who will pursue their private ends, and for which they will sacrifice the public good. Men of this character are generally artful and designing, and frequently possess brilliant talents and abilities. They commonly act in concert, and agree to share the spoils of their country among them; they will keep their object ever in view and follow it with constancy. To effect their purpose, they will assume any shape and, Proteus like, mold themselves into any form. Where they find members proof against direct bribery or gifts of offices, they will endeavor to mislead their minds by specious and false reasoning, to impose upon their unsuspecting honesty by an affectation of zeal for the public good. They will form juntos, and hold outdoor meetings: they will operate upon the good nature of their opponents by a thousand little attentions, and tease them into compliance by the earnestness of solicitation. Those who are acquainted with the manner of conducting business in public assemblies know how prevalent art and address are in carrying a measure, even over men of the best intentions and of good understanding. The firmest security against this kind of improper and dangerous influence, as well as all other, is a strong and numerous representation; in such a house of assembly, so great a number must be gained over before the private views of individuals could be gratified that there could be scarce a hope of success. But in the federal assembly, seventeen men are all that is necessary to pass a law. It is probable it will seldom happen that more than twenty-five will be requisite to form a majority; when it is considered what a number of places of honor and emolument will be in the gift of the executive, the powerful influence that great and designing men have over the honest and unsuspecting by their art and address, their soothing manners and civilities, and their cringing flattery, joined with their affected patriotism. When these different species of influence are combined, it is scarcely to be hoped that a legislature, composed of so small a number as the one proposed by the new constitution, will long resist their force.

Further objection against the feebleness of the representation is that it will not possess the confidence of the people. The execution of the laws in a free government must rest on this confidence, and this must be founded on the good opinion they entertain of the framers of the laws. Every government must be supported, either by the people having such an attachment to it as to be ready when called upon to support it, or by a force at the command of the government to compel obedience. The latter mode destroys every idea of a free government;

for the same force that may be employed to compel obedience to good laws might, and probably would, be used to wrest from the people their constitutional liberties. Whether it is practicable to have a representation for the whole union sufficiently numerous to obtain that confidence which is necessary for the purpose of internal taxation and other powers to which this proposed government extends is an important question. I am clearly of opinion it is not, and therefore I have stated this in my first number as one of the reasons against going into an entire consolidation of the states. One of the most capital errors in the system is that of extending the powers of the federal government to objects to which it is not adequate, which it cannot exercise without endangering public liberty, and which it is not necessary they should possess in order to preserve the union and manage our national concerns; of this, however, I shall treat more fully in some future paper. But, however this may be certain it is that the representation in the legislature is not so formed as to give reasonable ground for public trust.

In order for the people safely to repose themselves on their rulers, they should not only be of their own choice. But it is requisite they should be acquainted with their abilities to manage the public concerns with wisdom. They should be satisfied that those who represent them are men of integrity, who will pursue the good of the community with fidelity, and will not be turned aside from their duty by private interest, or corrupted by undue influence, and that they will have such a zeal for the good of those whom they represent, as to excite them to be diligent in their service. But it is impossible the people of the United States should have sufficient knowledge of their representatives, when the numbers are so few, to acquire any rational satisfaction on either of these points. The people of this state will have very little acquaintance with those who may be chosen to represent them; a great part of them will probably not know the characters of their own members, much less that of a majority of those who will compose the federal assembly. They will consist of men whose names they have never heard, and whose talents and regard for the public good they are total strangers to; and they will have no persons so immediately of their choice so near them, of their neighbors and of their own rank in life, that they can feel themselves secure in trusting their interests in their hands. The representatives of the people cannot, as they now do, after they have passed laws, mix with the people, and explain to them the motives which induced the adoption of any measure, point out its utility, and remove objections or silence unreasonable clamor against it. The number will be so small that but a very few of the most sensible and respectable yeomanry of the country can ever have any knowledge of them: being so far removed from the people, their station will be elevated and important, and they will be considered as ambitious and designing. They will not be viewed by the people as part of themselves, but as a body distinct from them, and having separate interests to pursue. The consequence will be that a perpetual jealousy will exist in the minds of the people against them; their conduct will be narrowly watched, their measures scrutinized, and their laws opposed, evaded, or reluctantly obeyed. This is natural, and exactly corresponds with the conduct of individuals towards those in whose hands they entrust important concerns. If the person confided in be a neighbor with whom his employer is intimately acquainted, whose talents he knows are sufficient to manage the business with which he is charged, his honesty and fidelity unsuspected, and his friendship and zeal for the service of this principal unquestionable, he will commit his affairs into his hands with unreserved confidence, and feel himself secure; all the transactions of the agent will meet with the most favorable construction, and the measures he takes will give satisfaction. But, if the person employed be a stranger whom he has never seen, and whose character for ability or fidelity he cannot fully learn; if he is constrained to choose him, because it was not in his power to procure one more agreeable to his wishes, he will trust him with caution, and be suspicious of all his conduct.

If then this government should not derive support from the good will of the people, it must be executed by force or not executed at all; either case would lead to the total destruction of liberty. The convention seemed aware of this, and have therefore provided for calling out the militia to execute the laws of the union. If this system was so framed as to command that respect from the people, which every good free government will obtain, this provision was unnecessary. The people would support the civil magistrate. This power is a novel one in free governments; these have depended for the execution of the laws on the Posse Comitatus, and never raised an idea that the people would refuse to aid the civil magistrate in executing those laws they themselves had made. I shall now dismiss the subject of the incompetency of the representation, and proceed as I promised to show that impotent as it is, the people have no security that they will enjoy the exercise of the right of electing this assembly, which at best, can be considered but as the shadow of representation.

By section four, article one, the Congress is authorized at any time by law to make or alter regulations respecting the time, place, and manner of holding elections for senators and representatives, except as to the places of choosing senators. By this clause the right of election itself, is in a great measure transferred from the people to their rulers. One would think that if anything was necessary to be made a fundamental article of the original compact, it would be that of fixing the branches of the legislature, so as to put it out of its power to alter itself by modifying the election of its own members at will and pleasure. When a people once resign the privilege of a fair election, they clearly have none left worth contending for.

It is clear that under this article the federal legislature may institute such rules respecting elections as to lead to the choice of one description of men. The weakness of the representation tends but too certainly to confer on the rich and *well born* all honors, but the power granted in this article may be so exercised as to secure it almost beyond a possibility of control. The proposed Congress may make the whole state one district, and direct that the capital (the city of New York, for instance) shall be the place for holding the election; the consequence would be that none but men of the most elevated rank in society would attend, and they would as certainly choose men of their own class as it is true what the *Apostle Paul* said, that "no man ever yet hated his own flesh, but nourisheth and cherisheth it." They may declare that those members who have the greatest number of votes shall be considered as duly elected; the consequence would be that the people who are dispersed in the interior parts of the state would give their votes for a variety of candidates, while any order or profession, residing in populous places, by uniting their interests, might procure whom they pleased to be chosen, and by this means the representatives of the state may be elected by one tenth part of the people who actually vote. This may be effected constitutionally, and by one of those silent operations which frequently takes place without being noticed, but which often produces such changes as entirely to alter a government, subvert a free constitution, and rivet the chains on a free people before they perceive they are forged. Had the power of regulating elections been left under the direction of the state legislatures where the people are not only nominally but substantially represented, it would have been secure; but if it was taken out of their hands, it surely ought to have been fixed on such a basis as to have put it out of the power of the federal legislature to deprive the people of it by law. Provision should have been made for marking out the states into districts, and for choosing by a majority of votes, a person out of each of them of permanent property and residence in the district which he was to represent.

If the people of America will submit to a constitution that will vest in the hands of any body of men a right to deprive them by law of the privilege of a fair election, they will submit to almost any thing. Reasoning with them will be in vain; they must be left until they are brought to reflection by feeling oppression. They will then have to wrest from their oppressors, by a strong hand, that which they now possess, and which they may retain if they will exercise but a moderate share of prudence and firmness.

I know it is said that the dangers apprehended from this clause are merely imaginary, that the proposed general legislature will be disposed to regulate elections upon proper principles, and to use their power with discretion, and to promote the public good. On this, I would observe that constitutions are not so necessary to regulate the conduct of good rulers as to restrain that of bad ones. Wise and good men will exercise power so as to promote the public happiness under any form of government. If we are to take it for granted that those who administer the government under this system will always pay proper attention to the rights and interests of the people, nothing more was necessary than to say who should be invested with the powers of government, and leave them to exercise it at will and pleasure. Men are apt to be deceived both with respect to their own dispositions and those of others. Though this truth is proven by almost every page of the history of nations; to wit, that power lodged in the hands of rulers to be used at discretion is almost always exercised to the oppression of the people and the aggrandizement of themselves, yet most men think if it was lodged in their hands they would not employ it in this manner. Thus when the prophet *Elisha* told *Hazael*, "I know the evil that thou wilt do unto the children of Israel; their strong holds wilt thou set on fire, and their young men wilt thou slay with the sword, and wilt dash their children, and rip up their women with child." Hazael had no idea that he ever should be guilty of such horrid cruelty and said to the prophet, "Is thy servant a dog that he should do this great thing." Elisha answered, "The Lord hath showed me that thou shalt be king of Syria." The event proved that Hazael only wanted an opportunity to perpetrate these enormities without restraint, and he had a disposition to do them, though he himself knew it not. . . .

The nature and extent of the judicial power of the United States, proposed to be granted by this constitution, claims our particular attention. Much has been said and written upon the subject of this new system on both sides, but I have not met with any writer, who has discussed the judicial powers with any degree of accuracy. And yet it is obvious that we can form but very imperfect ideas of the manner in which this government will work, or the effect it will have in changing the internal police and mode of distributing justice at present subsisting in the respective states, without a thorough investigation of the powers of the judiciary and of the manner in which they will operate. This government is a complete system, not only for making, but for executing laws. And the courts of law, which will be constituted by it, are not only to decide upon the constitution and the laws made in pursuance of it, but by officers subordinate to them to execute all their decisions. The real effect of this system of government will therefore be brought home to the feelings of the people through the medium of the judicial power. It is, moreover, of great importance to examine with care the nature and extent of the judicial power, because those who are to be vested with it are to be placed in a situation altogether unprecedented in a free country. They are to be rendered totally independent, both of the people and the legislature, both with respect to their offices and salaries. No errors they may commit can be corrected by any power above them, if any such power there be, nor can they be removed from office for making ever so many erroneous adjudications.

The only causes for which they can be displaced is conviction of treason, bribery, and high crimes and misdemeanors.

This part of the plan is so modeled as to authorize the courts, not only to carry into execution the powers expressly given, but where these are wanting or ambiguously expressed, to supply what is wanting by their own decisions.

That we may be enabled to form a just opinion on this subject, I shall, in considering it, first examine the nature and extent of the judicial powers and second, inquire whether the courts who are to exercise them are so constituted as to afford reasonable ground of confidence that they will exercise them for the general good.

With a regard to the nature and extent of the judicial powers, I have to regret my want of capacity to give that full and minute explanation of them that the subject merits. To be able to do this, a man should be possessed of a degree of law knowledge far beyond what I pretend to. A number of hard words and technical phrases are used in this part of the system, about the meaning of which gentlemen learned in the law differ.

Its advocates know how to avail themselves of these phrases. In a number of instances where objections are made to the powers given to the judicial, they give such an explanation to the technical terms as to avoid them.

Though I am not competent to give a perfect explanation of the powers granted to this department of the government, I shall yet attempt to trace some of the leading features of it, from which I presume it will appear, that they will operate to a total subversion of the state judiciaries, if not to the legislative authority of the states.

In article three, section two, it is said, "The judicial power shall extend to all cases in law and equity arising under this constitution, the laws of the United States, and treaties made, or which shall be made, under their authority, etc."

The first article to which this power extends is all cases in law and equity arising under this constitution.

What latitude of construction this clause should receive is not easy to say. At first view, one would suppose that it meant no more than this; that the courts under the general government should exercise, not only the powers of courts of law, but also that of courts of equity in the manner in which those powers are usually exercised in the different states. But this cannot be the meaning, because the next clause authorizes the courts to take cognizance of all cases in law and equity arising under the laws of the United States; this last article, I conceive, conveys as much power to the general judicial as any of the state courts possess.

The cases arising under the constitution must be different from those arising under the laws, or else the two clauses mean exactly the same thing.

The cases arising under the constitution must include such, as bring into question its meaning, and will require an explanation of the nature and extent of the powers of the different departments under it.

This article, therefore, vests the judicial with a power to resolve all questions that may arise on any case on the construction of the constitution, either in law or in equity.

First, they are authorized to determine all questions that may arise upon the meaning of the constitution in law. This article vests the courts with authority to give the constitution a legal construction, or to explain it according to the rules laid down for construing a law. These rules give a certain degree of latitude of explanation. According to this mode of construction, the courts are to give such meaning to the constitution as comports best with the common, and generally received acceptation of the words in which it is expressed, regarding their ordinary and popular use rather than their grammatical propriety. Where words are dubious, they will be explained by the context. The end of the clause will be attended to, and the words will be understood, as having a view to it; and the words will not be so understood as to bear no meaning or a very absurd one.

Second, the judicial are not only to decide questions arising upon the meaning of the constitution in law, but also in equity. By this they are empowered to explain the constitution according to the reasoning spirit of it, without being confined to the words or letter.

"From this method of interpreting laws (says Blackstone) by the reason of them, arises what we call equity;" which is thus defined by Grotius, "the correction of that, wherein the law, by reason of its universality, is deficient;" for since in laws all cases cannot be foreseen or expressed it is necessary that when the decrees of the law cannot be applied to particular cases, there should some where be a power vested of defining those circumstances which had they been foreseen the legislator would have expressed; and these are the cases, which according to Grotius, "lex non exacte definit, sed arbitrio boni viri permittet."

The same learned author observes, "That equity, thus depending essentially upon each individual case, there can be no established rules and fixed principles of equity laid down, without destroying its very essence, and reducing it to a positive law."

From these remarks, the authority and business of the courts of law under this clause may be understood.

They will give the sense of every article of the constitution that may from time to time come before them. And in their decisions they will not confine themselves to any fixed or established rules, but will determine, according to what appears to them, the reason and spirit of the constitution. The opinions of the supreme court, whatever they may be, will have the force of law, because there is no power provided in the constitution that can correct their errors or control their adjudications. From this court there is no appeal. And I conceive the legislature themselves cannot set aside a judgment of this court, because they are authorized by the constitution to decide in the last resort. The legislature must be controlled by the constitution, and not the constitution by them. They have therefore no more right to set aside any judgment pronounced upon the construction of the constitution, than they have to take from the president, the chief command of the army and navy, and commit it to some other person. The reason is plain; the judicial and executive derive their authority from the same source that the legislature do theirs; and therefore in all cases where the constitution does not make the one responsible to, or controllable by the other, they are altogether independent of each other.

The judicial power will operate to effect in the most certain, but yet silent and imperceptible manner, what is evidently the tendency of the constitution: an entire subversion of the legislative, executive and judicial powers of the individual states. Every adjudication of the supreme court, on any question that may arise upon the nature and extent of the general government, will affect the limits of the state jurisdiction. In proportion as the former enlarge the exercise of their powers will that of the latter be restricted.

That the judicial power of the United States will lean strongly in favor of the general government, and will give such an explanation to the constitution, as will favor an extension of its jurisdiction, is very evident from a variety of considerations.

First, the constitution itself strongly countenances such a mode of construction. Most of the articles in this system which convey powers of any considerable importance are conceived in general and indefinite terms, which are either equivocal, ambiguous, or which require long definitions to unfold the extent of their meaning. The two most important powers committed to any government, those of raising money and of raising and keeping up troops, have already been considered, and shown to be unlimited by anything but the discretion of the legislature. The clause which vests the power to pass all laws which are proper and necessary to carry the powers given into execution, has been shown [to] leave the legislature at liberty, to do everything which in their judgment is best. It is said, I know, that this clause confers no power on the legislature, which they would not have had without it. Though I believe this is not the fact, yet admitting it to be, it implies that the constitution is not to receive an explanation strictly, according to its letter; but more power is implied than is expressed. And this clause, if it is to be considered as explanatory of the extent of the powers given, rather than giving a new power, is to be understood as declaring that, in construing any of the articles conveying power, the spirit, intent and design of the clause should be attended to, as well as the words in their common acceptation.

This constitution gives sufficient color for adopting an equitable construction, if we consider the great end and design it professedly has in view; these appear from its preamble to be, "to form a more perfect union, establish justice, insure domestic tranquility, provide for the common defense, promote the general welfare, and secure the blessings of liberty to ourselves and posterity." The design of this system is here expressed, and it is proper to give such a meaning to the various parts, as will best promote the accomplishment of the end; this idea suggests itself naturally upon reading the preamble, and will countenance the court in giving the several articles such a sense, as will the most effectually promote the ends the constitution had in view. How this manner of explaining the constitution will operate in practice, shall be the subject of future inquiry.

Second, not only will the constitution justify the courts in inclining to this mode of explaining it, but they will be interested in using this latitude of interpretation. Every body of men invested with office are tenacious of power. They feel interested, and hence it has become a kind of maxim to hand down their offices, with all its rights and privileges, unimpaired to their successors; the same principle will influence them to extend their power, and increase their rights. This of itself will operate strongly upon the courts to give such a meaning to the constitution, in all cases where it can possibly be done, as will enlarge the sphere of their own authority. Every extension of the power of the general legislature, as well as of the judicial powers, will increase the powers of the courts; and the dignity and importance of the judges, will be in proportion to the extent and magnitude of the powers they exercise. I add [that] it is highly probable the emolument of the judges will be increased with the increase of the business they will have to transact and its importance. From these considerations the judges will be interested to extend the powers of the courts, and to construe the constitution as much as possible in such a way as to favor it; and that they will do it appears probable.

Third, because they will have precedent to plead to justify them in it. It is well known, that the courts in England have by their own authority, extended their jurisdiction far beyond the limits set them in their original institution, and by the laws of the land.

The court of exchequer is a remarkable instance of this. It was originally intended principally to recover the king's debts, and to order the revenues of the crown. It had a common law jurisdiction, which was established merely for the benefit of the king's accomptants. We learn from Blackstone that the proceedings in this court are grounded on a writ called quo minus, in which the plaintiff suggests that he is the king's farmer or debtor, and that the defendant has done him the damage complained of, by which he is less able to pay the king. These suits by the statute of Rutland are expressly directed to be confined to such matters as specially concern the king or his ministers in the exchequer. And by the articuli super cartas it is enacted, that no common pleas be thenceforth held in the exchequer contrary to the form of the great charter; but now any person may sue in the excheq-uer. The surmise of being debtor to the king being matter of form, and mere words of course, and the court is open to all the nation.

When the courts will have a precedent before them, of a court which extended its jurisdiction in opposition to an act of the legislature, is it not to be expected that they will extend theirs, especially when there is nothing in the constitution expressly against it? and they are author-ized to construe its meaning, and are not under any control?

This power in the judicial, will enable them to mold the government into almost any shape they please. The manner in which this may be effected we will hereafter examine . . .

In my last I showed that the judicial power of the United States, under the first clause of the second section of article eight, would be authorized to explain the constitution not only according to its letter but according to its spirit and intention; and having this power, they would strongly incline to give it such a construction as to extend the powers of the general government, as much as possible to the diminution and finally to the destruction of that of the respective states.

I shall now proceed to show how this power will operate in its exercise to effect these purposes. In order to perceive the extent of its influence, I shall consider first, how it will tend to extend the legislative authority, second, in what manner it will increase the jurisdiction of the courts and, third, the way in which it will diminish and destroy both the legislative and judicial authority of the United States.

First, let us inquire how the judicial power will effect an extension of the legislative authority. Perhaps the judicial power will not be able, by direct and positive decrees, ever to direct the legislature, because it is not easy to conceive how a question can be brought before them in a course of legal discussion, in which they can give a decision declaring that the legislature have certain powers which they have not exercised and which, in consequence of the determination of the judges, they will be bound to exercise. But it is easy to see that in their adjudications they may establish certain principles, which being received by the legislature, will enlarge the sphere of their power beyond all bounds.

It is to be observed that the supreme court has the power in the last resort to determine all questions that may arise in the course of legal discussion on the meaning and construction of the constitution. This power they will hold under the constitution and independent of the legislature. The latter can no more deprive the former of this right than either of them or both of them together can take from the president, with the advice of the senate, the power of making treaties or appointing ambassadors.

In determining these questions, the court must and will assume certain principles from which they will reason in forming their decisions. These principles, whatever they may be, when they become fixed by a course of decisions will be adopted by the legislature, and will be the rule by which they will explain their own powers. This appears evident from this consideration that if the legislature pass laws, which, in the judgment of the court, they are not authorized to do by the constitution, the court will not take notice of them; for it will not be denied that the constitution is the highest or supreme law. And the courts are vested with the supreme and uncontrollable power to determine in all cases that come before them what the constitution means; they cannot therefore execute a law which, in their judgment, opposes the constitution, unless we can suppose they can make a superior law give way to an inferior. The legislature, therefore, will not go over the limits by which the courts may adjudge they are confined. And there is little room to doubt but that they will come up to those bounds, as often as occasion and opportunity may offer, and they may judge it proper to do it. For as on the one hand, they will not readily pass laws which they know the courts will not execute; so on the other, we may be sure they will not scruple to pass such as they know they will give effect, as often as they may judge it proper.

From these observations it appears that the judgment of the judicial on the constitution will become the rule to guide the legislature in their construction of their powers.

What the principles are which the courts will adopt is impossible for us to say; but taking up the powers as I have explained them in my last number, which they will possess under this clause, it is not difficult to see that they may and probably will be very liberal ones.

We have seen that they will be authorized to give the constitution a construction according to its spirit and reason, and not to confine themselves to its letter.

To discover the spirit of the constitution, it is of the first importance to attend to the principal ends and designs it has in view. These are expressed in the preamble in the following words, viz. "We, the people of the United States, in order to form a more perfect union, establish justice, insure domestic tranquillity, provide for the common defense, promote the general welfare, and secure the blessings of liberty to ourselves and our posterity, do ordain and establish this constitution," etc. If the end of the government is to be learned from these words, which are clearly designed to declare it, it is obvious it has in view every object which is embraced by any government. The preservation of internal peace, the due administration of justice, and to provide for the defense of the community seem to include all the objects of government; but if they do not, they are certainly comprehended in the words, "to provide for the general welfare." If it be further considered that this constitution, if it is ratified, will not be a compact entered into by states in their corporate capacities, but an agreement of the people of the United States, as one great body politic, no doubt can remain, but that the great end of the constitution, if it is to be collected from the preamble in which its end is declared, is to constitute a government which is to extend to every case for which any government is instituted, whether external or internal. The courts, therefore, will establish this as a principle in expounding the constitution, and will give every part of it such an explanation as will give latitude to every department under it to take cognizance of every matter, not only that affects the general and national concerns of the union, but also of such as relate to the administration of private justice and to regulating the internal and local affairs of the different parts.

Such a rule of exposition is not only consistent with the general spirit of the preamble, but it will stand confirmed by considering more minutely the different clauses of it.

The first object declared to be in view is, "To form a perfect union." It is to be observed [that] it is not an union of states or bodies corporate; had this been the case, the existence of the state governments might have been secured. But it is a union of the people of the United States considered as one body who are to ratify this constitution, if it is adopted. Now to make a union of this kind perfect, it is necessary to abolish all inferior governments, and to give the general one complete legislative, executive and judicial powers to every purpose. The courts therefore will establish it as a rule in explaining the constitution to give it such a construction as will best tend to perfect the union or take from the state governments every power of either making or executing laws. The second object is "to establish justice." This must include not only the idea of instituting the rule of justice, or of making laws which shall be the measure or rule of right, but also of providing for the application of this rule or of administering justice under it. And under this the courts will in their decisions extend the power of the government to all cases they possibly can, or otherwise they will be restricted in doing what appears to be the intent of the constitution they should do; to wit, pass laws and provide for the execution of them, for the general distribution of justice between man and man. Another end declared is "to insure domestic tranquillity." This comprehends a provision against all private breaches of the peace, as well as against all public commotions or general insurrections; and to attain the object of this clause fully, the government must exercise the power of passing laws on these subjects, as well as of appointing magistrates with authority to execute them. And the courts will adopt these ideas in their expositions. I might proceed to the other clauses in the preamble, and it would appear by a consideration of all of them separately, as it does by taking them together, that if the spirit of this system is to be known from its declared end and design in the preamble, its spirit is to subvert and abolish all the powers of the state government, and to embrace every object to which any government extends.

As it sets out in the preamble with this declared intention, so it proceeds in the different parts with the same idea. Any person who will peruse with attention the eighth section in which most of the powers are enumerated, will perceive that they either expressly or by implication extend to almost every thing about which any legislative power can be employed. But if this equitable mode of construction is applied to this part of the constitution, nothing can stand before it.

This will certainly give the first clause in that article a construction which I confess I think the most natural and grammatical one, to authorize the Congress to do anything which in their judgment will tend to provide for the general welfare, and this amounts to the same thing as general and unlimited powers of legislation in all cases . . .

This same manner of explaining the constitution will fix a meaning, and a very important one too, to the twelfth clause of the same section, which authorizes the Congress to make all laws which shall be proper and necessary for carrying into effect the foregoing powers, etc. A voluminous writer in favor of this system has taken great pains to convince the public that this clause means nothing; for that the same powers expressed in this are implied in other parts of the constitution. Perhaps it is so, but still this will undoubtedly be an excellent auxilliary to assist the courts to discover the spirit and reason of the constitution, and when applied to any and every of the other clauses granting power, will operate powerfully in extracting the spirit from them.

I might instance a number of clauses in the constitution, which, if explained in an *equitable* manner, would extend the powers of the government to every case, and reduce the state legislatures to nothing; but I should draw out my remarks to an undue length, and I presume enough has been said to show, that the courts have sufficient ground in the exercise of this power to determine that the legislature have no bounds set to them by this constitution, by any supposed right the legislatures of the respective states may have to regulate any of their local concerns.

I proceed, second, to inquire in what manner this power will increase the jurisdiction of the courts. I would here observe that the judicial power extends expressly to all civil cases that may arise save such as arise between citizens of the same state, with this exception to those of that description, that the judicial of the United States have cognizance of cases between citizens of the same state, claiming lands under grants of different states. Nothing more, therefore, is necessary to give the courts of law under this constitution complete jurisdiction of all civil causes, but to comprehend cases between citizens of the same state not included in the foregoing exception.

I presume there will be no difficulty in accomplishing this. Nothing more is necessary than to set forth in the process, that the party who brings the suit is a citizen of a different state from the one against whom the suit is brought, and there can be little doubt but that the court will take cognizance of the matter, and if they do, who is to restrain them? Indeed, I will freely confess that it is my decided opinion that the courts ought to take cognizance of such causes under the powers of the constitution. For one of the great ends of the constitution is "to establish justice." This supposes that this cannot be done under the existing governments of the states; and there is certainly as good reason why individuals, living in the same state, should have justice, as those who live in different states. Moreover, the constitution expressly declares, that "the citizens of each state shall be entitled to all the privileges and immunities of citizens in the several states." It will therefore be no fiction, for a citizen of one state to set forth in a suit, that he is a citizen of another; for he that is entitled to all the privileges and immunities of a country is a citizen of that country. And in truth, the citizen of one state will, under this constitution, be a citizen of every state.

But supposing that the party, who alleges that he is a citizen of another state, has recourse to fiction in bringing in his suit; it is well known that the courts have high authority to plead, to justify them in suffering actions to be brought before them by such fictions. In my last number I stated that the court of exchequer tried all causes in virtue of such a fiction. The court of king's bench in England extended their jurisdiction in the same way. Originally, this court held pleas in civil cases only of trespasses and other injuries alleged to be committed *vi et armis*. They might likewise, says Blackstone, upon the division of the *aula regia*, have originally held pleas of any other civil action whatsoever (except in real actions which are now very seldom in use) provided the defendant was an officer of the court, or in the custody of the marshall or prison keeper of this court, for breach of the peace, etc. In process of time, by a fiction, this court began to hold pleas of any personal action whatsoever; it being surmised that the defendant has been arrested for a supposed trespass that "he has never committed, and being thus in the custody of the marshall of the court, the plaintiff is at liberty to proceed against him, for any other personal injury, which surmise of being in the marshall's custody, the defendant is not at liberty to dispute." By a much less fiction, may the pleas of the courts of the United States extend to cases between citizens of the same state. I shall add no more on this head, but proceed briefly to remark in what way this power will diminish and destroy both the legislative and judicial authority of the states.

It is obvious that these courts will have authority to decide upon the validity of the laws of any of the states in all cases where they come in question before them. Where the constitution gives the general government exclusive jurisdiction, they will adjudge all laws made by the states in such cases, void *ab initio*. Where the constitution gives them concurrent jurisdiction, the laws of the United States must prevail because they are the supreme law. In such cases, therefore, the laws of the state legislatures must be repealed, restricted, or so construed, as to give full effect to the laws of the union on the same subject. From these remarks it is easy to see that in proportion as the general government acquires power and jurisdiction, by the liberal construction which the judges may give the constitution, will those of the states lose its rights until they become so trifling and unimportant, as not to be worth having. I am much mistaken, if this system will not operate to effect this with as much celerity, as those who have the administration of it will think prudent to suffer it. The remaining objections to the judicial power shall be considered in a future paper . . .

I said in my last number that the supreme court under this constitution would be exalted above all other power in the government, and subject to no control. The business of this paper will be to illustrate this, and to show the danger that will result from it. I question whether the world ever saw, in any period of it, a court of justice invested with such immense powers, and yet placed in a situation so little responsible. Certain it is that in England and in the several states, where we have been taught to believe the courts of law are put upon the most prudent establishment; they are on a very different footing.

The judges in England, it is true, hold their offices during their good behavior, but then their determinations are subject to correction by the house of lords; and their power is by no means so extensive as that of the proposed supreme court of the union. I believe they in no instance assume the authority to set aside an act of parliament under the idea that it is inconsistent with their constitution. They consider themselves bound to decide according to the existing laws of the land, and never undertake to control them by adjudging that they are inconsistent with the constitution. Much less are they vested with the power of giving an *equitable* construction to the constitution.

The judges in England are under the control of the legislature, for they are bound to determine according to the laws passed by them. But the judges under this constitution will control the legislature, for the supreme court are authorized in the last resort to determine what is the extent of the powers of the Congress; they are to give the constitution an explanation, and there is no power above them to set aside their judgment. The framers of this constitution appear to have followed that of the British in rendering the judges independent by granting them their offices during good behavior, without following the constitution of England in instituting a tribunal in which their errors may be corrected; and without adverting to this that the judicial under this system have a power which is above the legislative, and which indeed transcends any power before given to a judicial by any free government under heaven.

I do not object to the judges holding their commissions during good behavior. I suppose it a proper provision provided they were made properly responsible. But I say this system has followed the English government in this, while it has departed from almost every other principle of their jurisprudence under the idea of rendering the judges independent, which, in the British constitution, means no more than that they hold their places during good behavior and have fixed salaries; they have made the judges *independent* in the fullest sense of the word. There is no power above them to control any of their decisions. There is no authority that can remove them, and they cannot be controlled by the laws of the legislature. In short, they are independent of the people, of the legislature, and of every power under heaven. Men placed in this situation will generally soon feel themselves independent of heaven itself. Before I proceed to illustrate the truth of these assertions, I beg liberty to make one remark. Though in my opinion the judges ought to hold their offices during good behavior, yet I think it is clear that the reasons in favor of this establishment of the judges in England do by no means apply to this country.

The great reason assigned why the judges in Britain ought to be commissioned during good behavior is this; that they may be placed in a situation, not to be influenced by the crown to give such decisions as would tend to increase its powers and prerogatives. While the judges held their places at the will and pleasure of the king, on whom they depended not only for their offices but also for their salaries, they were subject to every undue influence. If the crown wished to carry a favorite point, to accomplish which the aid of the courts of law was necessary, the pleasure of the king would be signified to the judges. And it required the spirit of a martyr for the judges to determine contrary to the king's will. They were absolutely dependent upon him both for their offices and livings. The king, holding his office during life and transmitting it to his posterity as an inheritance, has much stronger inducements to increase the prerogatives of his office than those who hold their offices for stated periods, or even for life. Hence, the English nation gained a great point in favor of liberty. When they obtained the appointment of the judges during good behavior, they got from the crown a concession which deprived it of one of the most powerful engines with which it might enlarge the boundaries of the royal prerogative and encroach on the liberties of the people. But these reasons do not apply to this country, we have no hereditary monarch. Those who appoint the judges do not hold their offices for life, nor do they descend to their children. The same arguments, therefore, which will conclude in favor of the tenure of the judge's offices for good behavior lose a considerable part of their weight when applied to the state and condition of America. But much less can it be shown that the nature of our government requires that the courts should be placed beyond all account more independent, so much so as to be above control.

I have said that the judges under this system will be *independent* in the strict sense of the word. To prove this I will show that there is no power above them that can control their decisions or correct their errors. There is no authority that can remove them from office for any errors or want of capacity or lower their salaries, and in many cases their power is superior to that of the legislature.

First. there is no power above them that can correct their errors or control their decisions. The adjudications of this court are final and irreversible, for there is no court above them to which appeals can lie, either in error or on the merits. In this respect it differs from the courts in England, for there the house of lords is the highest court to whom appeals, in error, are carried from the highest of the courts of law.

Second, they cannot be removed from office or suffer a dimunition of their salaries for any error in judgment or want of capacity. It is expressly declared by the constitution, "That they shall at stated times receive a compensation for their services which shall not be diminished during their continuance in office." The only clause in the constitution which provides for the removal of the judges from office is that which declares that "the president, vice-president, and all civil officers of the United States, shall be removed from office on impeachment for and conviction of treason, bribery, or other high crimes and misdemeanors." By this paragraph, civil officers, in which the judges are included, are removable only for crimes. Treason and bribery are named, and the rest are included under the general terms of high crimes and misdemeanors. Errors in judgement, or want of capacity to discharge the duties of the office, can never be supposed to be included in these words, *high crimes and misdemeanors*. A man may mistake a case in giving judgment, or manifest that he is incompetent to the discharge of the duties of a judge, and yet give no evidence of corruption or want of integrity. To support the charge, it will be necessary to give in evidence some facts that will show that the judges commited the error from wicked and corrupt motives.

Third. the power of this court is in many cases superior to that of the legislature. I have shown in a former paper that this court will be authorized to decide upon the meaning of the constitution, and that not only according to the natural and obvious meaning of the words, but also according to the spirit and intention of it. In the exercise of this power they will not be subordinate to but above the legislature. For all the departments of this government will receive their powers, so far as they are expressed in the constitution, from the people immediately who are the source of power. The legislature can only exercise such powers as are given them by the constitution. They cannot assume any of the rights annexed to the judicial, for this plain reason that the same authority which vested the legislature with their powers vested the judicial with theirs. Both are derived from the same source, both therefore are equally valid, and the judicial hold their powers independently of the legislature, as the legislature do of the judicial. The supreme court then have a right, independent of the legislature, to give a construction to the constitution and every part of it, and there is no power provided in this system to correct their construction or do it away. If, therefore, the legislature pass any laws inconsistent with the sense the judges put upon the constitution, they will declare it void; and therefore in this respect their power is superior to that of the legislature. In England the judges are not only subject to have their decisions set aside by the house of lords for error, but in cases where they give an explanation to the laws or constitution of the country, contrary to the sense of the parliament; though the parliament will not set aside the judgment of the court, yet, they have authority by a new law to explain a former one, and by this means to prevent a reception of such decisions. But no such power is in the legislature. The judges are supreme, and no law, explanatory of the constitution, will be binding on them.

From the preceding remarks which have been made on the judicial powers proposed in this system, the policy of it may be fully developed.

I have in the course of my observation on this constitution, affirmed and endeavored to show that it was calculated to abolish entirely the state governments, and to melt down the states into one entire government for every purpose as well internal and local, as external and national. In this opinion the opposers of the system have generally agreed, and this has been uniformly denied by its advocates in public. Some individuals indeed among them will confess that it has this tendency, and scruple not to say, it is what they wish; and I will venture to predict, without the spirit of prophecy, that if it is adopted without amendments, or some such precautions as will insure amendments immediately after its adoption, that the same gentlemen who have employed their talents and abilities with such success to influence the public mind to adopt this plan will employ the same to persuade the people that it will be for their good to abolish the state governments as useless and burdensome.

Perhaps nothing could have been better conceived to facilitate the abolition of the state governments than the constitution of the judicial. They will be able to extend the limits of the general government gradually, and by insensible degrees, and to accommodate themselves to the temper of the people. Their decisions on the meaning of the constitution will commonly take place in cases which arise between individuals, with which the public will not be generally acquainted; one adjudication will form a precedent to the next, and this to a following one. These cases will immediately affect individuals only; so that a series of determinations will probably take place before even the people will be informed of them. In the mean time, all the art and address of those who wish for the change will be employed to make converts to their opinion. The people will be told that their state officers, and state legislatures are a burden and expense without affording any solid advantage, for that all the laws passed by them might be equally well made by the general legislature. If to those who will be interested in the change be added those who will be under their influence, and such who will submit to almost any change of government which they can be persuaded to believe will ease them of taxes, it is easy to see the party who will favor the abolition of the state governments would be far from being inconsiderable. In this situation, the general legislature might pass one law after another, extending the general and abridging the state jurisdictions, and to sanction their proceedings would have a course of decisions of the judicial to whom the constitution has committed the power of explaining the constitution. If the states remonstrated, the constitutional mode of deciding upon the validity of the law is with the supreme court, and neither people nor state legislatures, nor the general legislature can remove them or reverse their decrees.

Had the construction of the constitution been left with the legislature, they would have explained it at their peril; if they exceed their powers, or sought to find in the spirit of the constitution more than was expressed in the letter, the people from whom they derived their power could remove them, and do themselves right. And indeed I can see no other remedy that the people can have against their rulers for encroachments of this nature. A constitution is a compact of a people with their rulers; if the rulers break the compact, the people have a right and ought to remove them and do themselves justice. But in order to enable them to do this with the greater facility, those whom the people choose at stated periods should have the power in the last resort to determine the sense of the compact. If they determine contrary to the understanding of the people, an appeal will lie to the people at the period when the rulers are to be elected, and they will have it in their power to remedy the evil. But when this power is lodged in the hands of men independent of the people, and of their representatives, and who are not constitutionally accountable for their opinions, no way is left to control them but *with a high hand and an outstretched arm.*

Chapter IV

In Support of Capitalism and Democracy

The Antifederalists were deeply suspicious of economic and political privilege. They viewed the majority of the citizenry to be composed of people of moderate wealth who secured their position by means of honesty and diligence. The danger of faction did not originate with the majority so constituted. Rather, the danger came from the ambition of the few who would use political offices to advance their own interests. They believed that the purpose of republican government was to protect all the interests of the citizenry. With respect to trade, the Antifederalists believed that would be best accomplished by leaving commerce free to pursue natural courses, a policy which would benefit all since none could enjoy the advantage of government support. They warned that the unlimited power over trade bestowed on Congress by the new Constitution would lead to the establishment of monopolies which, in turn, would give undue influence in government to the ambitious few. The Antifederalists considered the effect of monopolies on trade analogous to the effect of aristocracy on government. They felt that faction resulted from rewarding ambition with public place amid inadequate constitutional precautions, rather than from the viciousness of mankind or the necessity of historical development as argued in *The Federalist*. Minority faction encouraged and protected by government constituted the danger to be avoided.

The kind of capitalism favored by the Antifederalists was the kind articulated by Adam Smith in *The Wealth of Nations*. They asserted that the prosperity of the nation was best served when a large number of buyers and sellers pursued their self-interest in a market place free from the regulation and intrusion of a central government. In addition to warning about the creation of monopolies, the Antifederalists cautioned that the new plan gave Congress unlimited power over internal taxation. Such power not only distorted allocation decisions and enervated the enterprizing spirit, it also provided government with revenue for pursuing the aristocratic goals of international respect and grandeur. The Antifederalists saw a symbiotic relationship between monopoly capitalism and unlimited government. The solution to these twin dangers was free trade and restricted government.

The Antifederalists believed that substantial social equality prevailed in America and they wanted to preserve this equality. They admitted that in the nature of things certain inequalities were unavoidable. However, necessary inequalities were acceptable if they were compensated for by the elimination of unnecessary social inequality spilling over into the political realm which would, in turn, become the foundation for legitimizing both political and social inequality as natural. They accused the leading proponents of the Constitution with having a secret plan for the demise of social democracy and free commerce and the erection of a permanent political and economic aristocracy. Those governments which favor commerce seemed better suited to ameliorate the human condition, while those which *most* favor commerce seemed *best* of all.

A Georgian
An Essay
Gazette of the State of Georgia
15 November, 1787

Mr. Printer,

Through the channel of your paper we have lately been favored with the new Federal Constitution, the plan of which I must confess I like, and it is my heart's wish to see a federal constitution established agreeable to the principles of republican liberty and independence, and on the basis of a democratic government, meaning that of the people, being that very government intended by our glorious Declaration of Independence.

Though this new federal constitution, I believe, was framed and intended for the good of the United States, and, as we are well aware, was assented to by the political saviors of our country, to whom all deference and respect is due, yet the sacredness of these illustrious characters has not been sufficient nor able to prevent several articles from creeping into the said constitution, which, by their different constructions and great latitude given them, an American Sylla, or Augustus Octavianus, might one day or other make serviceable to his ambition, interest, and to the utter subversion of our SACRED FREEDOM And as mankind, upon the whole, is so depraved as, with pleasure, to trample upon the sacred rights and privileges of their fellow creatures, it is certainly one of our greatest cares, both for ourselves and our offspring, to frame such constitutional laws, thereby to prevent such designing tyrants (if ever they be) from grasping at a power, to our destruction, in the said federal constitution, within their reach; as also to guard with the safest care against all encroachments, and to bar them forever from paving the way to what is worse yet, an ARISTOCRATIC government, whereby about 70 nabobs would lord over three millions of people as slaves; as also to establish power, harmony, equality, and justice, for and among the whole of the United States.

I agree, as it may be said, that the Articles of the Confederation are defective; and, to make it answer effectually the purpose of a federal government, it is to be observed, delegates from all the states, except Rhode Island, were appointed by the legislatures, with this power only, "to meet in Convention, to join in devising and discussing all such ALTERATIONS and farther provisions as may be necessary to render the articles of the confederation adequate to the exigencies of the Union." This was the only power in them vested, and, in conformity to it, had they added to the articles of the confederation a power in Congress, *viz.*, to regulate foreign and internal trade, to lay and collect duties and imposts, uniform throughout the United States, to have the sole legislative power in maritime matters, to have a coercive power to enforce the payment of the quota of each delinquent state, but to leave internal taxation and excise to the management of each individual state, the legislature thereof being certainly best acquainted with that important business. Had they done this, all would have been well, and our federal government as good and fully adequate to its exigencies as could have been wished. But as this convention has thought fit to destroy such a useful fabric (as the Articles of Confederation with the before mentioned amendment and addition would have been) and, on the ruins of that, raised a new structure, rather favorable to aristocratic and destructive to democratic government; and as it seems not to have that equality and justice for its basis that it certainly ought to have among confederated, free, and independent states, I wish to point out the few articles inconsistent with such a constitution, and also to try the remedies thereof, hoping, by that means, that my fellow citizens will, by a candid second reading of said constitution, agree with me in the impropriety of such articles, and their united wisdom, in a Convention guided by the love of their country, and answering the benefit of the whole, will improve the remedies, and so establish a federal constitution capable of deterring any ambitious men from making a use of it to our destruction; as also to keep alive and in due harmony the confederation among the United Independent States, lately so dearly purchased from the government of Great Britain, because that meant "TO BIND US IN ALL CASES WHATSOEVER."

... Thus, fellow citizens, have I pointed out what I thought necessary to be amended in our federal constitution. I beg you to call to mind our glorious Declaration of Independence; read it, and compare it with the federal constitution; what a degree of apostasy will you not then discover. Therefore, guard against all encroachments upon your liberties so dearly purchased with the costly expense of blood and treasure. Show that you have yet that noble spirit, and provide remedies against the numberless evils of an unlimited taxation, against the fatal effects of a standing army in times of peace, against an unfair and too small representation. Let your suffrages at elections never be suffered to be regulated by laws at pleasure, but let it be stated and fixed. Let the trial by jury in civil and criminal cases, and the liberty of the press, be forever sacred and inviolable. Let Congress, for God's sake, not have that power of jurisdiction sought after to our destruction, but confine them to a territory of five miles only, and to only one supreme court, and allow them none extraordinary. Neither appeals in cases between citizens, whereby the rich may fly from justice, and the poor unable to follow them. And, at this rate, I am confident you will establish a government which will be lasting, and a blessing to ourselves and generations hereafter.

Having now discharged my duty, which as a citizen I owe to God, to my country, and myself, I leave you to judge for yourselves, and I hope you will act as becoming freemen and the guardians for your offspring.

Agrippa
Essays VII, IX, XII, XIV
(Boston) Massachusetts Gazette
18 and 28 December, 1787,
11, 14, and 18 January, 1788

To the People:

There cannot be a doubt, that, while the trade of this continent remains free, the activity of our countrymen will secure their full share. All the estimates for the present year, let them be made by what party they may, suppose the balance of trade to be largely in our favor. The credit of our merchants is, therefore, fully established in foreign countries. This is a sufficient proof, that when business is unshackled, it will find out that channel which is most friendly to its course. We ought, therefore, to be exceedingly cautious about diverting or restraining it. Every day produces fresh proofs, that people, under the immediate pressure of difficulties, do not, at first glance, discover the proper relief. The last year, a desire to get rid of embarrassments induced many honest people to agree to a tender act, and many others, of a different description, to obstruct the courts of justice. Both these methods only increased the evil they were intended to cure. Experience has since shown, that, instead of trying to lessen an evil by altering the present course of things, every endeavor should have been applied to facilitate the course of law, and thus to encourage a mutual confidence among the citizens, which increases the resources of them all, and renders easy the payment of debts. By this means one does not grow rich at the expense of another, but all are benefited. The case is the same with the states. Pennsylvania, with one port and a large territory, is less favorably situated for trade than Massachusetts, which has an extensive coast in proportion to its limits of jurisdiction. Accordingly a much larger proportion of our people are engaged in maritime affairs. We ought therefore to be particularly attentive to securing so great an interest. It is vain to tell us that we ought to overlook local interests. It is only by protecting local concerns, that the interest of the whole is preserved. No man when he enters into society, does it from a view to promote the good of others, but he does it for his own good. All men having the same view are bound equally to promote the welfare of the whole. To recur then to such a principle as that local interests must be disregarded, is requiring of one man to do more than another, and is subverting the foundation of a free government. Philadelphians would be shocked with a proposition to place the seat of general government and the unlimited right to regulate trade in Massachusetts. There can be no greater reason for our surrendering the preference to them. Such sacrifices, however we may delude ourselves with the form of words, always originate in folly, and not in generosity.

The perfection of government depends on the equality of its operation, as far as human affairs will admit, upon all parts of the empire, and upon all the citizens. Some inequalities indeed will necessarily take place. One man will be obliged to travel a few miles further than another man to procure justice. But when he has travelled, the poor man ought to have the same measure of justice as the rich one. Small inequalities may be easily compensated. There ought, however, to be no inequality in the law itself, and the government ought to have the same authority in one place as in another. Evident as this truth is, the most plausible argument in favor of the new plan is drawn from the inequality of its operation in different states. In Connecticut, they have been told that the bulk of the revenue will be raised by impost and excise, and therefore they need not be afraid to trust Congress with the power of levying a dry tax at pleasure. New York, and Massachusetts, are both more commercial states than Connecticut. The latter, therefore, hopes that the other two will pay the bulk of the continental expense. The argument is in itself delusive. If the trade is not overtaxed, the consumer pays it. If the trade is overtaxed, it languishes, and by the ruin of trade the farmer loses his market. The farmer has in truth no other advantage from imposts than that they save him the trouble of collecting money for the government. He neither gets nor loses money by changing the mode of taxation. The government indeed finds it the easiest way to raise the revenue; and the reason is that the tax is by this means collected where the money circulates most freely. But if the argument was not delusive, it ought to conclude against the plan, because it would prove the unequal operation of it, and if any saving is to be made by the mode of taxing, the saving should be applied towards our own debt and not to the payment of the part of a continental burden which Connecticut ought to discharge. It would be impossible to refute in writing all the delusions made use of to force this system through. Those respecting the public debt and the benefit of imposts are the most important, and these I have taken pains to explain. In one instance indeed, the impost does raise money at the direct expense of the seaports. This is when goods are imported subject to a duty and re-exported without a drawback. Whatever benefit is derived from this source surely should not be transferred to another state, at least till our own debts are cleared.

Another instance of unequal operation is that it establishes different degrees of authority in different states, and thus creates different interests. The lands in New Hampshire having been formerly granted by this state, and afterwards by that state, to private persons, the whole authority of trying titles becomes vested in a continental court, and that state loses a branch of authority, which the others retain over their own citizens. . . .

We come now to the second and last article of complaint against the present confederation, which is that Congress has not the sole power to regulate the intercourse between us and foreigners. Such a power extends not only to war and peace, but to trade and naturalization. This last article ought never to be given them; for though most of the states may be willing for certain reasons to receive foreigners as citizens, yet reasons of equal weight may induce other states, differently circumstanced, to keep their blood pure. Pennsylvania has chosen to receive all that would come there. Let any indifferent person judge whether that state in point of morals, education, energy is equal to any of the eastern states; the small state of Rhode Island only excepted. Pennsylvania in the course of a century has acquired her present extent and population at the expense of religion and good morals. The eastern states have, by keeping separate from the foreign mixtures, acquired their present greatness in the course of a century and a half and have preserved their religion and morals. They have also preserved that manly virtue which is equally fitted for rendering them respectable in war and industrious in peace.

The remaining power for peace and trade might perhaps be safely enough lodged with Congress under some limitations. Three restrictions appear to me to be essentially necessary to preserve the equality of rights to the states, which it is the object of the state governments to secure to each citizen. First, it ought not to be in the power of Congress either by treaty or otherwise to alienate part of any state without the consent of the legislature. Second, they ought not to be able by treaty or other law to give any legal preference to one part above another. Third, they ought to be restrained from creating any monopolies. Perhaps others may propose different regulations and restrictions. One of these is to be found in the old confederation, and another in the newly proposed plan. The third seems to be equally necessary.

After all that has been said and written on this subject, and on the difficulty of amending our old constitution so as to render it adequate to national purposes, it does not appear that anything more was necessary to be done than framing two new articles. By one a limited revenue would be given to Congress with a right to collect it, and by the other a limited right to regulate our intercourse with foreign nations. By such an addition we should have preserved to each state its power to defend the rights of the citizens, and the whole empire would be capable of expanding and receiving additions without altering its former constitution. Congress, at the same time, by the extent of their jurisdiction, and the number of their officers, would have acquired more respectability at home and a sufficient influence abroad. If any state was in such a case to invade the rights of the Union, the other states would join in defense of those rights, and it would be in the power of Congress to direct the national force to that object. But it is certain that the powers of Congress over the citizens should be small in proportion as the empire is extended; that in order to preserve the balance, each state may supply by energy what is wanting in numbers. Congress would be able by such a system as we have proposed to regulate trade with foreigners by such duties as should effectually give the preference to the produce and manufactures of our own country. We should then have a friendly intercourse established between the states upon the principles of mutual interest. A moderate duty upon foreign vessels would give an advantage to our own people, while it would avoid all the advantages arising from a prohibition, and the consequent deficiency of vessels to transport the produce of the southern states.

Our country is at present upon an average a thousand miles long from north to south, and eight hundred broad from the Mississippi to the Ocean. We have at least six millions of white inhabitants, and the annual increase is about two hundred and fifty thousand souls, exclusive of emigrants from Europe. The greater part of our increase is employed in settling the new lands, while the older settlements are entering largely into manufactures of various kinds. It is probable, that the extraordinary exertions of this state in the way of industry for the present year only, exceed in value five hundred thousand pounds. The new settlements, if all made in the same tract of country, would form a large state annually; and the time seems to be literally accomplished when a nation shall be born in a day. Such an immense country is not only capable of yielding all the produce of Europe, but actually does produce by far the greater part of the raw materials. The restrictions on our trade in Europe necessarily oblige us to make use of those materials, and the high price of labor operates as an encouragement to mechanical improvements. In this way we daily make rapid advancements towards independence in resources as well as in empire. If we adopt the new system of government we shall by one rash vote lose the fruit of the toil and expense of thirteen years, at the time when the benefits of that toil and expense are rapidly increasing. Though the imposts of Congress on foreign trade may tend to encourage manufactures, the excise and dry tax will destroy all the beneficial effects of the impost at the same time that they diminish our capital. Be careful then to give only a limited revenue and the limited power of managing foreign concerns. Once surrender the rights of internal legislation and taxation, and instead of being respected abroad, foreigners will laugh at us, and posterity will lament our folly. . .

To the Massachusetts Convention:

Suffer an individual to lay before you his contemplations on the great subject that now engages your attention. To you it belongs, and may Heaven direct your judgment, to decide on the happiness of all future generations as well as the present.

It is universally agreed that the object of every just government is to render the people happy, by securing their persons and possessions from wrong. To this end, it is necessary that there should be local laws and institutions; for a people inhabiting various climates will unavoidably have local habits and different modes of life, and these must be consulted in making the laws. It is much easier to adapt the laws to the manners of the people than to make manners conform to laws. The idle and dissolute inhabitants of the south require a different regimen from the sober and active people of the north. Hence, among other reasons, is derived the necessity of local governments, who may enact, repeal, or alter regulations as the circumstances of each part of the empire may require. This would be the case even if a very great state was to be settled at once. But it becomes still more needful, when the local manners are formed, and usages sanctified by the practice of a century and a half. In such a case, to attempt to reduce all to one standard is absurd in itself, and cannot be done but upon the principle of power, which debases the people and renders them unhappy, till all dignity of character is put away. Many circumstances render us an essentially different people from the inhabitants of the southern states. The unequal distribution of property, the toleration of slavery, the ignorance and poverty of the lower classes, the softness of the climate, and dissoluteness of manners, mark their character. Among us, the care that is taken of education, small and nearly equal estates, equality of rights, and the severity of the climate, renders the people active, industrious and sober. Attention to religion and good morals is a distinguishing trait in our character. It is plain, therefore, that we require for our regulation laws which will not suit the circumstances of our southern brethren, and the laws made for them would not apply to us. Unhappiness would be the uniform product of such laws; for no state can be happy when the laws contradict the general habits of the people, nor can any state retain its freedom while there is a power to make and enforce such laws. We may go further, and say, that it is impossible for any single legislature so fully to comprehend the circumstances of the different parts of a very extensive dominion as to make laws adapted to those circumstances. Hence arises in most nations of extensive territory, the necessity of armies to cure the defect of the laws. It is actually under the pressure of such an absurd government that the Spanish provinces have groaned for near three centuries; and such will be our misfortune and degradation, if we ever submit to have all the business of the empire done by one legislature. The contrary principle of local legislation by the representatives of the people, who alone are to be governed by the laws, has raised us to our present greatness; and an attempt on the part of Great Britain to invade this right brought on the revolution, which gave us a separate rank among the nations. We even declared that we would not be represented in the national legislature because one assembly was not adequate to the purposes of internal legislation and taxation.

The question then arises, what is the kind of government best adapted to the object of securing our persons and possessions from violence? I answer, a FEDERAL REPUBLIC. By this kind of government each state reserves to itself the right of making and altering its laws for internal regulation, and the right of executing those laws without any external restraint, while the general concerns of the empire are committed to an assembly of delegates, each accountable to his own constitutents. This is the happy form under which we live, and which seems to mark us out as a people chosen of God. No instance can be produced of any other kind of government so stable and energetic as the republican. The objection drawn from the Greek and Roman states does not apply to the question. Republicanism appears there in its most disadvantageous form. Arts and domestic employments were generally committed to slaves, while war was almost the only business worthy of a citizen. Hence arose their internal dissensions. Still they exhibited proofs of legislative wisdom and judicial integrity hardly to be found among their monarchic neighbors. On the other hand, we find Carthage cultivating commerce and extending her dominions for the long space of seven centuries, during which term the internal tranquility was never disturbed by her citizens. Her national power was so respectable, that for a long time it was doubtful whether Carthage or Rome should rule. In the form of their government they bore a strong resemblance to each other. Rome might be reckoned a free state for about four hundred and fifty years. We have then the true line of distinction between those two nations and a strong proof of the hardy materials which compose a republican government. If there were no other proofs we might with impartial judges risk the issue upon this alone. But our proof rests not here. The present state of Europe, and the vigor and tranquility of our own governments after experiencing this form for a century and a half, are decided proofs in favor of those governments which encourage commerce. A comparison of our own country, first with Europe and then with the other parts of the world, will prove, beyond a doubt, that the greatest share of freedom is enjoyed by the citizens, so much more does commerce flourish. The reason is that every citizen has an influence in making the laws, and thus they are conformed to the general interests of the state. But in every other kind of government they are frequently made in favor of a part of the community at the expense of the rest.

The argument against republics, as it is derived from the Greek and Roman states, is unfair. It goes on the idea that no other government is subject to be disturbed. As well might we conclude that a limited monarchy is unstable because that under the feudal system, the nobles frequently made war upon their king, and disturbed the public peace. We find, however, in practice that limited monarchy is more friendly to commerce, because more friendly to the rights of the subject than an absolute government; and that it is more liable to be disturbed than a republic, because less friendly to trade and the rights of individuals. There cannot, from the history of mankind, be produced an instance of rapid growth in extent, in numbers, in arts, and in trade, that will bear any comparison with our country. This is owing to what the friends of the new system, and the enemies of the revolution, for I take them to be nearly the same, would term *our extreme liberty*. Already, have our ships visited every part of the world, and brought us their commodities in greater perfection, and at a more moderate price than we ever before experienced. The ships of other nations crowd to our ports, seeking an intercourse with us. All the estimates of every party make the balance of trade for the present year to be largely in our favor. Already have some very useful, and some elegant manufactures got established among us, so that our country every day is becoming independent in her resources. Two thirds of the continental debt has been paid since the war, and we are in alliance with some of the most respectable powers of Europe. The western lands, won from Britain by the sword, are an ample fund for the principal of all our public debts; and every new sale excites that manly pride which is essential to national virtue. All this happiness arises from the freedom of our institutions and the limited nature of our government; a government that is respected from principles of affection, and obeyed with alacrity. The sovereigns of the old world are frequently, though surrounded with armies, treated with insult; and the despotic monarchies of the east, are the most fluctuating, oppressive, and uncertain governments of any form hitherto invented. These considerations are sufficient to establish the excellence of our own form, and the goodness of our prospects.

By section eight of article one, Congress is to have the unlimited right to regulate commerce, external and *internal*, and may therefore create monopolies which have been universally injurious to all the subjects of the countries that have adopted them, excepting the monopolists themselves. They have also the unlimited right to imposts and all kinds of taxes as well to levy as to collect them. They have indeed very nearly the same powers claimed formerly by the British parliament. Can we have so soon forgot our glorious struggle with that power, as to think a moment of surrendering it now? It makes no difference in principle whether the national assembly was elected for seven years or for six. In both cases we should vote to great disadvantage, and therefore ought never to agree to such an article. Let us make provision for the payment of the interest of our part of the debt, and we shall be fairly acquitted. Let the fund be an impost on our foreign trade, and we shall encourage our manufactures. But if we surrender the unlimited right to regulate trade and levy taxes, imposts will oppress our foreign trade for the benefit of other states, while excises and taxes will discourage our internal industry. The right to regulate trade, without any limitations, will, as certainly as it is granted, transfer the trade of this state to Pennsylvania. That will be the seat of business and of wealth, while the extremes of the empire will, like Ireland and Scotland, be drained to fatten an overgrown capital. Under our present equal advantages, the citizens of this state come in for their full share of commercial profits. Surrender the rights of taxation and commercial regulation, and the landed states at the southward will all be interested in draining our resources. For whatever can be got by impost on our trade and excises on our manufactures will be considered as so much saved to a state inhabited by planters. All savings of this sort ought surely to be made in favor of our own state; and we ought never to surrender the unlimited powers of revenue and trade to uncommercial people. If we do, the glory of the state from that moment departs, never to return.

The safety of our constitutional rights consists in having the business of government lodged in different departments, and in having each part well defined. By this means each branch is kept within the constitutional limits. Never was a fairer line of distinction than what may be easily drawn between the continental and state governments. The latter provide for all cases, whether civil or criminal, that can happen ashore, because all such cases must arise within the limits of some state. Transactions between citizens may all be fairly included in this idea, even though they should arise in passing by water from one state to another. But the intercourse between us and foreign nations properly forms the department of Congress. They should have the power of regulating trade under such limitations as should render their laws equal. They should have the right of war and peace, saving the equality of rights, and the territory of each state. But the power of naturalization and internal regulation should not be given them. To give my scheme a more systematic appearance, I have thrown it into the form of a resolve, which is submitted to your wisdom for amendment, but not as being perfect.

"Resolved, that the form of government proposed by the federal convention, lately held in Philadelphia, be rejected on the part of this commonwealth; and that our delegates in Congress are hereby authorized to propose on the part of this commonwealth, and, if the other states for themselves agree thereto, to sign an article of confederation, as an addition to the present articles, in the form following, provided such agreement be made on or before the first day of January, which will be in the year of our Lord 1790; the said article shall have the same force and effect as if it had been inserted in the original confederation, and is to be construed consistently with the clause in the former articles, which restrains the United States from exercising such powers as are not expressly given.

XIV. The United States shall have power to regulate, whether by treaty, ordinance, or law, the intercourse between these states and foreign dominions and countries, under the following restrictions. No treaty, ordinance, or law shall give a preference to the ports of one state over those of another; nor second, impair the territory or internal authority of any state; nor third, create any monopolies or exclusive companies; nor fourth, naturalize any foreigners. All their imposts and prohibitions shall be confined to foreign produce and manufactures imported, and to foreign ships trading in our harbor. All imposts and confiscations shall be to the use of the state where they shall accrue, excepting only such branches of impost, as shall be assigned by the separate states to Congress for a fund to defray the interest of their debt, and their current charges. In order the more effectually to execute this and the former articles, Congress shall have authority to appoint courts, supreme and subordinate, with power to try all crimes, not relating to state securities, between any foreign state, or subject of such state, actually residing in a foreign country, and not being an absentee or person who has alienated himself from these states on the one part, and any of the United States or citizens thereof on the other part; also all causes in which foreign ambassadors or other foreign ministers resident here shall be immediately concerned, respecting the jurisdiction or immunities only. And the Congress shall have authority to execute the judgment of such courts by their own affairs. Piracies and felonies committed on the high seas shall also belong to the department of Congress for them to define, try, and punish, in the same manner as the other causes shall be defined, tried, and determined. All the before mentioned causes shall be tried by jury and in some seaport town. And it is recommended to the general court at their next meeting to provide and put Congress in possession of funds arising from foreign imports and ships sufficient to defray our share of the present annual expenses of the continent."

To tell us that we ought to look beyond local interests, and judge for the good of the empire, is sapping the foundation of a free state. The first principle of a just government is that it shall operate equally. The report of the convention is extremely unequal. It takes a larger share of power from some, and from others, a larger share of wealth. Massachusetts will be obliged to pay nearly three times their present proportion towards continental charges. The proportion is now ascertained by the quantity of landed property, then it will be by the number of persons. After taking the whole of our standing revenue, by impost and excise, we must still be held to pay a sixth part of the remaining debt. It is evidently a contrivance to help the other states at our expense. Let us then be upon our guard, and do no more than the present confederation obliges. While we make that our beacon we are safe. It was framed by men of extensive knowledge and enlarged ability, at a time when some of the framers of the new plan were hiding in the forests to secure their precious persons. It was framed by men who were always in favor of a limited government, and whose endeavors Heaven has crowned with success. It was framed by men whose idols were not power and high life, but industry and constitutional liberty, and who are now in opposition to this new scheme of oppression. Let us then cherish the old confederation like the apple of our eye. Let us confirm it by such limited powers to Congress, and such an enlarged intercourse, founded on commerce and mutual want with the other states, that our union shall outlast time itself. It is easier to prevent an evil than to cure it. We ought therefore to be cautious of innovations. The intrigues of interested politicians will be used to seduce even the elect. If the vote passes in favor of the plan, the constitutional liberty of our country is gone forever. If the plan should be rejected, we always have it in our power by a fair vote of the people at large, to extend the authority of Congress. This ought to have been the mode pursued. But our antagonists were afraid to risk it. They knew that the plan would not bear examining. Hence we have seen them insulting all who were in opposition to it, and answering arguments only with abuse. They have threatened and they have insulted the body of the people. But I may venture to appeal to any man of unbiased judgment, whether his feelings tell him that there is any danger at all in rejecting the plan. I ask not the palsied or the jaundiced, nor men troubled with bilious or nervous affections, for they can see danger in everything.

But I apply to men who have no personal expectations from a change, and to men in full health. The answer of all such men will be that never was a better time for deliberation. Let us then, while we have it in our power, secure the happiness and freedom of the present and future ages. To accept the report of the convention, under the idea that we can alter it when we please, will be sporting with firebrands, arrows, and death. It is a system which must have an army to support it, and there can be no redress but by a civil war. If, as the federalists say, there is a necessity of our receiving it, for heaven's sake let our liberties go without our making a formal surrender. Let us at least have the satisfaction of protesting against it, that our own hearts may not reproach us for the meanness of deserting our dearest interests.

Our present system is attended with the inestimable advantage of preventing unnecessary wars. Foreign influence is assuredly smaller in our public councils, in proportion as the members are subject to be recalled. At present, their right to sit continues no longer than their endeavor to secure the public interest. It is therefore not an object for any foreign power to give a large price for the friendship of a delegate in Congress. If we adopt the new system, every member will depend upon thirty thousand people, mostly scattered over a large extent of country, for his election. Their distance from the seat of government will make it extremely difficult for the electors to get information of his conduct. If he is faithful to his constituents, his conduct will be misrepresented in order to defeat his influence at home. Of this we have a recent instance, in the treatment of the dissenting members of the late federal convention. Their fidelity to their constituents was their whole fault. We may reasonably expect similar conduct to be adopted, when we shall have rendered the friendship of the members valuable to foreign powers, by giving them a secure seat in Congress. We shall too have all the intrigues, cabals, and bribery practised, which are usual at elections in Great Britain. We shall see and lament the want of public virtue; and we shall see ourselves bought at a public market, in order to be sold again to the highest bidder. We must be involved in all the quarrels of European powers, and oppressed with expense, merely for the sake of being like the nations round about us. Let us then, with the spirit of freemen, reject the offered system, and treat as it deserves the proposition of men who have departed from their commission; and let us deliver to the rising generation the liberty purchased with our blood.

That the new system proposed for your adoption is not founded in argument, but in party spirit, is evident from the whole behavior of that party who favor it. The following is a short, but genuine specimen of their reasoning. The South Carolina legislature has established an unequal representation and will not alter it. Therefore, Congress should be invested with an unrestrained power to alter the time, manner and place of electing members into that body. Directly the contrary position should have been inferred. An elected assembly made an improper use of their right to control elections. Therefore such a right ought not to be lodged with them. It will be abused in ten instances for one in which it will serve any valuable purpose. It is said also that the Rhode Island assembly *intend* to abuse their power in this respect. Therefore we should put Congress in a situation to abuse theirs. Surely this is not a kind of reasoning that, in the opinion of any indifferent person, can vindicate the fourth section. Yet we have heard it publicly advanced as being conclusive.

The unlimited power over trade, domestic as well as foreign, is another power that will more probably be applied to a bad than to a good purpose. That our trade was for the last year much in favor of the commonwealth is agreed by all parties. The freedom that every man, whether his capital is large or small, enjoys, of entering into any branch that pleases him, rouses a spirit of industry and exertion that is friendly to commerce. It prevents that stagnation of business which generally precedes public commotions. Nothing ought to be done to restrain this spirit. The unlimited power over trade, however, is exceedingly apt to injure it.

In most countries of Europe, trade has been confined by exclusive charters. Exclusive companies are, in trade, pretty much like an aristocracy in government, and produce nearly as bad effects. An instance of it we have ourselves experienced. Before the revolution, we carried on no direct trade to India. The goods imported from that country came to us through the medium of an exclusive company. Our trade in that quarter is now respectable, and we receive several kinds of their goods at about half the former price. But the evil of such companies does not terminate there. They always, by the greatness of their capital, have an undue influence on the government.

In a republic, we ought to guard, as much as possible, against the predominance of any particular interest. It is the object of government to protect them all. When commerce is left to take its own course, the advantages of every class will be nearly equal. But when exclusive privileges are given to any class, it will operate to the weakening of some other class connected with them.

This appears to be the universal effect of such establishments. A point of such magnitude ought, then, to be particularly guarded. In some respects it is beneficial that a system of commerce should be established by national authority. But if it is found, as it will upon examination, that most governments establish those companies, from occasional and temporal motives, and that they produce ill effects on government and on trade, the power ought in this respect to be restrained. As we are situated at one extreme of the empire, two or three such companies would annihilate the importance of our seaports by transferring the trade to Philadelphia. With the decay of trade is connected the depreciation of lands and estates for want of a market for the produce. At present our exports are great and our manufactures are every day rising in importance. It seems to be agreed on all sides, that from the port of Boston only the balance was last year as much as a hundred and fifty thousand pounds in favor of the state; a comparison of that and former years is far from proving the distressed state of commerce. Complaints in that respect are about as well founded as in most others. They are made to serve a present purpose and when that is accomplished, there is no redress for the disappointment of the public expectation. It becomes us then to consider well of the powers before we surrender them. There is no recovering them when once given. It is vain to flatter ourselves with the idea that three quarters of the members of the new government will ever be for restraining their own power. If it was so easy as the federalists pretend to procure an alteration of the system after its adoption, I think that it is a circumstance not much in its favor. In order to be perfect a constitution should be permanent. The new system sets out with a violation of the compact between the states. While it is in discussion, we ought to consider, that injustice never can be the basis of a good government. I have met with an account of one government uniformly supported by that principle, and I do not wish even my antagonists to become the subjects of that kingdom.

In answer to the favorite remark of the federalists, that what is not given is reserved, it is sufficient to reply, that the framers of the proposed constitution have themselves thought it necessary to make an explicit reservation of the power to grant titles of nobility. Why did they reserve this point, if it would not otherwise have been given up? The conversation of the party is in direct opposition to any design ever to alter the system in favor of the liberties of the people. It is said that a constitution is itself a bill of rights. The fallacy of this position is easily shown, but the length of this paper makes it necessary to postpone that part of the argument. At present we shall only observe that a constitution does not necessarily point out any other dependencies than of the parts of the government upon each other, and not those between the government and people. Has Venice no constitution? Yet the people have no share in the government.

Centinel
Letters III, IV, VII, and VIII
(Philadelphia) Independent Gazette
8 and 30 November, 27 and 29 December, 1787

To the People of Pennsylvania:

> *"For every one that doeth evil, hateth the light, neither cometh to the light, lest his deeds should be reproved." John 3:20. But "there is nothing covered that shall not be revealed; neither hid that shall not be known. Therefore whatsoever ye have spoken in darkness, shall be heard in the light: and that which ye have spoken in the ear in closets, shall be proclaimed on the house tops." Luke 12:2–3.*

Friends, Countrymen, and Fellow-Citizens!

The formation of a good government is the greatest effort of human wisdom, actuated by disinterested patriotism. But such is the cursed nature of ambition, so prevalent in the minds of men, that it would sacrifice every thing to its selfish gratification. Hence the fairest opportunities of advancing the happiness of humanity are so far from being properly improved, that they are too often converted by the votaries of power and domination into the means of obtaining their nefarious ends. It will be the misfortune of America of adding to the examples of this kind, if the proposed plan of government should be adopted. But I trust, short as the time allowed you for consideration is, you will be so fully convinced of the truth of this, as to escape the impending danger. It is only necessary to strip the monster of its assumed garb, and to exhibit it in its native colors, to excite the universal abhorrence and rejection of every virtuous and patriotic mind.

For the sake of my dear country, for the honor of human nature, I hope and am persuaded, that the good sense of the people will enable them to rise superior to the most formidable conspiracy against the liberties of a free and enlightened nation that the world has ever witnessed. How glorious would be the triumph! How it would immortalize the present generation in the annals of freedom!

The establishment of a government is a subject of such momentous and lasting concern, that it should not be gone into without the clearest conviction of its propriety, which can only be the result of the fullest discussion, the most thorough investigation, and dispassionate consideration of its nature, principles, and construction. You are now called upon to make this decision, which involves in it not only your fate, but that of your posterity for ages to come. Your determination will either ensure the possession of those blessings which render life desirable, or entail those evils which make existence a curse. That such are the consequences of a wise or improper organization of government, the history of mankind abundantly testifies. If you viewed the magnitude of the object in its true light, you would join with me in sentiment that the new government ought not to be implicitly admitted. Consider then duly before you leap, for after the Rubicon is once passed, there will be no retreat.

If you were even well assured that the utmost purity of intention predominated in the production of the proposed government, such is the imperfection of human reason and knowledge, that it would not be wise in you to adopt it with precipitation *in toto*. For all former experience must teach you the propriety of a revision on such occasions, to correct the errors and supply the deficiencies that may appear necessary. In every government whose object is the public welfare, the laws are subjected to repeated revisions, in some by different orders in the governments, in others by an appeal to the judgments of the people and deliberative forms of procedure. A knowledge of this, as well as of other states, will show that in every instance where a law has been passed without the usual precautions, it has been productive of great inconvenience and evils, and frequently has not answered the end in view, a supplement becoming necessary to supply its deficiencies.

What then are we to think of the motives and designs of those men who are urging the implicit and immediate adoption of the proposed government? Are they fearful that if you exercise your good sense and discernment, you will discover the masked aristocracy that they are attempting to smuggle upon you under the suspicious garb of republicanism? When we find that the principal agents in this business are the very men who fabricated the form of government, it certainly ought to be conclusive evidence of their insidious design to deprive us of our liberties. The circumstances attending this matter are such as should in a peculiar manner excite your suspicion; it might not be useless to take a review of some of them.

In many of the states, particularly in this and the northern states, there are aristocratic juntos of the *well born few,* who had been zealously endeavoring since the establishment of their constitutions to humble that offensive *upstart, equal liberty.* But all their efforts were unavailing, the *ill bred churl* obstinately kept his assumed station.

However, that which could not be accomplished in the several states is now attempting through the medium of the future Congress. Experience having shown great defects in the present confederation, particularly in the regulation of commerce and maritime affairs, it became the universal wish of America to grant further powers, so as to make the federal government adequate to the ends of its institution. The anxiety on this head was greatly increased from the impoverishment and distress occasioned by the excessive importations of foreign merchandise and luxuries, and consequent drain of specie, since the peace. Thus the people were in the disposition of a drowning man, eager to catch at any thing that promised relief, however delusory. Such an opportunity for the acquisition of *undue* power has never been viewed with indifference by the ambitious and designing in any age or nation, and it has accordingly been too successfully improved by such men among us. The deputies from this state (with the exception of two), and most of those from the other states in the union, were unfortunately of this complexion, and many of them of such superior endowments that in an *exparte* discussion of the subject by specious glosses, they have gained the concurrence of some well disposed men, in whom their country have great confidence, which has given a great sanction to their scheme of power.

A comparison of the authority under which the convention acted and their form of government will show that they have despised their delegated power, and assumed sovereignty; that they have entirely annihilated the old confederation, and the particular governments of the several states, and instead thereof have established one general government that is to pervade the union, constituted on the most *unequal* principles, destitute of accountability to its constituents, and as despotic in its nature as the Venetian aristocracy; a government that will give full scope to the magnificent designs of the *well born;* a government where tyranny may glut its vengeance on the *low born,* unchecked by *an odious bill of rights* (as has been fully illustrated in my two preceding numbers); and yet as a blind upon the understandings of the people, they have continued the forms of the particular governments, and termed the whole a confederation of the United States, pursuant to the sentiments of that profound, but corrupt politician Machiavelli, who advises anyone who would change the constitution of a state to keep as much as possible to the old forms; for then the people seeing the same officers, the same formalities, courts of justice, and other outward appearances are insensible of the alteration, and believe themselves in possession of their old government. Thus Caesar, when he seized the Roman liberties, caused himself to be chosen dictator (which was an ancient office), continued the senate, the consuls, the tribunes, the censors, and all other offices and forms of the commonwealth, and yet changed Rome from the most free to the most tyrannical government in the world.

The convention, after vesting all the great and efficient powers of sovereignty in the general government, insidiously declare by section four of article four, "that the United States shall guarantee to every state in this union, a republican *form* of government." But of what avail will be the *form* without the *reality* of freedom?

The late convention in the majesty of its assumed omnipotence have not even condescended to submit the plan of the new government to the consideration of the people, the true source of authority, but have called upon them by their several conventions, 'to assent to and ratify' in toto, what they have been pleased to decree; just as the grand monarch of France requires the parliament of Paris to register his edicts without revision or alteration, which is necessary previous to their execution.

The authors and advocates of the new plan, conscious that its establishment can only be obtained from the ignorance of the people of its true nature, and their unbounded confidence in some of the men concurring, have hurried on its adoption with a precipitation that betrays their design. Before many had seen the new plan, and before any had time to examine it, they, by their ready minions, attended by some well disposed but mistaken persons, obtained the subscriptions of the people to papers expressing their entire approbation of it and their wish to have it established, thus precluding them from any consideration. But lest the people should discover the juggle, the elections of the state conventions are urged on at very early days. The proposition of electing the convention for this state in nine days after the date of the resolution for all the counties east of Bedford, and supported by three or four of the deputies of the convention, and who were also members of the then assembly, is one of the most extravagant instances of this kind. And even this was only prevented by the secession of nineteen virtuous and enlightened members. In order to put the matter beyond all recall, they have proceeded a step further. They have made the deputies nominated for the state convention of this city and elsewhere, pledge their sacred honor, previous to their election, that they would implicitly adopt the proposed government in toto; thus short as the period is before the final fiat is to be given, consideration is rendered nugatory, and conviction of its dangers or impropriety unavailable. A good cause does not stand in need of such means; it scorns all indirect advantages and borrowed helps, and trusts alone to its own native merit and intrinsic strength. The lion is never known to make use of cunning, nor can a good cause suffer by a free and thorough examination. It is knavery that seeks disguise. Actors do not care that any one should look into the tiring room, nor jugglers or sharpers into their hands or boxes.

Every exertion has been made to suppress discussion by shackling the press. But as this could not be effected in *this* state, the people are warned not to listen to the adversaries of the proposed plan, lest they should impose upon them, and thereby prevent the adoption of this blessed government. What figure would a lawyer make in a court of justice if he should desire the judges not to hear the counsel of the other side, lest they should perplex the cause and mislead the court? Would not every bystander take it for granted that he was conscious of the weakness of his client's cause, and that it could not otherwise be defended than by not being understood?

All who are friends to liberty are friends to reason, the champion of liberty, and none are foes to liberty but those who have truth and reason for their foes. He who has dark purposes to serve must use dark means; light would discover him, and reason expose him. He must endeavor to shut out both, and make them look frightful by giving them ill names.

Liberty only flourishes where reason and knowledge are encouraged; and wherever the latter are stifled, the former is extinguished. In Turkey printing is forbid, inquiry is dangerous, and free speaking is capital because they are all inconsistent with the nature of the government. Hence it is, that the Turks are all stupidly ignorant, and are all slaves. . .

It is a maxim that a government ought to be cautious not to govern over much, for when the cord of power is drawn too tight, it generally proves its destruction. The impracticability of complying with the requisitions of Congress has lessened the sense of obligation and duty in the people, and thus weakened the ties of the union. The opinion of power in a free government is much more efficacious than the exercise of it; it requires the maturity of time and repeated practice to give due energy and certainty to the operations of government, especially to such as affect the purses of the people.

The thirteen Swiss cantons, confederated by more general and weaker ties than these United States are by the present Articles of Confederation, have not experienced the necessity of strengthening their union by vesting their general diet with further or greater powers. This national body has only the management of their foreign concerns and in case of a war can only call by requisition on the several cantons for the necessary supplies, who are sovereign and independent in every internal and local exercise of government. And yet this rope of sand, as our confederation has been termed, which is so similar to that, has held together for ages without any apparent charm.

I am persuaded that a due consideration will evince that the present inefficacy of the requisitions of Congress is not owing to a defect in the confederation, but the peculiar circumstances of the times.

The wheels of the general government having been thus clogged and the arrearages of taxes still accumulating, it may be asked what prospect is there of the government resuming its proper tone, unless more compulsory powers are granted? To this it may be answered, that the produce of imposts on commerce which all agree to vest in Congress, together with the immense tracts of land at their disposal, will rapidly lessen and eventually discharge the present encumbrances. When this takes place, the mode by requisition will be found perfectly adequate to the extraordinary exigencies of the union. Congress has lately sold land to the amount of eight millions of dollars, which is a considerable portion of the whole debt.

It is to be lamented that the interested and designing have availed themselves so successfully of the present crisis, and under the specious pretence of having discovered a panacea for all the ills of the people, they are about establishing a system of government that will prove more destructive to them than the wooden horse filled with soldiers did in ancient times to the city of Troy. This horse was introduced by their hostile enemy the Grecians, by a prostitution of the sacred rites of their religion. In like manner, my fellow citizens are aspiring despots among yourselves prostituting the name of a Washington to cloak their designs upon your liberties.

I would ask how is the proposed government to shower down those treasures upon every class of citizens as is so industriously inculcated and so fondly believed? Is it by the addition of numerous and expensive establishments? Is it by doubling our judiciaries, instituting federal courts in every county of every state? Is it by a superb presidental court? Is it by a large standing army? In short, is it by putting it in the power of the future government to levy money at pleasure, and placing this government so independent of the people as to enable the administration to gratify every corrupt passion of the mind, to riot on your spoils, without check or control?

A transfer to Congress of the power of imposing imposts on commerce and the unlimited regulation of trade, I believe, is all that is wanting to render America as prosperous as it is in the power of any form of government to render her. This properly understood would meet the views of all the honest and well meaning.

What gave birth to the late continental convention? Was it not the situation of our commerce which lay at the mercy of every foreign power who from motives of interèst or enmity could restrict and control it, without risking a retaliation on the part of America, as Congress was impotent on this subject? Such indeed was the case with respect to Britain whose hostile regulations gave such a stab to our navigation as to threaten its annihilation. It became the interest of even the American merchant to give a preference to foreign bottoms; hence the distress of our seamen, shipwrights, and every mechanic art dependent on navigation.

By these regulations too we were limited in markets for our produce, our vessels were excluded from their West India Islands, and many of our staple commodities were denied entrance in Britain. Hence the husbandmen were distressed by the demand for their crops being lessened and their prices reduced. This is the source to which may be traced every evil we experience that can be relieved by a more energetic government. Recollect the language of complaint for years past, compare the recommendations of Congress founded on such complaints, pointing out the remedy, examine the reasons assigned by the different states for appointing delegates to the late convention, view the powers vested in that body. They all harmonize in one sentiment, that the due regulation of trade and navigation was the anxious wish of every class of citizens, was the great object of calling the convention.

This object being provided for, by the proposed Constitution, the people overlook and are not sensible of the needless sacrifice they are making for it. Of what avail will be a prosperous state of commerce, when the produce of it will be at the absolute disposal of an arbitrary and unchecked government, who may levy at pleasure the most oppressive taxes, who may destroy every principle of freedom, who may even destroy the privilege of complaining.

If you are in doubt about the nature and principles of the proposed government, view the conduct of its authors and patrons. That affords the best explanation, the most striking comment.

The evil genius of darkness presided at its birth, it came forth under the veil of mystery, its true features being carefully concealed, and every deceptive art has been and is practicing to have this spurious brat received as the genuine offspring of heaven-born liberty. So fearful are its patrons that you should discern the imposition that they have hurried on its adoption with the greatest precipitation. They have endeavored also to preclude all investigation. They have endeavored to intimidate all opposition. By such means as these have they surreptitiously procured a convention in this state favorable to their views. And here again investigation and discussion are abridged, the final question is moved before the subject has been under consideration; an appeal to the people is precluded even in the last resort, lest their eyes should be opened; the convention has denied the minority the privilege of entering the reasons of their dissent on its journals. Thus despotism is already triumphant, and the genius of liberty is on the eve of her exit, is about bidding an eternal adieu to this once happy people.

After so recent a triumph over British despots, after such torrents of blood and treasure have been spent, after involving ourselves in the distresses of an arduous war and incurring such a debt for the express purpose of asserting the rights of humanity, it is truly astonishing that a set of men among ourselves should have the effrontery to attempt the destruction of our liberties. But in this enlightened age to hope to dupe the people by the arts they are practicing is still more extraordinary. . .

The admiring world lately beheld the sun of liberty risen to meridian splendor in this western hemisphere, whose cheering rays began to dispel the glooms of even trans atlantic despotism. The patriotic mind, enraptured with the glowing scene, fondly anticipated a universal and eternal day to the orb of freedom; but the horizon is already darkened and the glooms of slavery threaten to fix their empire. How transitory are the blessings of this life! Scarcely have four years elapsed since these United States, rescued from the domination of foreign despots by the unexampled heroism and perseverance of its citizens, at such great expense of blood and treasure, when they are about to fall a prey to the machinations of a profligate junto at home, who seizing the favorable moment, when the temporary and extraordinary difficulties of the people have thrown them off their guard, and lulled that jealousy of power so essential to the preservation of freedom, have been too successful in the sacrilegious attempt. However I am confident that this formidable conspiracy will end in the confusion and infamy of its authors; that if necessary, the avenging sword of an abused people will humble these aspiring despots to the dust, and that their fate, like that of Charles the First of England, will deter such attempts in future and prove the confirmation of the liberties of America until time shall be no more.

One would imagine by the insolent conduct of these harpies of power that they had already triumphed over the liberties of the people, that the chains were riveted and tyranny established. They tell us all further opposition will be vain as this state has passed the rubicon. Do they imagine the freemen of Pennsylvania will be thus trepanned out of their liberties; that they will submit without a struggle? They must indeed be inebriated with the lust of dominion to indulge such chimerical ideas. Will the act of one sixth of the people, and this too founded on deception and surprise, bind the community? Is it thus that the altar of liberty, so recently crimsoned with the blood of our worthies, is to be prostrated and despotism reared on its ruins? Certainly not. The solemn mummery that has been acting in the name of the people of Pennsylvania will be treated with the deserved contempt; it has served indeed to expose the principles of the men concerned, and to draw a line of discrimination between the real and affected patriots.

Impressed with a high opinion of the understanding and spirit of my fellow citizens, I have in no stage of this business entertained a doubt of its eventual defeat. The momentary delusion, arising from an unreserved confidence placed in some of the characters whose names sanctioned this scheme of power did not discourage me. I foresaw that this blind admiration would soon be succeeded by rational investigation which, stripping the monster of its gilded covering, would discover its native deformity.

Already the enlightened pen of patriotism, aided by an able public discussion, has dispelled the mist of deception, and the great body of the people are awakened to a due sense of their danger and are determined to assert their liberty, if necessary by the sword; but this means need not be recurred to, for who are their enemies? A junto composed of the lordly and high minded gentry, of the profligate and the needy officehunters, of men principally who in the late war skulked from the common danger. Would such characters dare to face the majesty of a free people? No. All the conflict would be between the offended justice and generosity of the people, whether these sacrilegious invaders of their dearest rights should suffer the merited punishment, or escape with an infamous contempt.

However, as additional powers are necessary to Congress, the people will no doubt see the expediency of calling a convention for this purpose as soon as may be by applying to their representatives in assembly, at their next session, to appoint a suitable day for the election of such Convention.

* * *

Under the benign influence of liberty, this country, so recently a rugged wilderness and the abode of savages and wild beasts, has attained to a degree of improvement and greatness, in less than two ages, of which history furnishes no parallel. It is here that human nature may be viewed in all its glory; man assumes the station designed him by the creation; a happy equality and independency pervades the community; it is here the human mind, untrammeled by the restraints of arbitrary power, expands every faculty. As the field to fame and riches is open to all, it stimulates universal exertion and exhibits a lively picture of emulation, industry and happiness. The unfortunate and oppressed of all nations fly to this grand asylum where liberty is ever protected, and industry crowned with success.

But as it is by comparison only that men estimate the value of any good, they are not sensible of the worth of those blessings they enjoy, until they are deprived of them. Hence from ignorance of the horrors of slavery, nations that have been in possession of that rarest of blessings, liberty, have so easily parted with it. When groaning under the yoke of tyranny what perils would they not encounter, what consideration would they not give, to regain the inestimable jewel they had lost. But the jealously of despotism guards every avenue to freedom, and confirms its empire at the expense of the devoted people, whose property is made instrumental to their misery, for the rapacious hand of power seizes upon everything. Despair presently succeeds, and every noble faculty of the mind being depressed, and all motive to industry and exertion being removed, the people are adapted to the nature of the government and drag out a listless existence.

If ever America should be enslaved it will be from this cause, that they are not sensible of their peculiar felicity, that they are not aware of the value of the heavenly boon, committed to their care and protection, and if the present conspiracy fails, as I have no doubt will be the case, it will be the triumph of reason and philosophy, as these United States have never felt the iron hand of power, or experienced the wretchedness of slavery.

The conspirators against our liberties have presumed too much on the maxim that nations do not take the alarm, until they feel oppression. The enlightened citizens of America have on two memorable occasions convinced the tyrants of Europe that they are endued with the faculty of foresight, that they will jealously guard against the first introduction of tyranny, however speciously glossed over, or whatever appearance it may assume. It was not the mere amount of *the duty on stamps* or *tea* that America opposed. They were considered as signals of approaching despotism, as precedents whereon the superstructure of arbitrary sway was to be reared.

Notwithstanding such illustrious evidence of the good sense and spirit of the people of these United States, and contrary to all former experience of mankind, which demonstrates that it is only by gradual and imperceptible degrees that nations have hitherto been enslaved, except in case of conquest by the sword, the authors of the present conspiracy are attempting to seize upon absolute power at one grasp, impatient of dominion they have adopted a decisive line of conduct, which if successful, would obliterate every trace of liberty. I congratulate my fellow citizens that the infatuated confidence of their enemies has so blinded their ambition, that their defeat must be certain and easy, if imitating the refined policy of successful despots, they had attacked the citadel of liberty by sap, and gradually undermined its outworks, they would have stood a fairer chance of effecting their design. But in this enlightened age thus rashly to attempt to carry the fortress by storm, is folly indeed. They have even exposed some of their batteries prematurely, and thereby unfolded every latent view, for the unlimited power of taxation would alone have been amply sufficient for every purpose. By a proper application of this, the will and pleasure of the rulers would of course have become the supreme law of the land. Therefore there was no use in portraying the ultimate object by superadding the form to reality of supremacy in the following clause, *viz.*, that which empowers the new congress to make all laws that may be necessary and proper for carrying into execution any of their powers, by virtue of which every possible law will be constitutional, as they are to be the sole judges of the propriety of such laws; that which ordains that their acts shall be the supreme law of the land, any thing in the laws or constitution of any state to the contrary notwithstanding; that which gives Congress the absolute control over the time and mode of its appointment and election, whereby, independent of any other means, they may establish hereditary despotism; that which authorizes them to keep on foot at all times a standing army; and that which subjects the militia to absolute command; and to accelerate the subjugation of the people, trial by jury in civil cases and the liberty of the press are abolished.

So flagrant, so audacious a conspiracy against the liberties of a free people is without precedent. Mankind in the darkest ages have never been so insulted. Even then, tyrants found it necessary to pay some respect to the habits and feelings of the people, and nothing but the name of a Washington could have occasioned a moment's hesitation about the nature of the new plan, or saved its authors from the execration and vengeance of the people, which, eventually will prove an aggravation of their treason. For America will resent the imposition practiced upon the unsuspicious zeal of her *illustrious deliverer*, and vindicate her character from the aspersions of these enemies of her happiness and fame.

The advocates of this plan have artfully attempted to veil over the true nature and principles of it with the names of those respectable characters that by consummate cunning and address they have prevailed upon to sign it, and what ought to convince the people of the deception and excite their apprehensions, is that with every advantage which education, the science of government and of law, the knowledge of history and superior talents and endowments, furnish the authors and advocates of this plan with, they have from its publication exerted all their power and influence to prevent all discussion of the subject, and when this could not be prevented they have constantly avoided the ground of argument and recurred to declamation, sophistry, and personal abuse, but principally relied upon the magic of names. Would this have been their conduct, if their cause had been a good one? No. They would have invited investigation and convinced the understandings of the people.

But such policy indicates great ignorance of the good sense and spirit of the people. For if the sanction of every convention throughout the union was obtained by the means these men are practicing, yet their triumph would be momentary, the favorite object would still elude their grasp. For a good government founded on fraud and deception could not be maintained without an army sufficiently powerful to compel submission, which the *well born* of America could not speedily accomplish. However the complexion of several of the more considerable states does not promise even this point of success. The Carolinas, Virginia, Maryland, New York and New Hampshire have by their wisdom in taking a longer time to deliberate, in all probability saved themselves from the disgrace of becoming the dupes of this gilded bait, as experience will evince that it need only be properly examined to be execrated and repulsed.

The merchant, immersed in schemes of wealth, seldom extends his views beyond the immediate object of gain; he blindly pursues his seeming interest and sees not the latent mischief; therefore it is that he is the last to take the alarm when public liberty is threatened. This may account for the infatuation of some of our merchants who, elated with the imaginary prospect of an improved commerce under the new government, overlook all danger. They do not consider that commerce is the handmaid of liberty, a plant of free growth that withers under the hand of despotism, that every concern of individuals will be sacrificed to the gratification of the men in power, who will institute injurious monopolies and shackle commerce with every device of avarice, and that property of every species will be held at the will and pleasure of rulers.

If the nature of the case did not give birth to these well-founded apprehensions, the principles and characters of the authors and advocates of the measure ought. View the monopolizing spirit of the principal of them. See him converting a bank, instituted for common benefit, to his own and creatures' emolument, and by the aid thereof, controlling the credit of the state and dictating the measures of government. View the vassalage of our merchants, the thraldom of the city of Philadelphia, and the extinction of that spirit of independency in most of its citizens so essential to freedom. View this Collosus attempting to grasp the commerce of America and meeting with a sudden repulse, in the midst of his immense career, receiving a shock that threatens his very existence. View the desperate fortunes of many of his co-adjutors and dependents, particularly the bankrupt situation of the principal instrument under the *great man* in promoting the new government, whose superlative arrogance, ambition and rapacity would need the spoils of thousands to gratify. View his towering aspect, he would have no bowels of compassion for the oppressed, he would *overlook* all their sufferings. Recollect the strenuous and unremitted exertions of these men, for years past, to destroy our admirable constitution, whose object is to secure equal liberty and advantages to all, and the great obstacle in the way of their ambitious schemes, and then answer, whether these apprehensions are chimerical, whether such characters will be less ambitious, less avaricious, more moderate, when the privileges, property, and every concern of the people of the United States shall lie at their mercy, when they shall be in possession of absolute sway?

Maryland Farmer
Essays III (part II) and VII
(Baltimore) Maryland Gazette
18 March, 4 April, 1788

America is at present divided into three classes or descriptions of men, and in a few years there will be but two.

The first class comprehends all those men of fortune and reputation who stepped forward in the late revolution, from opposition to the administration, rather than the government of Great Britain: all those aristocrats whose pride disdains equal law; many men of very large fortune, who entertain real or imaginary fears for the security of property; those young men, who have sacrificed their time and their talents to public service, without any prospect of an adequate pecuniary or honorary reward; all your people of fashion and pleasure who are corrupted by the dissipation of the French, English, and American armies, and a love of European manners and luxury; the public creditors of the continent, whose interest has been heretofore sacrificed by their friends, in order to retain their services on this occasion; a large majority of the mercantile people, which is at present a very unformed and consequently dangerous interest; our old native merchants have been almost universally ruined by the receipt of their debts in paper during the war, and the payment in hard money of what they owed their British correspondents since peace; those who are not bankrupts, have generally retired and given place to a set of young men, who conducting themselves as rashly as ignorantly, have embarrassed their affairs and lay the blame on the government, and who are really unacquainted with the true mercantile interest of the country, which is perplexed from circumstances rather temporary than permanent. The foreign merchants are generally not to be trusted with influence in our government. They are most of them birds of passage, some perhaps British emissaries increasing and rejoicing in our political mistakes, and even those who have settled among us with an intention to fix themselves and their posterity in our soil, have brought with them more foreign prejudices than wealth. Time must elapse before the mercantile interest will be so organized as to govern themselves, much less others, with propriety. And lastly, to this class I suppose we may ultimately add the *tory interest* with the exception of very many respectable characters, who reflect with a gratification mixed with disdain that those principles are now become fashionable for which they have been persecuted and hunted down [and] which, although by no means so formidable as is generally imagined, is still considerable. They are at present wavering; they are generally, though with very many exceptions, openly for the proposed but secretly against any American government. *A burnt child dreads the fire.* But should they see any fair prospect of confusion arise, these gentry will be off at any moment for these five and twenty years to come. Ultimately should the administration promise stability to the new government, they may be counted on as the Janizaries of power, ready to efface all suspicion by the violence of their zeal. In general, all these various people would prefer a government as nearly copied after that of Great Britain as our circumstances will permit. Some would strain these circumstances; others still retain a deep rooted jealousy of the executive branch and strong republican prejudices as they are called. Finally, this class contains more aggregate wisdom and moral virtue than both the other two together. It commands nearly two-thirds of the property and almost one half the numbers of America, and has at present become almost irresistible from the name of the truly great and amiable man who, it has been said, is disposed to patronize it and from the influence which it has over the second class. This class is nearly at the height of their power; they must decline or moderate or another revolution will ensue, for the opinion of America is becoming daily more unfavorable to those radical changes which high-toned government requires. A conflict would terminate in the destruction of this class, or the liberties of their country. May the Guardian Angel of America prevent both!

The second class is composed of those descriptions of men who are certainly more numerous with us than in any other part of the globe. *First, those men* who are so wise as to discover that their ancestors and indeed all the rest of mankind were and are fools. We have a vast over proportion of these great men who, when you tell them that from the earliest period at which mankind devoted their attention to social happiness, it has been their uniform judgment that a government over governments cannot exist, *that is two governments* operating on the same individual; they assume the smile of confidence and tell you of two people travelling the same road, of a perfect and precise division of the duties of the individual. Still however, the political apothegm is as old as the proverb: *that no man can serve two masters*, and whoever will run their noddles against old proverbs will be sure to break them, however hard they may be. If they broke only their own, all would be right; but it is very horrible to reflect that all our numskulls must be cracked in concert. *Second,* the *trimmers* who from sympathetic indecision are always united with, and when not regularly employed, always fight under the banners of these great men. These people are forever at market and when parties are nearly equally divided, they get very well paid for their services. *Thirdly,* the *indolent,* that is almost every second man of independent fortune you meet with in America; *these are quite easy and can live under any government.* If men can be said to live who scarcely breathe; and if breathing was attended with any bodily exertion, would give up their small portion of life in despair. These men do not swim with the stream as the trimmers do, but are dragged like mud at the bottom. As they have no other weight than their fat flesh, they are hardly worth mentioning when we speak of the sentiments and opinions of America. As this second class never can include any of the yeomanry of the union, who never affect superior wisdom and can have no interest but the public good, it can be only said to exist at the birth of government, and as soon as the first and third classes become more decided in their views, this will divide with each and dissipate like a mist, or sink down into what are called moderate men, and become the tools and instruments of others. These people are prevented by a cloud from having *any* view; and if they are not virtuous, they at least preserve the appearance which in this world amounts to the same thing.

At the head of the third class appear the old rigid republicans, who although few in number, are still formidable. Reverence will follow these men in spite of detraction, as long as wisdom and virtue are esteemed among mankind. They are joined by the true *democrats*, who are in general fanatics and enthusiasts, and some few sensible, charming madmen. A decided majority of the *yeomanry* of America will, for a length of years, be ready to support these two descriptions of men; but as this last class is forced to act as a residuary legatee, and receive all the trash and filth. It is in some measure disgraced and its influence weakened, by, thirdly, the free-booters and plunderers, who infest all countries and ours perhaps as little as any other whatever; these men have that natural antipathy to any kind or sort of government that a rogue has to a halter. In number they are few indeed; such characters are the offspring of dissipation and want, and there is not that country in the world where so much real property is shared so equally among so few citizens, or where property is as easily acquired by fair means, very few indeed will resort to foul. Lastly, by the poor mob, *infoelix pecus!* [unhappy cattle] They are property of whoever will feed them and take care of them. Let them be spared! Let the burden of taxation sit lightly on their shoulders. But alas! This is not their fate. It is here that government forever falls with all its weight; it is here that the proposed government will press where it should scarcely be felt.

Oves bis mulget in hora, et succus pecori et lac subducitur agnis.

If ever a direct tax is laid by the general government it must, if not from necessity, at least from propriety, be laid on polls. It is the only one I believe to be practicable; there ought then to be some security that they avoid direct taxation where not absolutely indispensable, and some better security than the opinion of *Aristides*.

In this class may be counted men of the greatest mental powers and of as sublime virtue as any in America. They at present command nearly one-third of the property and above half the numbers of the United States, and in either event they must continue to increase in influence by great desertions from both the other classes. If the government is adopted, this class will be increased by the numerous, discontented and disappointed, and from that natural jealousy, which Englishmen and their descendants always will retain of their government and governors. If the government is not adopted, theirs will be the prevalent opinion. The object of this class either is or will be purely federal: a union of independent states, not a government of individuals. And should the proposed federal plan fail from the obstinacy of those who will listen to no *conditional* amendments, although such as they cannot disapprove; or should it ultimately in its execution upon a fair trial disappoint the wishes and expectations of our country then a union purely federal is what the reasonable and dispassionate patriots of America must bend their views to. My countrymen, preserve your jealousy, reject suspicion; it is the fiend that destroys public and private happiness. I know some weak, but very few if any wicked men in public confidence, and *learn* this most difficult and necessary lesson: that on the preservation of parties, public liberty depends. Whenever men are unanimous on great public questions, whenever there is but one party, freedom ceases and despotism commences. The object of a free and wise people should be so to balance parties, that *from the weakness of all you may be governed by the moderation of the combined judgments of the whole, not tyrannized ever by the blind passions of a few individuals.*

To examine and elucidate the great and leading principles of government, we must penetrate to the source of human action, and explore the heart and constitution of man; a consciousness of the equal rights of nature is a component part of that ethereal spirit, which we dignify with the appellation of soul. The ardent desire and unceasing pursuit of equality can therefore be no more destroyed by human power than the soul itself. The chains of terrestrial despotism may confine, afflict, and bow down to the earth this mold of flesh, but the soul more free than air quits this mortal frame, surrounded by ills no longer supportable and, after witnessing the final overthrow of all its hopes in this world, retires with indignation into a world unknown.

Let any people be personally and fairly consulted on the form of that government which is to rule them and their children, and they will establish the *law of equality* as its basis. The unequal division of property silently and gradually undermines this foundation almost as soon as society is formed; or before a new compact is confirmed, this equality is materially injured if not destroyed. Montesquieu justly observes that men, in the advanced stages of government, quit the equality of nature from the moment of their birth, never to re-enter it but by the force of equal law. The law then that is equally enforced on all ranks of society, to which the *great* and the *humble* are compelled to submit, is the next state of equality, to which this ever active principle of the mind aspires; with this it would be content as the most perfect state of liberty, which exists only in a just medium between two extremes; but in the attainment and preservation of this, the efforts of the human understanding never keep pace with the will.

Quicquid delirant reges, plectuntur achivi.

It is the poor people who suffer for the misrule of the great.

Laws are cobwebs, catching only the flies and letting the wasps escape. The great and powerful can easily bring to justice the *poor and humble offender;* but who is to lead to punishment the *great?* These lords of the earth who have extensive and powerful connections, who aim at no trifling larcenies, but who plunder a people of their liberties and put public revenues into their private purses under the sanction of laws made by themselves; these are the men who deprive their fellow mortals of their fondest hopes, and compel them to resort to the supreme aim of a monarch, to the authority of a single person, who exalted far above all may reduce them all, once more to that common level of equal law, of which mankind never loses sight. *Come, we will choose one man to rule over us!* is the cry of a people who are tired of the rule of the *elders.* The meaning of the word senate is an assembly of elders; but this the last and most fatal step is never retrieved until government returns through blood into that original chaos; from the discordant elements of which, new and equal forms of society arise, created upon first principles.

The corruption of the rule of one man is also regular and perhaps like every other progressive step of *mixed government,* unavoidable. He is at first limited and his hands tied; but as the powerful and strong are alone able to keep him confined, they are the checks which are necessarily imposed. The elders or the senate are always joined in power to guard against his usurpations. The people in this event find that instead of a protector of their equal rights, they have elected a patron for the rich and powerful, who, under the sanction of his name and authority, plunder and oppress with still greater security. If a weak Prince should attempt to curb their insolence, he generally becomes himself the sacrifice to his own temerity; the proud chiefs rebel, put new shackles on their principal, until at length tired of his own uneasy and dependent situation, disgusted at sheltering evil and his incapacity to do good, some able and politic chieftain breaks the bonds of restraint. Perhaps with the manly boldness of a Gustavus Erickson, he may demand of the representatives of the nation, to take back that power which is only a cloak for vice and which is too weak to do good. He may request them to deprive him of the authority he had received, or give him that which would enable him to secure the public prosperity and private happiness. Let him leave the legislature with a stern firmness, retire to an army who adore him, the submission must follow; or let such a chief pursue the more usual route to power. Let him profit of the discontents of the multitude, and he will quickly fasten the cords of authority around the necks of the great.

The chief magistrate is now clothed with full authority to *do good*. If he does so, he confirms a solid tyranny for his degenerate successors. For if power does not corrupt him it certainly will those that follow. In this view, the best elected magistrates have only entailed misery on mankind. The wise and moderate administration of Augustus (who was appointed commander in chief of the established forces, and was annually elected consul during the whole period of his life) secured the power and gave full scope to the vices of Tiberious, Caligula, and Nero in whom the Julian line ended. A veneration for the memory of Titus enabled his brother Domitian to sink the spirit of the world, and the divine Marcus Aurelius found that the luster of his own virtues would frustrate every endeavor of his disinterested and patriot head to set aside the election of that monster, his son, or rather his wife's son, Commodus. Marcus Aurelius could never have been the father of such a son, and the latter end of this all-accomplished mortal was embittered with the prospect of the misery of his fellow citizens under the administration of a brute. As to hereditary chief magistrates, I perfectly agree with the Marquis Mirabeau, and what he says of France may be justly extended to the whole world. He says, if I recollect right, that in 1100 years there have been but four Princes on the French throne that did not deserve the gallows. In England, Henry the Second was succeeded by a brute, a coward, and a fool: Richard, John, and Henry. The valiant and just Edward the First made way for the mean and despicable Edward the Second. The Great Edward the Third and his adored son, the Black Prince, crowned the English throne with laurels to be lavished away by the profuse and injudicious hand of Richard the Second; and the valiant Henry the Fifth transmitted his glory and authority to be tarnished by his weak son, Henry the Sixth. In fine, there is no general truth more fully established than that human beings entrusted with power will abuse it, from the Prince who fills the throne down to the degraded negro, who beats his poor plowhorses and oxen so unmercifully. There is a humane and benevolent saying of an illustrious Prince, the Marshal Vendome, which deserves to be imprinted on our minds in indelible characters. He said that in a long march he listened attentively to the quarrels between the muleteers and the mules, and that he found the mules always in the right. Thus the possession and the abuse of power seem inseparably connected.

The rule of any one man who is elevated to a pre-eminence of power is always surrounded by those vile minions and favorites, who bask in the sunshine of courts, deify the object of their adoration with the venal incense of flattery, intercept every avenue to truth, and who never can be satisfied until they reduce the people to the slavery of the ancient Persians, who, when their Prince ordered them to be well bastinadoed, were obliged to fall down upon their knees and say, *We thank you most gracious Sovereign for deigning to recollect us.*

But it will be asked can this happen in America? My countrymen, you will yet discover before your day is cold, a truth long established by every political inquiry; that in all governments in which there is sown the smallest seed of the rule of one man, no checks, no bars can prevent its growing into a monarchy, or a despotism if the empire is extensive. And that to attempt to form a virtuous republic on the unqualified principles of representation is as vain as to expect a carriage to run with wheels only on one side. Wheels will be added on the other, and the machine once set in motion downhill will never stop until it carries us to the *bottom.* Let us not set off without every necessary check.

It is true the proposed national system guarantees to each State a republican form of government. Whoever will look into Coxe's Northern Travels will find that in the treaty, whereby the three arch despots of Russia, Germany, and Prussia divided that poor distracted country, Poland, they solemnly guarantee (in express words) to the said Poland a *republican government forever.*

Federal Farmer
Letters VII, VIII, IX
(Poughkeepsie) Country Journal
31 December, 1787, 3 and 4 January, 1788

In viewing the various governments instituted by mankind, we see their whole force reducible to two principles: the important springs which alone move the machines and give them their intended influence and control are force and persuasion; by the former men are compelled, by the latter they are drawn. We denominate a government despotic or free, as the one or other principle prevails in it. Perhaps it is not possible for a government to be so despotic, as not to operate persuasively on some of its subjects; nor is it, in the nature of things, I conceive, for a government to be so free, or so supported by voluntary consent, as never to want force to compel obedience to the laws. In despotic governments one man or a few men, independent of the people, generally make the laws, command obedience, and enforce it by the sword. One-fourth part of the people are armed, and obliged to endure the fatigues of soldiers, to oppress the others and keep them subject to the laws. In free governments the people or their representatives make the laws; their execution is principally the effect of voluntary consent and aid. The people respect the magistrate, follow their private pursuits, and enjoy the fruits of their labor with very small deductions for the public use. The body of the people must evidently prefer the latter species of government, and it can be only those few who may be well paid for the part they take in enforcing despotism that can, for a moment, prefer the former. Our true object is to give full efficacy to one principle, to arm persuasion on every side, and to render force as little necessary as possible. Persuasion is never dangerous, not even in despotic governments. But military force, if often applied internally, can never fail to destroy the love and confidence and break the spirits of the people, and to render it totally impracticable and unnatural for him or them who govern and yield to this force against the people to hold their places by the peoples' elections.

I repeat my observation that the plan proposed will have a doubtful operation between the two principles; and whether it will preponderate towards persuasion or force is uncertain.

Government must exist. If the persuasive principle be feeble, force is infallibly the next resort. The moment the laws of congress shall be disregarded they must languish, and the whole system be convulsed; that moment we must have recourse to this next resort, and all freedom vanish.

It being impracticable for the people to assemble to make laws, they must elect legislators and assign men to the different departments of the government. In the representative branch we must expect chiefly to collect the confidence of the people, and in it to find almost entirely the force of persuasion. In forming this branch, therefore, several important considerations must be attended to. It must possess abilities to discern the situation of the people and of public affairs, a disposition to sympathize with the people, and a capacity and inclination to make laws congenial to their circumstances and condition. It must afford security against interested combinations, corruption and influence; it must possess the confidence, and have the voluntary support of the people.

I think these positions will not be controverted, nor the one I formerly advanced, that a fair and equal representation is that in which the interests, feelings, opinions and views of the people are collected, in such manner as they would be were the people all assembled. Having made these general observations, I shall proceed to consider further my principal position, *viz.*, that there is no substantial representation of the people provided for in a government in which the most essential powers, even as to the internal police of the country, are proposed to be lodged; and to propose certain amendments as to the representative branch, first, that there ought to be *an increase of the numbers of representatives* and, second, that the elections of them ought to be better secured.

The representation is unsubstantial and ought to be increased. In matters where there is much room for opinion, you will not expect me to establish my positions with mathematical certainty; you must only expect my observations to be candid and such as are well founded in the mind of the writer. I am in a field where doctors disagree; and as to genuine representation, though no feature in government can be more important, perhaps no one has been less understood, and no one that has received so imperfect a consideration by political writers. The ephori in Sparta and the tribunes in Rome were but the shadow; the representation in Great Britain is unequal and insecure. In America we have done more in establishing this important branch on its true principles than, perhaps, all the world besides: yet even here I conceive that very great improvements in representation may be made. In fixing this branch, the situation of the people must be surveyed, and the number of representatives and forms of election apportioned to that situation. When we find a numerous people settled in a fertile and extensive country, possessing equality, and few or none of them oppressed with riches or wants, it ought to be the anxious care of the constitution and laws, to arrest them from national depravity, and to preserve them in their happy condition. A virtuous people make just laws, and good laws tend to preserve unchanged a virtuous people. A virtuous and happy people by laws uncongenial to their characters may easily be gradually changed into servile and depraved creatures. Where the people or their representatives make the laws, it is probable they will generally be fitted to the national character and circumstances, unless the representation be partial and the imperfect substitute of the people. However the people may be electors, if the representation be so formed as to give one or more of the natural classes of men in the society an undue ascendancy over the others, it is imperfect; the former will gradually become masters, and the latter slaves. It is the first of all among the political balances to preserve in its proper station each of these classes. We talk of balances in the legislature, and among the departments of government; we ought to carry them to the body of the people. Since I advanced the idea of balancing the several orders of men in a community in forming a genuine representation, and seen that idea considered as chimerical, I have been sensibly struck with a sentence in the Marquis Beccaria's treatise. This sentence was quoted by congress in 1774, and is as follows: "In every society there is an effort continually tending to confer on one part the height of power and happiness, and to reduce the others to the extreme of weakness and misery; the intent of good laws is to oppose this effort, and to diffuse their influence universally and equally." Add to this Montesquieu's opinion, that "in a free state every man, who is supposed to be a free agent, ought to be concerned in his own government: therefore, the legislative should reside in the whole body of the people, or their representatives." It is extremely clear that these writers had in view the several orders of men in society, which we call aristocratic, democratic, merchantile, mechanic, *etc.*, and perceived the efforts they are constantly, from interested and ambitious views, disposed to make to elevate themselves and oppress others. Each order must have a share in the business of legislation actually and efficiently. It is deceiving a people to tell them they are electors, and can choose their legislators, if they cannot in the nature of things, choose men from among themselves and genuinely like themselves. I wish you to take another idea along with you. We are not only to balance these natural efforts, but we are also to guard against accidental combinations, combinations founded in the connections of offices and private interests; both evils which are increased in proportion as the number of men, among which the elected must be, are decreased.

To set this matter in a proper point of view, we must form some general ideas and descriptions of the different classes of men, as they may be divided by occupations and politically. The first class is the aristocratic. There are three kinds of aristocracy spoken of in this country; the first is a constitutional one, which does not exist in the United States in our common acceptation of the word. Montesquieu, it is true, observes, that where a part of the persons in a society, for want of property, age, or moral character, are excluded any share in the government, the others, who alone are the constitutional electors and elected, form this aristocracy. This, according to him, exists in each of the United States, where a considerable number of persons, as all convicted of crimes, under age, or not possessed of certain property, are excluded any share in the government. The second is an aristocratic faction; a junto of unprincipled men, often distinguished for their wealth or abilities, who combine together and make their object their private interests and aggrandizement. The existence of this description is merely accidental, but particularly to be guarded against. The third is the natural aristocracy; this term we use to designate a respectable order of men, the line between whom and the natural democracy is in some degree arbitrary. We may place men on one side of this line, which others may place on the other, and in all disputes between the few and the many, a considerable number are wavering and uncertain themselves on which side they are, or ought to be. In my idea of our natural aristocracy in the United States, I include about four or five thousand men; and among these I reckon those who have been placed in the offices of governors, of members of Congress, and state senators generally, in the principal officers of Congress, of the army and militia, the superior judges, the most eminent professional men, etc. and men of large property. The other persons and orders in the community form the natural democracy; this includes in general the yeomanry, the subordinate officers, civil and military, the fishermen, mechanics and traders, many of the merchants and professional men. It is easy to perceive that men of these two classes, the aristocratic, and democratic, with views equally honest, have sentiments widely different, especially respecting public and private expenses, salaries, taxes, *etc.* Men of the first class associate more extensively, have a high sense of honor, possess abilities, ambition, and general knowledge; men of the second class are not so much used to combining great objects, [but] they possess less ambition, and a larger share of honesty. Their dependence is principally on middling and small estates, industrious pursuits, and hard labor, while that of the former is principally on the emoluments of large estates, and of the chief offices of government. Not only the efforts of these two great parties are to be balanced, but other interests and parties also, which do not always oppress each other merely for want of power, and for fear of the consequences; though they, in fact, mutually depend on each other. Yet such are their general views that the merchants alone would never fail to make laws favorable to themselves and oppressive to the farmers, *etc.* The farmers alone would act on like principles; the former would tax the land, the latter the trade. The manufacturers are often disposed to contend for monopolies, buyers make every exertion to lower prices, and sellers to raise them; men who live by fees and salaries endeavor to raise them, and the part of the people who pay them, endeavor to lower them: the public creditors to augment the taxes, and the people at large to lessen them. Thus, in every period of society, and in all the transactions of men, we see parties verifying the observation made by the Marquis; and those classes which have not their centinels in the government, in proportion to what they have to gain or lose, must infallibly be ruined.

Efforts among parties are not merely confined to property; they contend for rank and distinctions. All their passions in turn are enlisted in political controversies. Men elevated in society are often disgusted with the changeableness of the democracy, and the latter are often agitated with the passions of jealousy and envy. The yeomanry possess a large share of property and strength, [and] are nervous and firm in their opinions and habits. The mechanics of towns are ardent and changeable, honest and credulous; they are inconsiderable for numbers, weight and strength, not always sufficiently stable for the supporting free governments. The fishing interest partakes partly of the strength and stability of the landed, and partly of the changeableness of the mechanic interest. As to merchants and traders, they are our agents in almost all money transactions, give activity to government, and possess a considerable share of influence in it. It has been observed by an able writer that frugal industrious merchants are generally advocates for liberty. It is an observation, I believe well founded, that the schools produce but few advocates for republican forms of government; gentlemen of the law, divinity, physic, etc. probably form about a fourth part of the people, yet their political influence perhaps is equal to that of all the other descriptions of men. If we may judge from the appointments to Congress, the legal characters will often, in a small representation, be the majority; but the more the representatives are increased, the more of the farmers, merchants, *etc.*, will be found to be brought into the government.

These general observations will enable you to discern what I intend by different classes, and the general scope of my ideas, when I contend for uniting and balancing their interests, feelings, opinions, and views in the legislature; we may not only so unite and balance these as to prevent a change in the government by the gradual exaltation of one part to the depression of others, but we may derive many other advantages from the combination and full representation. A small representation can never be well informed as to the circumstances of the people; the members of it must be too far removed from the people in general to sympathize with them, and too few to communicate with them. A representation must be extremely imperfect where the representatives are not circumstanced to make the proper communications to their constituents, and where the constituents in turn cannot, with tolerable convenience, make known their wants, circumstances, and opinions, to their representatives. Where there is but one representative to 30,000 or 40,000 inhabitants it appears to me he can only mix and be acquainted with a few respectable characters among his constituents, even double the federal representation, and then there must be a very great distance between the representatives and the people in general represented. On the proposed plan, the state of Delaware, the city of Philadelphia, the state of Rhode Island, the province of Maine, the county of Suffolk in Massachusetts will have one representative each; there can be but little personal knowledge or but few communications, between him and the people at large of either of those districts. It has been observed that mixing only with the respectable men, he will get the best information and ideas from them; he will also receive impressions favorable to their purposes particularly. Many plausible shifts have been made to divert the mind from dwelling on this defective representation, these I shall consider in another place.

Could we get over all our difficulties respecting a balance of interests and party efforts, to raise some and oppress others, the want of sympathy, information and intercourse between the representatives and the people, an insuperable difficulty will still remain; I mean the constant liability of a small number of representatives to private combinations. The tyranny of the one, or the licentiousness of the multitude, are, in my mind, but small evils, compared with the factions of the few. It is a consideration well worth pursuing, how far this house of representatives will be liable to be formed into private juntos, how far influenced by expectations of appointments and offices, how far liable to be managed by the president and senate, and how far the people will have confidence in them. To obviate difficulties on this head, as well as objections to the representative branch, generally, several observations have been made. These I will now examine, and if they shall appear to be unfounded, the objections must stand unanswered.

That the people are the electors, must elect good men, and attend to the administration.

It is said that the members of Congress, at stated periods, must return home, and that they must be subject to the laws they may make, and to a share of the burdens they may impose.

That the people possess the strong arm to overawe their rulers, and the best checks in their national character against the abuses of power, that the supreme power will remain in them.

That the state governments will form a part of, and a balance in the system.

That Congress will have only a few national objects to attend to, and the state governments many and local ones.

That the new Congress will be more numerous than the present, and that any numerous body is unwieldy and mobbish.

That the states only are represented in the present Congress, and that the people will require a representation in the new one that in fifty or an hundred years the representation will be numerous.

That congress will have no temptation to do wrong; and that no system to enslave the people is practicable.

That as long as the people are free they will preserve free governments; and that when they shall become tired of freedom, arbitrary government must take place.

It has lately been often observed, that the power or body of men entrusted with the national defense and tranquillity, must necessarily possess the purse unlimitedly, that the purse and sword must go together. This is new doctrine in a free country, and by no means tenable. In the British government the king is particularly entrusted with the national honor and defense, but the commons solely hold the purse. I think I have amply shown that the representation in congress will be totally inadequate in matters of taxation, *etc.*, and therefore, that the ultimate control over the purse must be lodged elsewhere.

We are not to expect even honest men rigidly to adhere to the line of strict impartiality, where the interest of themselves or friends is particularly concerned; if we do expect it, we shall deceive ourselves, and make a wrong estimate of human nature.

But it is asked how shall we remedy the evil, so as to complete and perpetuate the temple of equal laws and equal liberty? Perhaps we never can do it. Possibly we never may be able to do it in this immense country under any one system of laws however modified; nevertheless, at present, I think the experiment worth a making. I feel an aversion to the disunion of the states, and to separate confederacies; the states have fought and bled in a common cause, and great dangers too may attend these confederacies. I think the system proposed capable of very considerable degrees of perfection, if we pursue first principles. I do not think that De Lolme or any writer I have seen has sufficiently pursued the proper inquiries and efficient means for making representation and balances in government more perfect; it is our task to do this in America. Our object is equal liberty, and equal laws diffusing their influence among all orders of men; to obtain this we must guard against the bias of interest and passions, against interested combinations, secret or open. We must aim at a balance of efforts and strength.

Clear it is, by increasing the representation we lessen the prospects of each member of congress being provided for in public offices; we proportionably lessen official influence and strengthen his prospects of becoming a private citizen, subject to the common burdens, without the compensation of the emoluments of office. By increasing the representation we make it more difficult to corrupt and influence the members; we diffuse them more extensively among the body of the people, perfect the balance, multiply information, strengthen the confidence of the people, and consequently support the laws on equal and free principles. There are two other ways, I think, of obtaining in some degree the security we want; the one is by excluding more extensively the members from being appointed to offices, the other is by limiting some of their powers.

Brutus
Essay III
New York Journal
15 November, 1787

To the Citizens of the State of New York:

In the investigation of the constitution under your consideration, great care should be taken that you do not form your opinions respecting it, from unimportant provisions or fallacious appearances.

On a careful examination, you will find that many of its parts of little moment are well formed; in these it has a specious resemblance of a free government. But this is not sufficient to justify the adoption of it; the gilded pill is often found to contain the most deadly poison.

You are not however to expect a perfect form of government, any more than to meet with perfection in man; your views, therefore, ought to be directed to the main pillars upon which a free government is to rest. If these are well placed, on a foundation that will support the superstructure, you should be satisfied, although the building may want a number of ornaments which, if your particular tastes were gratified, you would have added to it. On the other hand, if the foundation is insecurely laid, and the main supports are wanting or not properly fixed, however the fabric may be decorated and adorned, you ought to reject it.

Under these impressions it has been my object to turn your attention to the principal defects in this system.

I have attempted to show that a consolidation of this extensive continent under one government, for internal as well as external purposes, which is evidently the tendency of this constitution, cannot succeed without a sacrifice of your liberties; and therefore that the attempt is not only preposterous, but extremely dangerous. I have shown, independent of this that the plan is radically defective in a fundamental principle, which ought to be found in every free government; to wit, a declaration of rights.

I shall now proceed to take a nearer view of this system, to examine its parts more minutely, and show that the powers are not properly deposited for the security of public liberty.

The first important object that presents itself in the organization of this government is the legislature. This is to be composed of two branches; the first to be called the general assembly, and is to be chosen by the people of the respective states, in proportion to the number of their inhabitants, and is to consist of sixty-five members, with powers in the legislature to increase the number, not to exceed one for every thirty thousand inhabitants. The second branch is to be called the senate, and is to consist of twenty-six members, two of which are to be chosen by the legislatures of each of the states.

In the former of these there is an appearance of justice, in the appointment of its members, but if the clause which provides for this branch, be stripped of its ambiguity, it will be found that there is really no equality of representation even in this house.

The words are "representatives and direct taxes shall be apportioned among the several states, which may be included in this union, according to their respective numbers, which shall be determined by adding to the whole number of free persons, including those bound to service for a term of years, and excluding Indians not taxed, three fifths of all other persons." What a strange and unnecessary accumulation of words are here used to conceal from the public eye what might have been expressed in the following concise manner: Representatives are to be proportioned among the states respectively, according to the number of freemen and slaves inhabiting them, counting five slaves for three free men.

"In a free state," says the celebrated Montesquieu, "every man who is supposed to be a free agent ought to be concerned in his own government, therefore the legislature should reside in the whole body of the people, or their representatives." But it has never been alleged that those who are not free agents can upon any rational principle have anything to do in government, either by themselves or others. If they have no share in government, why is the number of members in the assembly to be increased on their account? Is it because in some of the states, a considerable part of the property of the inhabitants consists in a number of their fellow men who are held in bondage in defiance of every idea of benevolence, justice, and religion, and contrary to all the principles of liberty, which have been publicly avowed in the late glorious revolution? If this be a just ground for representation, the horses in some of the states and the oxen in others ought to be represented, for a great share of property in some of them consists in these animals; and they have as much control over their own actions as these poor unhappy creatures who are intended to be described in the above recited clause by the words, "all other persons." By this mode of apportionment, the representatives of the different parts of the union will be extremely unequal; in some of the southern states, the slaves are nearly equal in number to the free men. And for all these slaves, they will be entitled to a proportionate share in the legislature; this will give them an unreasonable weight in the government which can derive no additional strength, protection, nor defense from the slaves, but the contrary. Why then should they be represented? What adds to the evil is that these states are to be permitted to continue the inhuman traffic of importing slaves until the year 1808; and for every cargo of these unhappy people, which unfeeling, unprincipled, barbarous, and avaricious wretches may tear from their country, friends and tender connections and bring into those states, they are to be rewarded by having an increase of members in the general assembly.

There appears at the first view a manifest inconsistency in the apportionment of representatives in the senate upon the plan of a consolidated government. On every principle of equity and propriety, representation in a government should be in exact proportion to the numbers or the aids afforded by the persons represented. How unreasonable and unjust then is it that Delaware should have a representation in the senate equal to Massachusetts, or Virginia, the latter of which contains ten times her numbers and is to contribute to the aid of the general government in that proportion? This article of the constitution will appear the more objectionable, if it is considered that the powers vested in this branch of the legislature are very extensive, and greatly surpass those lodged in the assembly, not only for general purposes, but in many instances, for the internal police of the states. The other branch of the legislature, in which, if in either a faint spark of democracy is to be found, should have been properly organized and established; but upon examination you will find that this branch does not possess the qualities of a just representation, and that there is no kind of security, imperfect as it is, for its remaining in the hands of the people.

It has been observed that the happiness of society is the end of government, that every free government is founded in compact, and that, because it is impracticable for the whole community to assemble, or when assembled, to deliberate with wisdom and decide with dispatch, the mode of legislating by representation was devised.

The very term representative implies that the person or body chosen for this purpose should resemble those who appoint them; a representation of the people of America, if it be a true one, must be like the people. It ought to be so constituted, that a person who is a stranger to the country, might be able to form a just idea of their character by knowing that of their representatives. They are the sign; the people are the thing signified. It is absurd to speak of one thing being the representative of another upon any other principle. The ground and reason of representation in a free government implies the same thing. Society instituted government to promote the happiness of the whole, and this is the great end always in view in the delegation of powers. It must then have been intended that those who are placed instead of the people should possess their sentiments and feelings, and be governed by their interests; or, in other words, should bear the strongest resemblance of those in whose room they are substituted. It is obvious that for an assembly to be a true likeness of the people of any country, they must be considerably numerous. One man or a few men cannot possibly represent the feelings, opinions, and characters of a great multitude. In this respect, the new constitution is radically defective. The house of assembly, which is intended as a representation of the people of America will not, nor cannot, in the nature of things, be a proper one. Sixty-five men cannot be found in the United States who hold the sentiments, possess the feelings, or are acquainted with the wants and interests of this vast country. This extensive continent is made up of a number of different classes of people, and to have a proper representation of them, each class ought to have an opportunity of choosing their best informed men for the purpose; but this cannot possibly be the case in so small a number. The state of New York on the present apportionment will send six members to the assembly. I will venture to affirm that number cannot be found in the state who will bear a just resemblance to the several classes of people who compose it. In this assembly, the farmer, merchant, mechanic, and other various orders of people ought to be represented according to their respective weight and numbers; and the representatives ought to be intimately acquainted with the wants, understand the interests of the several orders in the society, and feel a proper sense and becoming zeal to promote their prosperity. I cannot conceive that any six men in this state can be found properly qualified in these respects to discharge such important duties. But supposing it possible to find them; is there the least degree of probability that the choice of the people will fall upon such men? According to the common course of human affairs, the natural aristocracy of the country will be elected. Wealth always creates influence, and this is generally much increased by large family connections. This class in society will for ever have a great number of dependents; besides, they will always favor each other [as] it is their interest to combine. They will therefore constantly unite their efforts to procure men of their own rank to be elected; they will concenter all their force in every part of the state into one point, and by acting together will most generally carry their election. It is probable that but few of the merchants, and those the most opulent and ambitious, will have a representation from their body; few of them are characters sufficiently conspicuous to attract the notice of the electors of the state in so limited a representation. The great body of the yeomen of the country cannot expect any of their order in this assembly; the station will be too elevated for them to aspire to. The distance between the people and their representatives will be so very great, that there is no probability that a farmer, however respectable, will be chosen. The mechanics of every branch must expect to be excluded from a seat in this body. It will and must be esteemed a station too high and exalted to be filled by any but the first men in the state in point of fortune; so that in reality there will be no part of the people represented but the rich, even in that branch of the legislature which is called the democratic. The well born and highest orders in life, as they term themselves, will be ignorant of the sentiments of the middling class of citizens, strangers to their ability, wants, and difficulties, and void of sympathy, and fellow feeling. This branch of the legislature will not only be an imperfect representation, but there will be no security in so small a body against bribery and corruption. It will consist at first of sixty-five, and can never exceed one for every thirty thousand inhabitants; a majority of these, that is, thirty-three, are a quorum, and a majority of which, or seventeen, may pass any law; so that twenty-five men will have the power to give away all the property of the citizens of these states. What security therefore can there be for the people, where their liberties and property are at the disposal of so few men? It will literally be a government in the hands of the few to oppress and plunder the many. You may conclude with a great degree of certainty that it, like all others of a similar nature, will be managed by influence and corruption, and that the period is not far distant when this will be the case, if it should be adopted. For even now there are some among us whose characters stand high in the public estimation, and who have had a principal agency in framing this constitution, who do not scruple to say that this is the only practicable mode of governing a people who think with that degree of freedom which the Americans do. This government will have in their gift a vast number of offices of great honor and emolument. The members of the legislature are not excluded from appointments; and twenty-five of them, as the case may be, being secured, any measure may be carried.

The rulers of this country must be composed of very different materials from those of any other, of which history gives us any account, if the majority of the legislature are not before many years entirely at the devotion of the executive; and these states will soon be under the absolute domination of one or a few, with the fallacious appearance of being governed by men of their own election.

The more I reflect on this subject, the more firmly am I persuaded that the representation is merely nominal, a mere burlesque; and that no security is provided against corruption and undue influence. No free people on earth, who have elected persons to legislate for them, ever reposed that confidence in so small a number. The British house of commons consists of five hundred and fifty-eight members; the number of inhabitants in Great Britain is computed at eight million. This gives one member for a little more than fourteen thousand, which exceeds double the proportion this country can ever have. And yet we require a larger representation in proportion to our numbers than Great Britain, because this country is much more extensive, and differs more in its productions, interests, manners, and habits. The democratic branch of the legislatures of the several states in the union consists, I believe at present, of near two thousand; and this number was not thought too large for the security of liberty by the framers of our state constitutions. Some of the states may have erred in this respect, but the difference between two thousand and sixty-five is so very great that it will bear no comparison.